"In *The Gospels of the Weekday Lectionary*, John Craghan offers readers both succinct exegetical insight and pertinent pastoral reflection. While this work is especially helpful for preachers who wish to offer a brief, yet substantial, word during the weekday homily, it also provides other listeners or readers of the weekday gospel texts with food for prayer and meditation. Craghan's work calls all hearers of the Word to a sacramental vision of life that sees more deeply from a faith perspective."

> —James A. Wallace, CSsR
> Professor of Homiletics
> Washington Theological Union
> Author of *Preaching to the Hunger*.

"Regular weekday Mass-goers relish thoughtful comments on the readings, especially the Gospel passages. Celebrants wish to oblige. John Craghan offers a practical and welcome service. His analysis of the text is enlightening, his reflections relevant and pithy. First class."

> —Wilfrid Harrington, OP
> Professor of Scripture
> Priory Institute, Dublin, Ireland

"John Craghan's expertise as a biblical scholar is evident on every page of this book. He not only captures the essence of the gospel message, but he also challenges us with its implications for our present-day lives. These insightful reflections will be warmly received by those who, in addition to other pressing ministerial responsibilities, are called on to preach on weekdays. They will also provide readers seeds that can grow into a rich biblical spirituality."

> —Dianne Bergant, CSA
> Professor of Biblical Studies
> Catholic Theological Union

"John Craghan has provided a precious instrument for all who make the Gospels the core of their daily liturgical and prayer life. He not only states concisely and reliably what the ancient texts say but also helps people today to appreciate more fully the person of Jesus and to face up to the challenges he places before those who seek to follow him."

> —Reverend Daniel J. Harrington, SJ
> Boston College School of Theology and Ministry

Discard

MAY 14 '24

Discard

The Gospels of the
Weekday Lectionary

Commentary and Reflections

LIBRARY
ST. VINCENT DE PAUL
REGIONAL SEMINARY
10701 SO. MILITARY TRAIL
BOYNTON BEACH, FL. 33436

John F. Craghan

LITURGICAL PRESS
Collegeville, Minnesota

www.litpress.org

Cover design by David Manahan, OSB.

Some materials in this book first appeared in *Scripture in Church*, a quarterly published by Dominican Publications, Dublin, Ireland. www.dominicanpublications.com. The author and publishers acknowledge permission granted by Dominican Publications.

Daily Scripture excerpts in this work are from the *Lectionary for Mass for Use in the Dioceses of the United States.* Copyright © 2001, 1998, 1997, 1992, 1986, and 1970, Confraternity of Christian Doctrine, Washington, D.C. Used with permission. All rights reserved. No portion of this text may be reproduced by any means and without permission in writing from the copyright owner.

Other Scripture texts in this work, unless otherwise noted, are taken from the *New Revised Standard Version Bible* © 1989, Division of Christian Education of the National Council of the Churches of Christ in the United States of America. Used by permission. All rights reserved.

© 2010 by Order of Saint Benedict, Collegeville, Minnesota. All rights reserved. No part of this book may be reproduced in any form, by print, microfilm, microfiche, mechanical recording, photocopying, translation, or by any other means, known or yet unknown, for any purpose except brief quotations in reviews, without the previous written permission of Liturgical Press, Saint John's Abbey, PO Box 7500, Collegeville, Minnesota 56321-7500. Printed in the United States of America.

1   2   3   4   5   6   7   8   9

Library of Congress Cataloging-in-Publication Data

Craghan, John F.
   The gospels of the weekday lectionary : commentary and reflections / John F. Craghan.
      p.   cm.
   "Lectionary for Mass for Use in the Dioceses of the United States."
   Includes index.
   ISBN 978-0-8146-3338-0 — ISBN 978-0-8146-3933-7 (e-book)
      1. Church year meditations.   2. Bible. N.T. Gospels—Meditations.
   3. Catholic Church. Ordo lectionum Missae (2nd ed., 1998)   I. Title.
BX2170.C55C73 2010
242'.3—dc22
                                                        2010017076

For

Barbara Lynne

"Ubi enim est thesaurus tuus, ibi est et cor tuum."

(Matt 6:21)

Table of Contents

Preface

Why only the gospels of the weekday Lectionary and not the first readings? This is indeed a very legitimate question since these readings (mainly from the Old Testament) are also designed to nourish the faith of participants. The simple answer is volume or size. When one considers that there are separate weekday first readings for Year 1 and Year 2, commentary and reflection on them would obviously create an exceedingly bulky tome. Without disparaging the first readings, the gospels enjoy pride of place in the Liturgy of the Word. According to the instruction on the Lectionary, the gospels constitute the high point of the proclamation of the word (13, 36).

While many authors have written on the three-year Sunday cycle along with the appropriate solemnities and feasts, relatively few have devoted attention to the gospels of the weekday Lectionary. To a certain extent this is a lacuna that the present work seeks to address. This is in line with the instruction on the Lectionary that declares that the weekday readings complement the message of salvation presented in the three-year Sunday-Festal Lectionary (65). Thus weeks one through nine cover the Gospel of Mark, weeks ten through twenty-one the Gospel of Matthew, and weeks twenty-two through thirty-four the Gospel of Luke, while the Easter season focuses on the Gospel of John. As a result, the faithful have ample time to absorb the message of each evangelist.

In commenting and reflecting on the gospels of the weekday Lectionary, I have at least three groups in mind. First, I consider the busy parish priest who may wish to develop the message of the evangelists but may not have sufficient time to prepare. Second, I think of the leaders of the Liturgy of the Word with communion service who may wish to apply the gospel message to their congregations. Third, I envision those people, both religious and lay, who use the weekday gospels for their daily meditation. I hope that both the commentary and reflections will assist them, to some degree, in their prayer life.

Seize the text. It is absolutely imperative to begin with reading the actual biblical text in question. This is based on the conviction that there is no substitute for knowing what the text says. Commentary and reflections presuppose that one has devoted sufficient time to what the four evangelists have written.

A significant number of the commentaries and reflections in this work originally appeared in *Scripture in Church*, a quarterly put out by Dominican Publications of Dublin, Ireland. I am grateful to this publishing house and especially to Fr. Bernard Treacy, OP, the managing editor of *Scripture in Church*, for permission to use them in this work in a somewhat different format.

I dedicate this book to my wife, Barbara Lynne Wenzel Craghan, who gently but firmly challenges me each day to live the Good News. This work, therefore, is a small tribute to her indomitable spirit.

John F. Craghan
Darboy, Wisconsin

The Advent Season

The First Week of Advent

Monday: Matthew 8:5-11   In this episode Jesus reaches out once again to an "outsider" (see the leper in the preceding pericope [8:1-4]). This time the outsider is a Gentile military officer who seeks a cure for his paralyzed servant from Jesus. Having learned proper military discipline in the Roman army, the officer does not require Jesus' visit to the sick servant—only a word of command is necessary. It is hardly surprising, therefore, that Jesus is astonished at the centurion's faith. It is a faith that Jesus has not found among his own people (the "insiders").

Reflection. It is precisely this type of faith that must give believers pause. Here they are provided with a conspicuous example of faith in the approach taken by the Gentile officer. He recognizes that Jesus possesses such power that only a word of command suffices to heal the paralyzed servant. This passage challenges believers to assess their own approach to faith. They must ask the question: who is this Jesus? They must reach deep within themselves and affirm that this Jesus demonstrates divine power and compassion to a world all too paralyzed by self-love. The pagan centurion urges modern followers of this same Jesus to revive their faith and readmit him into their daily concerns.

Tuesday: Luke 10:21-24   Here Luke has Jesus react to the success of the disciples' mission in 10:17-20. His reaction is twofold: (1) praise of God as his Father, and (2) a statement about the unique standing of the disciples as witnesses to his ministry and teaching. In the first reaction, Luke has Jesus focus attention on the nature of the Father and the Son. This underlines not only God as Father but also Jesus as his Son.

1

Jesus thus emerges as the revealer because of this unique relationship with the Father. In the second reaction, Luke has Jesus praise the disciples not merely for seeing and hearing in general but for the special revelation that they have seen and heard.

Reflection. The intimacy expressed by Jesus must rivet the attention of believers. There is, first of all, the intimacy that exists between the Father and Jesus. Second, there is the intimacy that exists between Jesus and the disciples. This twofold intimacy clearly shows that to accept Jesus is to belong to the family of Jesus. As Jesus will point out in 11:2-4, disciples have the right to address God as "Father." This God, therefore, is not a remote celestial being shielded from the concerns of human life. Rather, this God is the Father who involves himself in human problems. In addition, Jesus and his disciples enjoy a special bond by sharing a common mission and a common revelation. As members of Jesus' extended family, believers possess not only a unique status but also the obligation to live up to the family name. Intimacy means both rights and duties.

Wednesday: Matthew 15:29-37   This passage contains two scenes that highlight Jesus' compassion: (1) the healing of the sick and (2) the feeding of the four thousand. In the first scene, Jesus ascends the mountain—a geographical setting that implies a revelation. The various kinds of sick persons (the lame, blind, maimed, etc.) remind the reader of passages such as Isaiah 35:5-6 in which the glory of God manifests itself in the healing of such people. It is hardly surprising that the crowds not only are astonished but also break out into praise of the God of Israel. In the second scene, it is Jesus' compassion that explicitly moves him to feed the crowds. The disciples' question about their inability to feed such a multitude serves only to heighten Jesus' concern for the people's needs.

Reflection. This dimension of compassion must provoke not only admiration but also imitation. To be sure, miracle working after the manner of Jesus surpasses human capability. Nonetheless compassion easily adopts a multitude of shapes and forms. A word of encouragement to the depressed, a visit to the homebound, a gift to the financially strapped, etc., manifest Jesus' ongoing concern for these and similar people. For believers, the mountain must serve as the place of revelation.

Where followers of Jesus provide for others, his revelation or message becomes all too evident.

Thursday: Matthew 7:21, 24-27   In the opening verse Matthew contrasts saying and doing. He categorically states that to utter the name of the Lord is patently inadequate. Believers must also do the will of the Father. Doing thus becomes the condition for entering the kingdom. Matthew next states this opposition in terms of hearing and doing. He contrasts the wise man and the foolish man. The wise man builds his house on rock so that it can withstand all the forces of nature. The foolish man, however, builds his house on sand and so is unable to survive the fury of nature.

Reflection. This conclusion to Matthew's Sermon on the Mount speaks volumes to believers even today. It is so easy to mouth pious platitudes and recite the teachings of the faith. It is another matter, however, to reduce them to action. This gospel passage leaves believers with lingering questions: will they build on solid rock and thus become doers or will they build on sand and thus become only hearers? Advent provides a special time for reflecting on such methods of construction.

Friday: Matthew 9:27-31   In this miracle story Matthew underlines once again the compassionate mission of Jesus. By having the two blind men address Jesus as "Son of David," Matthew reminds his audience of the ideal Messiah King who "has pity on the weak and the needy, and saves the lives of the needy" (Ps 72:13). After the two men have persevered in following Jesus, he raises the question of their faith. For Matthew, faith in the power of Jesus is the absolute condition for healing.

Reflection. This account must remind believers that faith consists in much more than a list of propositions that one accepts and can recite on the proper liturgical occasion. Faith is, first and foremost, the acceptance of a person. Believers ground themselves in the person of their God and are thus prepared to accept articles of faith. Who finally is this person to whom believers commit themselves entirely? Perhaps the two blind men serve as the fitting response to this question. They are rooted in the person of Jesus, the Lord and Son of David, who can overcome their blindness merely by his touch. The faith approach taken by these two blind men must encourage believers to do likewise.

Saturday: Matthew 9:35–10:1, 5a, 6-8   The concluding verses in chapter 9 look forward to the missionary discourse in chapter 10. The sight of the crowds moves Jesus to compassion. They resemble helpless, exhausted sheep deprived of a shepherd. Jesus reads this scene in terms of a great harvest in which his disciples will play a key role by bringing the Good News to others. At the same time, given the scarcity of laborers, one must beg the Father, the lord of the harvest, to provide. By summoning the twelve disciples and sharing his mission with them, Jesus provides an answer to this prayer. Limiting themselves to the lost sheep of the house of Israel, they are to announce the arrival of the kingdom as Jesus did.

Reflection. This passage in Matthew may strike believers as the sole prerogative of the Twelve. Their temptation is thus to exempt themselves from bringing the Good News to others. By their baptism, however, believers become priests, prophets, and kings or queens. They are not only entitled to preach the Good News but also compelled to do so. Such proclamation of the Gospel message is not confined to pulpits and places of worship. In the seemingly insignificant events of daily living believers discover the setting for extending Jesus' mission. This missionary discourse is both the challenge and the inspiration to exercise the ministry of preaching the Good News.

The Second Week of Advent

Monday: Luke 5:17-26   In this episode, some men, having heard of Jesus' healing power, attempt to bring their paralyzed friend to Jesus. They awkwardly ascend the roof, carrying the paralytic on his mat—a mode of transportation that no doubt provokes considerable grumbling from the crowd. At this point Luke remarks that Jesus, on witnessing the faith of the mat bearers, not the faith of the paralytic, offers forgiveness to the sick man. To demonstrate that he possesses the power to forgive sins, Jesus then heals the paralytic, commanding him to take up his mat and return home.

Reflection. What must capture the attention of believers is that Jesus eventually cures the paralytic because of the faith of others, namely, the mat bearers. Genuine faith, therefore, has the capacity to touch others to such a point that the seemingly unimaginable (a miracle) becomes possible. Believers demonstrate such faith in what may seem to be the monotonous events of everyday life. At home, at work, at play, at social events, etc., believers have the capacity to transform society. The world stands in dire need of such infectious faith.

Tuesday: Matthew 18:12-14   In this discourse Matthew insists that the community must provide for the little ones, namely, those un-important disciples who can all too easily go astray because they are neglected. To make his point, Matthew introduces the parable of the shepherd who leaves the ninety-nine sheep on the mountains and searches for the one sheep that has gone astray. In turn, disciples must search for the Christian sheep that has wandered away from the fold and thus violate purely human calculations by leaving the ninety-nine. The one endangered sheep takes precedence over the rest. Such relent-less care for one sheep does not spring from an impersonal command but from the will of the Father.

Reflection. Such neglected disciples are to be found in every com-munity. Matthew appears to urge believers to lay aside their cold objec-tive calculations in order to focus on the one that has strayed. In the final analysis, salvation hinges, not on purely personal holiness, but on a communal holiness that envisions everyone as worthy of one's time and attention. In this parable, therefore, the role of community is clearly paramount. Disciples are not isolated individuals linked egotistically to their God. Rather, disciples are community members who see themselves as inexorably bound to their God in the company of others, particularly the more fragile ones.

Wednesday: Matthew 11:28-30   In this passage Jesus offers a share in the unique relationship he has outlined in 11:25-27 (the mutual knowledge of the Father and Son in which the disciple shares). Speaking like Lady Wisdom (see Prov 8–9), he invites all who find the Pharisaic law a heavy yoke (see Matt 23:4) to accept his own yoke. He appeals to the religious outsiders whom the Pharisees criticize for not keeping the law. The yoke proposed here is bound up with the very person of Jesus—the yoke is Jesus himself. He offers himself as the embodiment of gentleness and humility. To accept Jesus is to attain that final rest that the weekly Sabbath symbolizes.

Reflection. In seeking guides for Christian living, some disciples occasionally bypass Christ. They explore the world of power and prestige but conclude they are not the genuine article. They extrapolate models from the entertainment world but soon realize that they are at least ersatz and, at worst, self-destructive. Today's passage identifies the scribes and the Pharisees as seeking to find the norm for living in the law. Disregarding the personal thrust of Israel's covenant faith, they concentrate on obligations and prohibitions—on things, not a person. For Matthew, Jesus is the message. He seeks to root people in his person. To accept his person is to know peace. To acknowledge his person is to learn humility and gentleness. The law simply will not do. Accept no substitutes—only Jesus will do.

Thursday: Matthew 11:11-15   For Matthew, while there is no greater human being than John the Baptist, those who commit themselves to Jesus in the coming of the kingdom will enjoy a higher status. It is not that John is excluded but that the Lord is free to give. Those who oppose this kingdom, however, attempt to thwart its coming and block out those who would like to receive it. Significantly, John belongs not to the old age of prophecy but to the new age of the kingdom. Both the Prophets and the Law find their fulfillment in John as he, being more than a prophet, prepares God's people for the coming of the Messiah and final judgment.

Reflection. As believers observe in the Our Father, the kingdom is still in the process of coming. Hence they must also participate in this process. Like John the Baptist, through their special gifts and talents, they attempt to make the kingdom a greater reality. In effect, this passage in Matthew is the clarion call to action—believers cannot sit idly by and merely yearn for the coming of the kingdom. They must heed Jesus' summons to join forces with figures such as the Baptist and make the kingdom a greater reality with each passing day.

Friday: Matthew 11:16-19   In this episode Matthew presents Jesus as complaining that his contemporaries have not listened and acted appropriately. Like the children in the marketplace, they have declined the gift of salvation offered by John the Baptist and Jesus. The Baptist practiced asceticism, but they interpreted his noneating and nondrinking as nothing less than diabolical possession. Jesus displays a more congenial type of table fellowship, but they reject it as gluttony and drunkenness. Both John the Baptist and Jesus, therefore, experience rejection. Nonetheless Jesus as God's wisdom will be eventually vindicated.

Reflection. This passage addresses modern believers and their capacity to interpret and judge correctly. God works out the plan of salvation in everyday life. Believers must choose between what is genuine and what is phony. Will they accept as models those who flaunt power, prestige, and status, or will they opt to emulate those who exhibit compassion, thoughtfulness, and justice? Will Jesus and those who imitate him emerge as their only viable option?

Saturday: Matthew 17:9a, 10-13   This scene captures the descent of Jesus and the disciples from the mount of the transfiguration. The disciples quote the opinion of the scribes that Elijah will return from heaven before the Messiah comes. Jesus responds by citing the text of Malachi and seeing its fulfillment in the person of John the Baptist. Unfortunately Israel did not recognize the Baptist as the returning Elijah and subsequently put him to death. Jesus adds that he too will experience the same fate. The transfigured Jesus is also the Suffering Son of Man.

Reflection. This great paradox of suffering and death as the condition for glory must energize modern believers. Although for Jesus' audience a crucified Messiah is a contradiction in terms, for Jesus as well as for all disciples only suffering and death can usher in the transformation of the resurrection. For today's disciples it may not be the expectation of actual physical martyrdom that confronts them. Rather, the reality of the cross emerges in everyday life. There are always the conflicts between Jesus' values and those of a hostile and unbelieving world. In opting for Jesus' values, disciples will experience pain and frustration. Paradoxically such experiences are the raw material for birth into glory.

The Third Week of Advent

Monday: Matthew 21:23-27   In this episode the Jewish authorities ask Jesus about the nature and origin of his authority. Responding with a counterquestion, Jesus asks them about the origin and hence the authority of John's baptism. This counterquestion dumbfounds his opponents. If they acknowledge that his baptism came from heaven (God), they accuse themselves of refusing to repent. If they admit that his baptism was purely human, they provoke the anger of the common people who revered John as a martyred prophet. Not surprisingly the Jewish authorities refuse to take a stand on Jesus' question. Jesus, Israel's genuine teacher, has triumphed over its false teachers.

Reflection. For modern disciples this passage raises troubling questions about the source of a person's authority. All too often, it seems, people look to extrinsic proof for authority, e.g., academic degrees or the commendation of superiors. This episode, however, may force them to consider the genuineness of a person's words and deeds as the basis of authority. Clearly the common people recognized John the Baptist's authority from his message and especially his death as a martyr. Do modern followers of Jesus dare to recognize his presence and his authority in what they say and do? Personal honesty has its own way of vindicating itself.

Tuesday: Matthew 21:28-32   In the parable Matthew contrasts the sayers but non-doers (the second son) with the non-sayers but doers (the first son). Matthew then has Jesus speak about the social outcasts (the tax collectors and prostitutes). The outcasts reacted to the manner and message of the Baptist and thus repented. The Jewish leaders, however, remained recalcitrant and so did not repent. From Matthew's perspective the sayers but non-doers are the Jewish community represented by its leaders (the chief priests and elders). The non-sayers but doers are the Gentiles represented by the social outcasts. The parable may originally have defended Jesus' preaching of the Good News to outcasts. But as the text now reads, there is a clear dichotomy between those who reject and those who accept outcasts.

Reflection. Matthew's message urges today's disciples to accept his standard for admission into the kingdom: welcome all, reject no one.

Imperceptibly people appear to establish criteria whereby only certain categories of people are really "good" people—the rest do not merit their attention or consideration. Nonetheless Matthew maintains that believers should dismantle such criteria and thus view all people from Jesus' vantage point. Final selection is God's prerogative, not theirs.

Wednesday: Luke 7:18b-23   The imprisoned John the Baptist sends disciples to Jesus to inquire if he is the expected Messiah ("the one who is to come"). Probably the Baptist believes that the stories of Jesus' compassion and his message of love and forgiveness do not match his own preaching of fire and damnation. Significantly John's disciples arrive at the very moment when Jesus is performing miracles for the sick and distressed. Jesus replies to John's messengers that his actions fulfill the time of messianic deliverance foreseen by the prophet Isaiah (see Isa 35:5-6). This is what the messengers must report to the Baptist. The episode concludes with the statement that truly blessed is the person who is not scandalized by Jesus.

Reflection. This passage contains two different views about the role of the Messiah. For the Baptist, the Messiah must thunder hell and damnation; for Jesus, the Messiah must perform works of mercy. No one will dispute the role of rigorous preaching of the absolute need to repent. Jesus, however, chooses to provoke God's kingdom by deeds of compassion whereby especially the marginalized become the beneficiaries. Modern believers can take Jesus' view to heart by demonstrating God's involvement with the world (the kingdom) by assisting those in need. In so doing, they will not be scandalized by Jesus' modus agendi.

Thursday: Luke 7:24-30   Jesus' testimony clearly relates John the Baptist to God's plan of salvation. John is neither a reed shaken by the wind nor one dressed in elegant clothes. Rather, he is a prophet— indeed, much more than prophet. In fact, he is: (1) Elijah who has returned; (2) one greater than all other human beings; and (3) Jesus' precursor, the messenger sent ahead of him. All the people, including the tax collectors, by listening to John's message and receiving his baptism, approved God's plan of salvation. The Pharisees and the lawyers, on the contrary, rejected John's baptism and thus frustrated that plan.

Reflection. This passage focuses attention on God's plan of salvation by contrasting the response of all the people, on the one hand, and that of the Pharisees and the lawyers, on the other hand. Nevertheless, this divine plan is not limited to the time of Jesus—it involves all followers of Jesus here and now. Specifically one's vocation in life forms an essential element of that plan. Whether married, single, widowed, divorced, etc., followers of Jesus by faithfully carrying out their vocation join the ranks of all the people in the gospel passage. Unlike the Pharisees and the lawyers, they choose not to thwart God's plan by duly acknowledging their commitment to God and one another.

Friday: John 5:33-36   The background for this discourse is Jesus' defense of his healing on the Sabbath. In this particular section Jesus presents the following witnesses for his action: (1) John the Baptist and (2) his own works. John witnessed to Jesus as the Lamb of God and the Son of God. John is here described as a burning and shining lamp whose light Jesus' audience rejoiced in for a while. But that audience now refuses to accept the one to whom John witnessed. At this point Jesus refers to a testimony greater than John's, namely, his own works whose accomplishment demonstrates that the Father has indeed sent him.

Reflection. This passage speaks of credentials, witnesses, and testimony. While the Baptist's testimony and Jesus' own works provide more than ample proof that the Father sent him, believers may raise the question of the credibility of their own testimony. How do they show a hostile and unbelieving world that Jesus has sent them as witnesses? To be sure, they cannot appeal to the works or miracles they have performed. They can perhaps, however, point to their lifestyles. Service to others in whatever form over a period of time is indeed a significant credential. For example, to offer hope to the discouraged and a sense of future to the depressed is no mean achievement.

December 17–24: The Weekdays of Advent

December 17: Matthew 1:1-17   Matthew's genealogy explains the identity of Jesus: son of David (embracing Jewish members of the community) and son of Abraham (including Gentile members; see Gen

22:18). Matthew thus demonstrates how God has provided for all of humanity. He works this out artistically by arranging three sections of fourteen generations. He also introduces five women into the genealogy where the combination of irregularity and divine intervention is central. Thus Tamar, a Canaanite outsider, pretending to be a prostitute, committed incest with her father-in-law Judah but nonetheless continued the line of the Messiah. Rahab, another Canaanite outsider and a real prostitute, provided the help whereby Joshua ultimately conquered Jericho. Ruth, a Moabite outsider and a widow, contributed to God's plan by becoming the great-grandmother of David. Bathsheba, the wife of Uriah the Hittite, committed adultery with David but also bore him Solomon, thus continuing the Messiah's line. Finally there is Mary, the wife of Joseph and a virgin, who becomes the mother of the Messiah.

Reflection. It is a question of roots. In his genealogy Matthew informs his audience that Jesus belongs to a history and a people. Believers also have their own history and national heritages. They think automatically of their families and the people from whom they are descended. Nonetheless Matthew's genealogy challenges them to think of other roots. Specifically they too are part of the genealogy that includes Jesus. As believers, they have, therefore, not only a history but also a destiny. That destiny implies that they live up to the family name by their ongoing fidelity to Jesus' message, even though some of their forebears may have tarnished the family name. Ultimately they are to view themselves as members of a community of believers who must reach out to others and thus share their patrimony with them. The genealogy must mean Good News for everyone.

December 18: Matthew 1:18-25 This passage is an expanded footnote that explains the irregularity in the genealogy. If Jesus has no human father, then how can he be called "son of David" (1:1)? This footnote explains that Joseph was perplexed but that because of the angel's revelation he was willing to accept legal paternity. Hence in 1:20 Joseph is addressed as "son of David." Rereading the Greek text of Isaiah 7:14, Matthew indicates that Jesus will be Emmanuel ("God is with us"), a theme that he picks up at the very end of the gospel (28:20) where Jesus assures the community: "I am with you always . . . ."

Joseph's generous response makes this abiding presence initially possible.

Reflection. In this account Matthew has Joseph demonstrate that human response does make a difference. Instead of dropping out of the marriage and thus refusing legal paternity, Joseph opts to be the catalyst for realizing God's plan of salvation. Followers of Jesus are challenged to emulate Joseph's example. In the circumstances of their daily lives they have the opportunity to respond to God's plan by developing married love, by caring for their families, by demanding justice in their jobs, etc. Joseph is indeed a man for all seasons, a model for all ages.

December 19: Luke 1:5-25   In preparing his readers for the future mission of the Baptist, Luke adds a distinctively Old Testament flavor to this account by presenting the barren couple (Zechariah and Elizabeth) as a latter-day model of Abraham and Sarah as well as Elkanah and Hannah. In this announcement of birth Zechariah experiences fear when Gabriel informs him of the birth of a son. Overwhelmed by such news, Zechariah asks the angel how all this is possible, given his and his wife's advanced ages. Gabriel replies that, because Zechariah does not believe this message, he will be unable to speak until the blessed event takes place. Here response to God's message plays the pivotal role—a role that Luke will develop in the annunciation to Mary.

Reflection. In this episode faith makes all the difference in the world. It demands that disciples open themselves up to God's world of surprises. In essence, it requires followers of Jesus to trust their God, even and especially when the divine message appears to make no sense in the face of purely human calculations. Believers today can sense Zechariah's bewilderment and reluctance to believe. They are bidden, however, not to follow Zechariah's example by accepting a God of surprises who does not operate according to typically human equations. To believe in this God is to ground oneself in a God of surprises who can overcome not only barrenness but also any and all obstacles that people experience. To believe or not to believe—that is the question!

December 20: Luke 1:26-38   In this annunciation of birth Luke clearly contrasts Mary's response to that of Zechariah. Many components are similar, e.g., the recipient's fear, the message (here Jesus as

Son of God and Davidic Messiah), and the question (the apparent impossibility of compliance because of Mary's virginal status). Gabriel replies that this conception will take place through God's creative Spirit. After receiving a sign (Elizabeth's conception) that she does not request, Mary in contrast to Zechariah opens herself up completely to God's will: "Behold, I am the handmaid of the Lord" (1:38). Mary's faith and her role as the Lord's servant will receive greater attention as Luke proceeds with his account.

Reflection. It is Mary's openness to God's will that must command attention. Luke presents her as initially perplexed by Gabriel's message. After Gabriel's revelation about the virginal conception, however, Luke portrays Mary of Nazareth as totally committed to God's plan for her. In saying yes, she becomes an integral part of the great plan of salvation. It is this openness that must speak to the situation of modern disciples. All human beings experience collision of wills, namely, what God wants and what they want. They seem to see only part of the intricate divine plan and prefer to choose that. In this scene, however, Mary urges modern believers to dare to trust that God's will for them involves a much larger picture. This handmaid of the Lord continues to make this appeal: look beyond yourselves and dare to be open.

December 21: Luke 1:39-45   Mary's haste in going into the hill country to visit Elizabeth reflects her obedience to God's plan. She hears Elizabeth's Spirit-filled exclamation that she is blessed among women and the fruit of her womb is blessed. These blessings are indeed appropriate because of the child in her womb. Elizabeth, however, follows up such blessings with a beatitude. She states that Mary is indeed fortunate since she accepts in faith the fulfillment of what God told her. Once again Luke accentuates the faith of this woman. She receives blessings because of her child but she receives a beatitude from Elizabeth because of a personal quality, namely, a deep and abiding faith.

Reflection. For Luke, Mary's journey into the hill country is more than a matter of a family visit. It follows upon Gabriel's message of Elizabeth's pregnancy and thus reveals Mary as an active participant in the plan of God. Having opened herself up entirely to that plan, Mary inexorably pursues it. This visitation scene speaks to disciples' own involvement in God's Providence. Instead of being idle onlookers, they are called upon to play their part in God's destiny for themselves and others. By living out the implications of their vocation, they find themselves involved, like Mary, in a journey. Only the geography is different. Theirs is not a trek into the hill country. Rather, it is the relentless, almost restless, movement of meeting their obligations to others whether at home, at play, at work, or wherever. Their openness to God's directives will ensure the success of their journey.

December 22: Luke 1:46-56   The *Magnificat* is a psalm of declarative praise or thanksgiving that serves as a mosaic of Old Testament passages focusing on Jesus' coming. (The canticle of Hannah in 1 Samuel 2:1-10 that follows upon the birth of her son Samuel greatly influences this composition.) After an introduction underlining Mary's limitless joy, the canticle provides motives for praising God, e.g., the overcoming of her lowliness (virginity is tantamount to barrenness) and the Exodus-like accomplishments ("great things"). Verses 51-52 anticipate the victory to be won by Jesus' death and resurrection, namely, the time of the manifestation of God's power and Jesus' exaltation to God's right hand. Verse 53 emphasizes reversal strategy ("the hungry" versus "the rich"). The conclusion (v. 55) states that God has acted in accordance with the promises made to Abraham and his descendants.

Reflection. In her *Magnificat* Mary reveals in her exuberant praise the ability to break free from the restraints of egoism and to advance beyond the perimeters of focus on self. This extraordinary capacity to praise must impact modern disciples. While they may not find it overly difficult to praise God, they may find it much more challenging to praise the accomplishments of others. For some strange reason many judge the time of death to be the appropriate occasion to laud the goodness and generosity of others. The *Magnificat*, however, encourages them to battle the insidious forces of their ego and break out now into the hymn of creation: "It is good, very good."

December 23: Luke 1:57-66   In this account of the birth and naming of John the Baptist, Elizabeth's delivery smacks of the Old Testament where the once barren wives of the patriarchs bear a child (or children) and thus provoke an atmosphere of intense joy. When the neighbors and relatives come to learn of the divinely arranged conception and birth, they begin to surmise the future greatness of the Baptist by the couple's agreement on the unexpected name of John. Zechariah's regained speech directs the reader to Gabriel's prediction in 1:20. However, the miracle obviously enhances the amazement of all those present. This is Luke's device for foreshadowing John's greatness (yet a greatness subordinate to that of Jesus).

Reflection. In addition to the intense joy of the couple's neighbors and relatives there are two other reactions: amazement (v. 63) and fear (v. 65). Such reactions speak volumes in today's world where hope is too often in short supply. Amazement conjures up the image of an event that shatters human expectations. Fear connotes the dimension of awe, a situation in which one is simply overwhelmed by God's intervention. Given all the circumstances surrounding the Baptist's birth and naming, these reactions of amazement and fear merit much more than passing attention. As believers approach the birth and naming of Jesus, such reactions assume even greater significance. In these events God overwhelms and bewilders believers. Although the word "awesome" is bandied about all too freely these days, nonetheless, the events of the birth and naming of Jesus are truly awesome.

December 24: Luke 1:67-79 Like the *Magnificat*, the *Benedictus* is a hymn of declarative praise or a thanksgiving in which Zechariah blesses God for the gift of his son. However, Luke adds in verses 76-77 that God's present involvement in Israel stems from the Lord whose way the Baptist will prepare. The two strophes in the piece (vv. 68-71 and vv. 72-73) announce what God has accomplished for his people Israel and what God has done "for us" (vv. 69, 73), fulfilling the promises to both Abraham and David. This canticle, therefore, relives the narrative of the great ancestors of Israel and its hopes but moves on to see these expectations fulfilled in Jesus. The language of praise serves as the appropriate medium for linking hope (Abraham and David) and realization (Jesus).

Reflection. This account of exuberant praise at the birth and naming of the Baptist may speak to the celebration of Christian baptism. On such an occasion believers rejoice at the birth of the child and his or her new name. Essentially they celebrate the incorporation of the newly baptized into the family of the church. He or she has become heir to the promises to Israel and their fulfillment in Jesus. As a new member of this family, the newly baptized assumes obligations through the sponsors that he or she will live up to the family name and honor—a commitment symbolized by the baptismal garment and candle. The *Benedictus* is an appropriate expression of divine praise and human involvement on such an occasion.

The Christmas Season

December 26–31

December 26 (St. Stephen): Matthew 10:17-22   In this part of his missionary discourse Matthew discusses the issue of future opposition, a reality that will eventually confront all the disciples. Just as missionaries participate in Jesus' mission and authority, so they will also experience his persecution and martyrdom. Similar to their Master, the disciples will be handed over to the local Jewish courts and be scourged in their synagogues. Once again like Jesus, they will be haled before the civil authorities. Such occasions, however, will provide the opportunities to witness to their Lord before Jews and Gentiles. In these circumstances disciples must exhibit no fear about the manner or substance of their speech since the Spirit of their Father will provide the proper words to speak. Even though their closest family members will kill them, their heavenly Father will not desert them. In the face of universal opposition disciples who withstand such immense pressure will know salvation.

Reflection. On the feast of St. Stephen, the first martyr, the gospel (together with the account of Stephen's martyrdom in Acts 7) emphasizes the need for courage and strength in the face of persecution. In most situations today, believers do not encounter the threat of physical death. Nevertheless, they constantly face the reality of persecution in manifold subtle ways. When issues such as justice in the workplace, compassion for the marginalized, or defense of the sanctity of all human life emerge, disciples can expect no little opposition. By courageously clinging to their Christian code of honor and value system, such followers bear witness to the charge laid on them in this missionary discourse.

December 27 (St. John the Evangelist): John 20:1a, 2-8   John's account of the empty tomb consists of two parts: (1) Mary Magdalene's arrival and subsequent report (vv. 1-2) and (2) the arrival of the Beloved Disciple and Peter whose reactions differ markedly (vv. 3-8). For John, the Beloved Disciple explains the meaning of the empty tomb. The burial clothes point to the resurrection of Jesus: "he saw and believed" (v. 8). In contrast to Peter, the Beloved Disciple comes to faith. For John, therefore, the Beloved Disciple, not Peter, becomes the model to be followed. His love for Jesus has led him to believe the mystery of Jesus. Death could not be the Father's last gesture.

Reflection. The drudgery of daily existence, the discovery of a debilitating disease, the death of a loved one, etc., overwhelm believers on a regular basis. The disturbing question is: will they imitate Peter or the Beloved Disciple? Peter observes the wrappings and the piece of cloth but remains on the level of Good Friday. The Beloved Disciple sees the same objects but advances to the level of Easter Sunday—he believes! He discovers in the mystery of the empty tomb God's transforming action in the life of Jesus and in his own life. Believers are encouraged to emulate the Beloved Disciple by viewing tragic experiences as faith opportunities. As the resurrection of Jesus shows, God has the capacity to take what is evil and convert it into what is good.

December 28 (Holy Innocents): Matthew 2:13-18   According to Matthew Jesus relives and thus embodies the story of Israel. Like Jacob/Israel, he must leave the land of Israel and go down to Egypt. Like Jacob/Israel, he must leave Egypt and go up to the land of Israel. Jesus is also a new Moses. Like Moses, a new pharaoh (Herod) threatens his life and thus he is forced to flee (see Exod 2:15). Just as Pharaoh ordered the killing of the baby boys of the Hebrews (Exod 1:22), so his later counterpart orders the killing of the all the baby boys two years old or under in and around Bethlehem. Matthew relates Herod's tragic command to the experience of Rachel, the wife of Jacob/Israel who laments her slaughtered children, namely, the Judeans forced into Babylonian exile (Jer 31:15).

Reflection. At Christmastime believers usually anticipate the hymns and carols celebrating the birth of Jesus. This gospel message, however, introduces a somber, jarring note, namely, the slaughter of the innocent children in and around Bethlehem. Clearly Matthew is considering the fate of Jesus who will suffer an ignominious death at the hands of the civil and religious authorities. In this account innocent children must die in order to save Jesus' life. Their death, therefore, enables Jesus to survive so that he, innocent as well, may eventually die. In so doing, Jesus lives out the shocking meaning of his name: "he will save his people from their sins" (Matt 1:21). His death is not a tragic mistake but a painful yet saving moment in God's overall plan for humanity.

December 29 (The Fifth Day in the Octave of Christmas): Luke 2:22-35   Although only the purification (see Lev 12:1-8) required going to the sanctuary, Luke mentions the offering of the firstborn male since this leads to the meeting with Simeon, the Eli figure who confronts the latter-day Elkanah and Hannah, namely, Joseph and Mary. Luke indicates the greatness of Jesus by dwelling on the law, the prophetic spirit, and the temple cult. In the *Nunc Dimittis* Luke anticipates the Acts of the Apostles in which the Gentiles are also recognized as God's people. In the second oracle (vv. 34-35) Luke has Simeon anticipate: (1) the Jewish rejection of Jesus during the ministry and the passion, and (2) the overture to the Gentiles in Acts. In the process of discrimination (the sword) Mary will also experience pain as Israel as a whole fails to respond.

Reflection. Like Matthew, Luke also provides a dimension of opposition to Jesus as well as persecution: (1) Jesus as a sign of contradiction; (2) one destined for the fall of many in Israel; and (3) the occasion for a sword passing through Mary's soul. At Christmastime Luke (as well as Matthew) prepares for the harsh consequences affecting not only Jesus but also his followers. Luke presents Simeon as one who foresees rejection and catastrophe. This episode poses the following question for believers: how will they cope with pain and sorrow? They can adopt a stiff upper lip approach and accept such misfortunes with Stoic apathy. They can also choose, however, to follow the example of the Lukan Mary. In Luke 2:19 she treasures and ponders the mystery of Jesus' birth and in Luke 2:51 she treasures the abrupt question of her twelve-year-old son in the temple. Like all disciples, Mary is searching for the meaning of such events. She challenges disciples to respond as she did at the annunciation and thus to be open to the initially baffling and disturbing experiences of life.

December 30 (The Sixth Day in the Octave of Christmas): Luke 2:36-40   In Anna the prophetess (together with Simeon) Luke probably refers to the gift of the Spirit at Pentecost. As soon as Anna enters the scene, she breaks out into praise and announces the Good News about Jesus "to all who were awaiting the redemption of Jerusalem" (v. 38). Her life devoted to worship, fasting, and prayer enables her to recognize Jesus and speak about him. As a widow, she reminds the reader of the heroine Judith who did not remarry after her husband's death and spent her time in prayer and observance of the law (see Jdt 8:1-8). In closing this episode, Luke has Mary and Joseph return to Nazareth with Jesus who grows and becomes strong. The ending recalls the return of Samuel's parents (Elkanah and Hannah) to their home and their son's growth in stature and favor with God (see 1 Sam 2:20-21, 26).

Reflection. Today's hectic, fast-paced world allows relatively little time for prayer and reflection. Believers are so caught up in this frantic chase after security and pleasure that they do not slow down and make time for prayer. They are thus unlike Anna in today's gospel. Devoted to worship, fasting, and prayer, she evinces no trouble in recognizing Jesus and in speaking about him. This episode challenges disciples to adjust and revise their schedules and allow time for prayer. Prayer provides the opportunity to make contact with God and perceive things from a divine point of view. Prayer frees disciples from the shackles of egoism and energizes them to focus on their God and their God's extended family. The example of Anna deserves to become contagious in their daily lives.

December 31 (The Seventh Day in the Octave of Christmas): John 1:1-18   This hymn opens with the period before creation and the relationship of the Word (Jesus) to God. Through creation ("in the beginning"; see Gen 1:1), that is, an act of revelation, the Word has a claim on all. What emerges from God's creative Word is the gift of eternal life. In keeping with Genesis 1:3, the light shines on in darkness, even though humans have sinned. Verses 10-12 treat the Word incarnate in the ministry of Jesus: (1) the rejection of the Word and (2) the acceptance of the Word. In verse 14 the Word is bound up with human history and human destiny. "To dwell" refers to God's tabernacling at Sinai where his glory fills the tent (see Exod 40:34). It may also suggest, however, Lady Wisdom's tabernacling in the midst of Israel (see Sir 24:8). At several points the roles of the Word and John the Baptist are distinguished. For example, in verse 8 John is not the light but a witness to the light.

Reflection. John's prologue compels believers to ponder the reality of God's bonding with humans. Such bonding reaches a crescendo when Jesus/the Word becomes flesh and pitches his tent in their midst. To put it succinctly, God does not say it with flowers—God says it with his Son. At Christmastime this divine gift giving must provoke a special pause. Humanity's history and destiny are radically changed when the Word becomes one of them. In turn, this newness must prompt them to see everything from a completely new perspective. In essence, they are bidden to transform their world. They are called upon to make justice, love, and compassion the transforming components in this quest. Anything less is unworthy of the gift of the Word.

January 2–7: Before Epiphany

January 2: John 1:19-28   There are two sets of interrogations in this passage. In the first (vv. 19-23) the Baptist responds negatively, rejecting identification with the traditional figures of the end time, namely, the Messiah, Elijah, and the Prophet (see Deut 18:15-18). He then responds positively, identifying himself as the herald of Isaiah 40:3. In the second set (vv. 24-27) the priests and the Levites seek the Baptist's reason for baptizing. He replies that he baptizes only with water and makes reference to the hidden Messiah. Such a figure remains unknown until he suddenly appears among his people. The Baptist thus defends the practice of baptizing as a means of preparing for the one to come.

Reflection. This passage focuses on the issue of identity. Here the Baptist experiences no identity crisis. He rejects the titles of the Messiah, Elijah, and the Prophet, only to settle for the designation "herald."

John identifies himself simply in terms of the one who is to come. The Baptist's manner of identity pursuit speaks to modern followers of Jesus. Though tempted to find their identity solely within themselves, they are asked to cast a wider net. They are challenged to identify themselves in relation to others. Thus spouses, children, other family members, coworkers, colleagues, etc., must frame their search for identity. Only service to these others is an adequate form of identification.

January 3: John 1:29-34   The author of John has skillfully combined the sayings of the Baptist with his own theological viewpoint. Here the Baptist identifies Jesus as the Lamb of God (v. 29), the Preexistent One (v. 30), and the giver of the Spirit (vv. 32-34). While the Baptist probably understands the lamb to mean the apocalyptic lamb who will wipe out God's enemies (see Rev 7:17; 17:14), the author most likely takes it to mean the Suffering Servant and/or the Passover lamb (see John 19:14, 36). Although the author does not mention the baptism of Jesus itself, he does speak of the Spirit. While the Baptist may be thinking in terms of the fiery eschatological preacher of judgment, the author probably understands the Spirit as the Holy Spirit that Jesus will communicate to all believers at the moment of his exaltation. According to John 5:31-37 there are different channels through which God's testimony to Jesus is conveyed. Here the Baptist figures prominently as the first such channel.

Reflection. This passage deals with the Baptist's perception of Jesus. But it raises the question of a larger issue: how do believers perceive other people? To be sure, they are usually not engaged in discovering the personality and character of unique figures such as Jesus. Nonetheless, they are constantly (perhaps unwittingly) assessing the character of others in everyday life. They are usually tempted to judge them by externals, e.g., their looks, their financial status, their rank in the community, etc. Today's gospel message encourages them to look more deeply. These "amorphous" others are people created in God's own image and likeness. They are valuable persons for whom Christ suffered, died, and rose again. Ultimately they are their sisters and brothers—hence deserving of profound respect and honor. Believers must always learn to readjust their lenses when assessing such "others."

January 4: John 1:35-42   This passage is the Johannine account of the call of the first disciples. Here the Baptist's disciples become Jesus' disciples. The use of the verb "to follow" underlines the dedication of the disciples. Here Jesus takes the initiative by inquiring into the object of their quest. That object is God and the verb "to stay" suggests a permanent, not a temporary, commitment. In John the verbs "to come" and "to see" are often linked with the process of coming to faith (see 5:50; 6:40). In this passage the author uses the motif of Lady Wisdom. For example, in Wisdom 6:16 Lady Wisdom makes her rounds, seeking those who are worthy of her. To find Wisdom is to find life (see Prov 8:35). The stay with Jesus leads the two disciples to a deeper insight as to who Jesus really is.

Reflection. The Johannine account of the call of the first disciples must make believers ever more aware of their status as disciples. Like the disciples in this episode, they too receive the call to follow Jesus. They also experience seeing Jesus, i.e., sharing more intimately with him. They also seek Jesus—hence they are involved in a search that ultimately leads to the revelation of the cross. They also stay or abide with Jesus. Such staying or abiding is permanent. To understand where Jesus abides, that he abides in the Father and the Father in him, is to abide with Jesus. As in the allegory of the vine and the branches (John 15:1-11), while they abide with Jesus, they are also called to fruitful service.

January 5: John 1:43-51   In this passage disciples no longer find Jesus. Rather, Jesus actively pursues Philip. Next, Jesus' journey to Galilee leads to the call of Nathanael by Philip. On learning of Jesus' background, Nathanael inquires about anything good coming from the insignificant town of Nazareth. At this juncture Philip invites Nathanael to come and see. Jesus then greets Nathanael as an Israelite without guile. After Nathanael's question about the source of knowledge concerning himself, Jesus responds that he saw him under a fig tree. Such awareness moves Nathanael to confess Jesus as the Son of God and the King of Israel. Jesus then reassures him that despite his limited perception of his identity Nathanael will see yet greater things. The reference to Jacob's ladder (Gen 28:10-17) shows that Jesus himself is this awesome place and the gate of heaven. Hence disciples will see the revelation of the heavens in Jesus himself.

Reflection. This passage highlights the gradual process of coming to faith in Jesus. What is more important perhaps is that the gift of faith, though incipient, becomes a contagious reality. Faith in Jesus can never be reduced to a purely personal and individualistic gift. Rather, disciples must share this gift with others. In this episode Jesus finds Philip but Philip finds Nathanael. This passage must prompt modern disciples to look beyond themselves to those countless others whom they can evangelize. This need not mean mounting a pulpit and formally proclaiming the Good News. The communication of faith often occurs in simpler and more subtle modes, e.g., a word of encouragement, a kind deed, a reassuring smile, etc. Whatever the medium, believers must hand on the message of Jesus to others.

January 6: Mark 1:7-11 (Luke 3:23-38 [long form] or Luke 3:23, 31-34, 36, 38 [short form] may also be used)   After John's avowal of himself as the slave of the more powerful One who will baptize with the Holy Spirit, the passage focuses on the baptism itself. Mark's account, like those of Matthew and Luke, interprets the event to reveal different facets of Jesus' person and mission. The address as God's Son recalls Psalm 2:7, thus identifying Jesus as the Davidic Messiah. "Beloved" may possibly allude to Isaac, Abraham's beloved son (Gen 22:2), and thus anticipate Good Friday. The phrase "with you I am well pleased" borrows from the first Suffering Servant song (Isa 42:1) and pictures Jesus as empowered by God's Spirit to regather and regroup a scattered Israel. The tearing apart of the heavens comes from Isaiah 64:1—a rending that permits God to descend and rejoin his people. The passage as a whole, therefore, announces that Jesus, the Son of God and royal Davidic Messiah, enters upon a ministry as the final prophet and servant for the benefit of sinful Israel.

Reflection. The baptism of Jesus signals a turning point in his career whereby he leaves his family and occupation to embrace a new calling. Like Jesus, believers also have their careers including marriage, remarriage, single parenthood, life as a single person, etc. Part of their response to these vocations must be rooted in their own baptism. On that occasion they also receive the Spirit to assist them in fulfilling their calling. As with Jesus at the Jordan, they must see their Spirit-driven careers as faith opportunities to serve others. In different ways, perhaps, they carry out the tasks of prophetic spokespersons and suffering servants for others. Jesus at the Jordan and believers in the twenty-first century have no little in common.

January 7: John 2:1-11   The approximately 120 gallons of wine interpret the person and mission of Jesus. Here Jesus brings to fulfillment the meaning of Jewish feasts and ceremonies (in this case the prescriptions of Jewish purification) with an overabundance of wine. The wedding feast conjures up the messianic days, e.g., the future marriage between the Lord and Jerusalem (see Isa 62:4-5). Amos 9:13-14 also speaks of the coming days when "the mountains shall drip sweet wine, and all the hills shall flow with it." In this scene the mother of Jesus plays a conspicuous role. "Do whatever he tells you" (v. 5) illustrates her faith that she then shares with Jesus' disciples. As a result, the episode closes with the author's statement that Jesus' disciples believed in him (v. 11).

Reflection. Mary's function in this scene may help modern disciples in their journey of faith. Sensing the embarrassment of the couple at the lack of wine (v. 3), she responds to the family's needs. After Jesus' reply about the priority of his hour (v. 4), however, she directs the servants to follow his instructions. In so doing, Mary advances from family embarrassment to the priority of the Father's will for Jesus. In their journey of faith disciples may also encounter opportunities for similar growth. They can move beyond banal everyday events, whether embarrassing or not, to a level where they perceive God's will unfolding for them. Their first reactions, seen from a human perspective, are neither negative nor trivial. Rather, they become the raw material for seeing things from a wholly new dimension.

January 7–12: The Weekdays after Epiphany

January 7 (or Monday after Epiphany): Matthew 4:12-17, 23-25
Learning of John the Baptist's death, Jesus continues his mission in Galilee in the face of opposition. Like the Baptist, Jesus also will be handed over to suffering and death. Here Matthew exploits the text of Isaiah 8:23–9:1 ("Galilee of the Gentiles") to intimate the beginning

of the Gentile mission in Jesus' ministry, although with rare exceptions he focused only on Israel. Pursuing the link with John, Matthew presents Jesus repeating and fulfilling his mission of repentance, i.e., a radical change of thinking that leads to a radical change in lifestyle. The reason for such a change derives from the notion of the kingdom of heaven, namely, that God is beginning his kingly rule over the world. At the end of the passage Matthew adds a summary of Jesus' ministry that prepares for his first great sermon, the Sermon on the Mount.

Reflection. For most believers repentance evokes the notion of sorrow for sin. The biblical concept, however, involves a great deal more. It embraces the prophetic summons for Israel to return to the Lord after its infidelity. It involves a profound change of thinking that necessarily leads to an all-encompassing change of lifestyle. In other words, one's way of living is so drastically altered that one can prepare for and advance the coming of the kingdom of heaven. It suggests that the petition in the Our Father ("thy kingdom come") must be more than an idle wish—it must bring about a total reshaping and intensification of lifestyle. The message of the Baptist and Jesus proves to be as timely as ever.

January 8 (or Tuesday after Epiphany): Mark 6:34-44   Mark initially directs his audience to two Old Testament allusions: (1) a desert place (v. 35), evoking the image of the manna (Exod 16); and (2) the role of the good shepherd who provides for his sheep (Ezek 34). The disciples' complaint about the limited provisions also reminds the reader of Elisha who fed 120 men with twenty barley loaves (2 Kgs 4:42-44). This passage also anticipates life in God's kingdom as a banquet at which the Messiah presides. The language of blessing, breaking, and giving points to the celebration of the Eucharist at the Last Supper. Interestingly the scene concludes without any mention of wonder typical of a miracle story. Clearly the feeding account reflects a messianic interpretation touching the person of Jesus.

Reflection. Eucharist and compassion belong together. In this passage compassion moves Jesus to feed the crowd. Sitting down to eat and drink with Jesus at Eucharist, however, must also prompt believers to show compassion for others. According to 1 Corinthians 11:26 disciples proclaim the dying of Jesus at Eucharist. Such self-giving must seek out the concerns of others and make efforts to remedy them. A Eucharist devoid of compassion is a sham since it fails to embrace the needs of the community. Ultimately Eucharist involves a call to action whereby the followers of Jesus the Shepherd celebrate a sacrament of compassion.

January 9 (or Wednesday after Epiphany): Mark 6:45-52 In the Old Testament the sea often symbolizes destructive power. God's power expresses itself, however, in the control of such turbulent, unruly waters as in the act of delivering the people of Israel from the ravages of the Red Sea. Mark links this sea imagery with the theme of the disciples' misunderstanding, a lack of comprehension rendered more acute by the preceding scene of the loaves and fish. Paradoxically, although God wills such lack of understanding and hardness of heart, still the disciples cannot grasp the unity of Jews and Gentiles. They fail to see that Jesus is the one loaf (see Mark 8:14) who, through his power over the elements, opens up the way to the Gentiles.

Reflection. This episode brings together two basic themes: (1) the Eucharist (Jesus as the provider of food) and (2) unity (a community that embraces both Jews and Gentiles). Today's disciples may also fail to understand that the role of the Eucharist is to foster unity in another direction, namely, unity among Christians themselves. Such followers must admit that peaceful coexistence with members of the same worshiping community is patently inadequate. They must dispel their incomprehension and hardness of heart by seeing Jesus as the one loaf who demands the conquest of the unruly waters of human ego. Accepting others as genuine sisters and brothers in Christ and acting accordingly captures the meaning of Eucharist. Sharing the bread and the cup involves becoming food and drink for others.

January 10 (or Thursday after Epiphany): Luke 4:14-22 Unlike Mark and Matthew, Luke presents the rejection of Jesus at the start of his ministry, not later. This scene in the Nazareth synagogue, therefore, anticipates the fame of the Spirit-filled prophet. In the synagogue service Jesus reads the text of Isaiah 61:1-2 but omits the phrase "bind up the brokenhearted," substituting Isaiah 58:6, i.e., "liberty to captives." Jesus' prophetic message thus entails bringing good news to the poor and announcing the jubilee year (see Lev 25:8-55), namely, a time when all debts are cancelled and all property restored to the original owners.

Jesus states that he has fulfilled the message of Isaiah through his Spirit-filled presence. This synagogue scene is, in effect, his inaugural address but ironically the initial positive reaction of the listeners soon turns to persecution.

Reflection. At their baptism followers of Jesus receive an anointing that constitutes them prophets. As such, they do not predict events that will occur in the distant future. Rather, they become God's spokespersons who share the Good News with others. To that extent their mission overlaps with that of the Spirit-driven Jesus in the synagogue. Similarly their mission embraces the poor, the captives, the blind, and the oppressed of their time and place. Also, like Jesus, they function as the heralds of the jubilee year. Admittedly the poor, the captives, etc., assume different forms and shapes. Nonetheless, modern followers must show a skeptical world that the same Spirit of the Lord is upon them as well because he has anointed them.

January 11 (or Friday after Epiphany): Luke 5:12-16   In this scene Luke reveals Jesus breaking through social conventions by reaching out to the ostracized leper (leprosy involved a variety of skin disorders, not just Hansen's disease). Without fear of contamination Jesus touches the man (a feature of his healing ministry) and directs him to report to the priest to have his cure properly examined whereupon he can duly return to society and engage once again in public worship. Because of this cure Jesus' notoriety increases to such a point that crowds gather around him to hear him and be healed of their illnesses. Significantly Luke adds that Jesus would break away to deserted places to pray.

Reflection. In Luke's presentation Jesus strikes a balance between his ministry of preaching and healing and his need to seek out the privacy of deserted places to commune with his Father. Such a balance commends itself to modern disciples. Theirs is a notoriously rapid-paced society that cannot entertain the notion of occasionally slowing down. While people cannot neglect heavy schedules because of their families and the like, they dare not forget their need to decelerate and smell the roses. In the midst of their feverish activity they must find time for prayer. Such time affords opportunities for reassessing their careers and realigning them in accord with God's plan. Prayer thus enables disciples to think the thoughts of God, not just those of humans. As someone once remarked, "If you're too busy to pray, you're too busy."

January 12 (or Saturday after Epiphany): John 3:22-30 This passage highlights the proper relationship that must exist between Jesus and the Baptist. The simple fact is that Jesus, once a disciple of the Baptist, is attracting more attention than his erstwhile mentor. A discussion of purification sets the stage for pursuing that relationship. Against the background of Jesus' increasing popularity, John responds to his disciples that, as the friend of the bridegroom (the best man), he greatly rejoices at the bridegroom's voice. Because he hears his voice, the Baptist is prepared to decrease as Jesus occupies center stage. He thus shows himself open to the word of God by his willingness to abdicate the scene. The reader now perceives that John serves as an exemplar of genuine faith by opening himself up to that word (v. 27: "what has been given from heaven").

Reflection. This passage reflects a problem in the Johannine community about the rank and position of John the Baptist in relation to Jesus. In both secular and ecclesiastical worlds ambition and power play less than subtle roles. All too many people long to be the biggest and the best in these ego-infested worlds. Without eliminating the need for leadership roles, this scene offers a healthy balance. The Baptist shows genuine faith by positioning himself in accord with the word of God. As a result, he must decrease. To act according to "what has been given from heaven" becomes the norm for rank and authority. John the Baptist clearly functions as "a man for all seasons" in this regard.

The First to the Ninth Weeks of the Year

The First Week of the Year

Monday: Mark 1:14-20   In the opening verses Mark begins the public ministry of Jesus with a summary. He notes the fate of the Baptist and suggests that the cross cannot be divorced from a consideration of the person and work of Jesus. In Jesus, God's kingdom has finally dawned and a new age has begun. The audience is then invited to change their lives radically ("repent") and "believe in the Gospel" (v. 15). After this announcement Mark relates the call of the first disciples to demonstrate Jesus' invitation and the believer's response. Following Jesus means total dedication to him and radical renunciation. The first pair of brothers illustrates this total dedication while the second pair highlights the radical renunciation (see 1 Kgs 19:19-21). For Mark, the person of Jesus is the core reality in discipleship.

Reflection. The messenger must become the message. In becoming followers of Jesus, the two pairs of brothers ultimately commit themselves to realizing Jesus' message in their own lives. Dedication to Jesus makes them messengers and embarks them on a mission of actually becoming Jesus' message. The situation of the modern disciple/messenger does not differ essentially from that of Peter, Andrew, James, and John. Though in a different setting, modern messengers face the same reality, namely, that of incorporating the message of Jesus in their very persons. This does not necessarily entail waving flags and creating a din. Rather, it involves self-giving to the nth degree, coping with pain and rejection, displaying gentleness in the midst of strife, etc. Just as Jesus embodies the message of the kingdom in his preaching and healing, modern messengers must do the same. Their way of life must demonstrate that they are making the kingdom come near. In so doing, they embody the message of Jesus.

Tuesday: Mark 1:21-28   Together with 1:29-31 (the cure of Peter's mother-in-law) and 1:32-34 (the healings in the evening), this episode consisting of teaching and exorcism provides a typical picture of Jesus' early ministry. Here Mark shows Jesus teaching in the synagogue. His style of teaching, however, is decidedly different from the traditionalism of the scribes—it is a new teaching backed up with authority. Mark then presents Jesus' exorcism as a frontal attack on the realm of the demons. The unclean spirit acknowledges such a frontal attack by asking: "Have you come to destroy us?" (v. 24). The demon also seeks to overpower Jesus by recognizing him as the Holy One of God. In this way the demon is much more perceptive than the crowd. Eschewing the more elaborate rites of contemporary exorcism, Jesus simply issues a command and the unclean spirit obeys.

Reflection. Mark presents Jesus as a prophetic figure who is shocked by everything that oppresses and depresses the human spirit. As a result, he teaches and exorcises. The episode must pose this question for today's believers: do they dare to be shocked by everything that dehumanizes people? In the comfort of their homes they peruse their sanitized newspapers and watch their "objective" TV reporters. So much of what they see is truly shocking news ranging from crimes against humanity to gross forms of injustice and violence. They may rightly observe that they constitute an army of only one and hence will have little impact on these forces of evil. Nonetheless, to focus on relatively small aspects of evil in their everyday lives (e.g., gossip or unkind words) and to seek to eradicate them is to share the company of Jesus the exorcist.

Wednesday: Mark 1:29-39   In this presentation of Jesus' typical day of ministry, Mark notes that Jesus' exorcisms and miracles witness the impact of the arrival of the kingdom and hence salvation. For Mark's audience, Peter's mother-in-law symbolizes the believer whom Jesus has raised and who is then commissioned to serve. In verses 32-34 Mark concludes Jesus' typical day with more exorcisms and healings. "[B]ecause they knew him" (v. 34) is the first instance of the so-called messianic secret, namely, the identity of Jesus' real status as Son of God.

For Mark, that real status can only be proclaimed in the wake of Jesus' suffering and death (9:9). In the final section Mark depicts the disciples as popularity seekers who are upset because Jesus loses a great chance to display his powers. In verse 38 Jesus corrects this misconception—his purpose is not to satisfy the curiosity of the Capernaum crowds but to carry out the mission of his Father. He must move elsewhere so that others will benefit.

Reflection. In the healing of Peter's mother-in-law Mark provides a capsule description of the meaning of discipleship. Jesus *raises* her *up*—this is the same verb used for Jesus' resurrection (16:6). After this action Mark relates that she begins to serve them—this is the same verb that captures the focus of Jesus' ministry (10:45: "not to be served but to serve"). In baptism disciples share in that transforming act whereby the Father raised Jesus from the dead. As a result of that participation, disciples are empowered to serve others. Peter's mother-in-law is thus a perfect example of genuine discipleship.

Thursday: Mark 1:40-45 The cleansing of the leper is a significant scene in the beginning of Mark. While leprosy results in loss of community, Mark shows that Jesus' kingdom is accessible to all and hence his kingdom means the overthrow of everything that impedes true community. Where the Jewish community can only erect barriers against the disease, Jesus is ready to tear them down by readmitting the leper to community. The conclusion (v. 45) reveals the popular acceptance of Jesus' intent. The reaction of the cured man merits attention—he proclaims the word. Here the audience of Mark is invited to see itself. That audience has been cleansed in baptism and consequently called upon to proclaim the word. Jesus' miracle thus continues to live on in the daily proclamation of such Christians.

Reflection. Cleansing and proclamation go hand in hand. The cleansing from sin that takes place in baptism generates a movement outward that articulates itself in proclamation. This passage challenges believers to follow the example of the leper. Recognizing his cleansing, the former leper goes out, proclaims this freely, spreads the word, and thereby enhances Jesus' notoriety. Obviously the man cannot contain his enthusiasm. In turn, modern believers are bidden to follow suit. While the mode of proclamation may differ today, e.g., compassion for the marginalized, defense of human life, honesty in business dealings, etc., the fact of proclamation remains imperative. The leper and modern disciples must lock arms in the relentless task of proclamation.

Friday: Mark 2:1-12   This passage is part of a larger complex of conflict stories (2:1–3:6). This complex explains in part the hostility toward Jesus that culminates in his death. Each segment, however, is not only a debate with enemies but also a pronouncement story, i.e., one that focuses on a declaration or statement by Jesus. This account of the healing of the paralytic consists of two different components: (1) a miracle story (vv. 1-5a, 11-12) and (2) a conflict story (vv. 5b-10) that focuses on Jesus' pronouncement in verse 10a.

Forgiveness of sins is apparently a burning issue in Mark's community. Mark highlights this by showing the scribes asking themselves (v. 6) and harboring thoughts (v. 8). Since for them only God can forgive sins, Jesus' usurpation of this prerogative is blasphemy pure and simple. Mark's community, however, contends that, as believers, they share in the exaltation of Jesus and hence his prerogatives, in this case the forgiveness of sins.

Reflection. Believers are only too happy to ask God to forgive their sins. Since God never gets in their way, approaching him for pardon becomes a relatively easy procedure. To offer forgiveness to those who have hurt them, however, is a different kettle of fish. Their bruised ego bristles at the thought of digging deep within themselves to formulate the good tidings of forgiveness. At this juncture they are urged to follow the lead of Mark's community by breaking free from the centripetal force of ego and engage in the centrifugal power of love through forgiveness. Whenever they dare to reach out and pardon, they manifest the enormous energy of mutual care and concern.

Saturday: Mark 2:13-17   The call of Levi functions as the introduction to Jesus' pronouncement story in verses 15-17. Here Mark depicts Jesus' attitude to outsiders (sinners and tax collectors) that constitutes a scandal for the religious authorities. In the preceding account of the paralytic (2:1-12) Jesus' authority to forgive sins takes center stage. Here Jesus' role as physician to heal the sick becomes the pivotal issue. By sharing table fellowship with sinners and tax collectors, Jesus declares that these "sick" have need of his medical services. By eating with these outsiders, Jesus announces that his community is necessarily composed of sinners.

Reflection. For some reason people like to erect barriers that keep the "good" people inside and the "bad" people outside. They automatically rule out any thought of dialogue or the possibility of rapprochement. They conclude that this uneasy situation must prevail because they are healthy and the "others" are sick. This scene at Levi's dinner party, however, offers a totally opposite perspective, a perspective that demands the obliteration of such barriers. This episode compels Jesus' followers to dialogue with and befriend those who do not share their theological outlook. To refuse to talk is to refuse to throw open the kingdom to these less than beautiful people. Believers must recall that the community is always an aggregate of sinners who must reach out to other sinners.

The Second Week of the Year

Monday: Mark 2:18-22   This passage is the fourth conflict story in 2:1–3:6. It consists of: (1) a pronouncement story (vv. 18-20) and (2) two added sayings (vv. 21-22). The story shows that the messianic age (the bridegroom) has arrived with Jesus. Originally the story dealt with the differences between the disciples of the Baptist and the disciples of Jesus, but it was later expanded to include the Pharisees because of the complex of conflict stories.

Since only Yahweh, not the Messiah, was the bridegroom in the Old Testament and subsequent Jewish literature, Mark implies that Jesus is on a par with Yahweh. He will suffer death, however, an event that will legitimate the practice of fasting. Until that time, joy, not sorrow, is the proper response. The two sayings clearly show that this radically new message demands a radically new container. The message is not a piece of cloth added to the old or a mixture poured into the old. The person of Jesus implies that the kingdom is a radically new event.

Reflection. Believers must cope with the tension between the old and the new. To be sure, times and conditions change, but values endure. For example, on most Fridays Catholics are no longer obliged to abstain from meat. Nonetheless, the value, namely, the imposition of some penance in recollection of Jesus' suffering and death, continues. Hence instead of abstinence from meat believers may choose to spend more time in prayer, visit a sick person, volunteer for some worthy cause, etc. In this way disciples recall the value of Good Friday but express it in different ways.

Tuesday: Mark 2:23-28 This passage, the disciples and the Sabbath, is the fifth conflict story in the complex of 2:1–3:6. It contains: (1) a pronouncement story (vv. 23-26) and (2) two attached sayings (vv. 27-28). In its present context, namely, the Sabbath, the story centers on Jesus' freedom with regard to the law. Thus Jesus enjoys the same freedom that the Old Testament grants David (see 1 Sam 21:2-7). Sabbath observance must respect human needs. The attached sayings demonstrate that the institution exists for the people, not vice versa. As a day of freedom, the Sabbath means freedom not only *from* every kind of work but also *for* certain kinds of work. Jesus, therefore, as Lord of the Sabbath, liberates the Sabbath from the limitations imposed on it by nonliberated humans.

Reflection. Sabbath observance poses not a few problems for modern disciples. Does the celebration of the Eucharist suffice for keeping holy the Sabbath? This episode in Mark may offer some help by suggesting that Sabbath observance implies freedom *for* certain practices. Such freedom may recommend spending more time in prayer or helping others. It may also suggest that disciples take time out to enjoy the beauty and magnificence of God's creative work. To enjoy them is to enter into the rhythm of creation whereby disciples truly rest on the Sabbath. In this way they imitate the Lord of creation: "and on the seventh day he rested, and was refreshed" (Exod 31:17).

Wednesday: Mark 3:1-6 In this final conflict story of 2:1–3:6 the cure of the man with the withered hand revolves around the concern of the Christian community in its celebration of the Lord's Day rather than the Jewish Sabbath. Verse 4 elaborates priorities for that celebration: good over evil, life over death. For Jesus, the real question is: how much good can one do on the Sabbath? Not: how much good can one refrain from doing? Mark goes on to show Jesus' reaction to Pharisaic blindness. His anger expresses his displeasure with the warped human values of his opponents. The indignation of the Pharisees is such that they align themselves with the supporters of Roman rule (the Herodians)—odd partners indeed!

Reflection. This episode poses, in part, the following question: what are the values that drive believers' everyday lives? Do they accept how much good they should refrain from doing or how much good they can actually accomplish? These questions reflect a more troubling perspective. Do they honestly judge others as made in God's image and likeness and, therefore, deserving of their service? The Pharisees in today's episode do not accept such a perspective by compartmentalizing humans within such rigid categories of time (healing limited to six days per week). The scene urges believers to take time out and reassess their value system. In the final analysis, they are called upon to adopt Jesus' value system wherein service knows no timetable or specific categories of people. All are God's extended family, dependent on one another for timely service.

Thursday: Mark 3:7-12   After so much hostility in the conflict complex of 2:1–3:6 this passage offers a ray of light and hope in the people's enthusiasm and the evil spirits' discernment. A great crowd gathers not only from the friendly confines of Galilee but even from the Gentile regions of Tyre and Sidon. In Mark Jesus entertains a response of faith from non-Jews as well. Because of the overly enthusiastic crowds that threaten to crush him, Jesus requires a boat at his disposal. In this setting the evil spirits play a crucial role. They grasp the true nature of Jesus as the Son of God—an identification that neither the crowds nor the disciples make.

Reflection. Tragedy will not be God's last word. The evil spirits' perception of Jesus as the Son of God recalls his baptism (1:11) and the Christian use of Psalm 2. In that psalm the newly anointed Davidic king is recognized as God's son. Though he faces opposition from enemies, he will eventually triumph. The title "Son of God" also foreshadows Jesus' trial and crucifixion (see 14:62; 15:39). But believers derive hope and comfort from God's vindication in the resurrection. While hope is unfortunately all too often in short supply, the title "Son of God" assures believers that the bleakness of Calvary will give way to the radiance of the empty tomb. Hope still remains disciples' most important product.

Friday: Mark 3:13-19   Out of the enthusiastic crowds Jesus chooses the Twelve. Since Jesus comes as a prophet to renew Israel, this number of special disciples obviously brings to mind the twelve sons of Jacob/ Israel, i.e., the very constitution of God's chosen people. (Jesus selects only males because of the twelve sons of Jacob/Israel.) The Twelve have two specific functions: (1) to be with Jesus and (2) to be sent out to proclaim the message and have authority to cast out demons. By being with Jesus, they enjoy a close bond of personal friendship with him. They are also entrusted with the mystery of the kingdom (see 4:11). By proclaiming the message of that kingdom, they continue Jesus' mission. Significantly Jesus does not call perfect, sinless disciples. Peter will later deny him and Judas will betray him. These disciples are indeed a very fragile community.

Reflection. While the Twelve make up a special group of disciples, they remain disciples whose twofold task remains being with Jesus and doing the things of Jesus. Modern disciples constitute part of that long gray line that traces its origins back to Jesus' choice. As members of the church, the believing community, today's disciples continue to be with Jesus. By the character of their lives and their opposition to all forms of evil they do the things of Jesus. The fragility of the Twelve, however, must remind them that opposition, misunderstanding, and failure will dog them as well. Their ability to cling to Jesus and his ongoing mission will determine the quality of their discipleship.

Saturday: Mark 3:20-21   This episode forms part of Mark's "sandwiching" technique. Between the sections treating Jesus' family (3:20-21, 31-35) Mark has introduced ("sandwiched") the scene about the scribes from Jerusalem and their allegation of Jesus' diabolical possession (3:22-30). The discipleship theme in the family segment (who are Jesus' true relatives?) and the christological theme in the insertion (who is Jesus?) complement each other. The sandwiching device thus develops the parallel between the religious authorities and Jesus' own family. Both proffer wrong explanations of his work and, therefore, cannot see the truth. In the first family section (vv. 20-21) his relatives express concern over his conduct and come out to seize him. They believe that he is mentally ill, a state often associated with possession by the devil. It is worth observing that both Matthew and Luke omit the family's comment about Jesus' mental imbalance.

Reflection. In this scene Jesus' own family has misunderstood him. In their view his way of acting perforce leads to the conclusion that he is mentally unbalanced. Yet Jesus holds fast to the will of the Father. Not even family objections can deter him from completing his mission. Such resolve must speak to the situation of believers. All too often they are tempted to capitulate and satisfy the expectations of family and friends, even though they are false. The standard of discipleship is nothing less than wholehearted commitment to what they acknowledge to be honest and true. If Jesus had problems with kith and kin, they should expect nothing less.

The Third Week of the Year

Monday: Mark 3:22-30 In this "sandwiched" scene the Jerusalem scribes make two accusations against Jesus: (1) he is possessed by an evil spirit (specifically: Beelzebul), and (2) he effects his exorcisms by the power of Satan. Jesus replies to these charges by way of parables (vv. 23-25). A divided kingdom or household implies civil war. But Jesus' works are a frontal attack on the power of Satan—there is absolutely no evidence of civil strife. Verse 27 is another saying in which Satan is the strong man and Jesus "the stronger one" (see 1:7). By his exorcisms Jesus has overpowered Satan. Verse 30 shows that the mention of blasphemy against the Holy Spirit functions as Jesus' reply to the Beelzebul accusation. Whatever may have been the origin of the unforgivable sin saying, it is used here to indicate that, by attributing the exorcisms to the power of Satan, one puts oneself outside God's kingdom. It is fundamentally the refusal to acknowledge Jesus and the Spirit at work in him.

Reflection. In this scene the scribes from Jerusalem cannot deny Jesus' ability to perform miracles. Hence they conclude that some supernatural power operates within him. Since, in their judgment, his teaching violates the law, the source of his supernatural power must be demonic. Jesus' modern disciples face a similar quandary at times. They observe, in their judgment, that very ordinary people do extraordinary things, e.g., gain leadership positions, display marvelous judgment in difficult situations, defuse potentially dangerous conflicts, etc. The question arises: what is the source of such accomplishments? Rather than acknowledge the talent and giftedness of these ordinary people, followers of Jesus may be tempted to think that all this is pure luck or happenstance. Such disciples, however, must learn to applaud human attainments. To acknowledge human success is ultimately to acknowledge the Giver of gifts.

Tuesday: Mark 3:31-35   Mark links this passage to Jesus' family in 3:20-21 that believes him to be demented. Here Mark intends to establish Jesus' genuine criteria for discipleship. Are they merely family relationships or something else? Jesus' mother and brothers act rather abruptly by sending for him and calling him. The geography here is telling. In verses 31-32 Mark mentions twice that the family has positioned itself outside in contrast to the crowd sitting around Jesus. When he learns that his family is asking for him, he poses the question about the real identity of his mother and brothers and sisters. Glancing at the crowd surrounding him, Jesus solemnly pronounces his mother, brother, and sister to be anyone who does the will of God. Although rejected by his own physical family and the religious authorities, Jesus finds acceptance among the family of disciples who in obedience to God await the kingdom.

Reflection. The criterion for discipleship has remained constant over the centuries, namely, doing the will of God. Stronger than any physical ties, carrying out the will of God constitutes a person as Jesus' mother, brother, or sister. The problem, of course, emerges in the collision of wills, namely, God's or one's own. Once God's will becomes clear, however, disciples must acknowledge its priority over their own. Such an option enables believers to sit among the crowd of disciples surrounding Jesus rather than be relegated to the periphery where the physical family huddles in their rejection.

Wednesday: Mark 4:1-20 This complex consists of: (1) an introduction providing a setting for Jesus in a boat on the sea (vv. 1-2); (2) the parable of the sower (vv. 3-9); (3) the purpose of the parables (vv. 10-12); and (4) the explanation of the parable of the sower (vv. 13-20). Parables can include similes, metaphors, maxims, proverbs, riddles, etc. Parables both reveal and conceal. For those prepared to hear, they communicate the Good News of the kingdom. For those refusing to listen, they sound obscure, meaningless. The original parable focuses on Jesus' ministry. While there are three cases of failure to respond (seed on the path, seed on rocky ground, and seed among thorns), there is one case of great success (seed on good ground) that yields thirty, sixty, and a hundredfold. Verse 9 captures the challenge of the parable, namely, the need to hear.

In verses 10-12 Mark discusses the purpose of the parables in view of the Jewish rejection of Jesus' message. Mark distinguishes the insiders (the Twelve and the other disciples) and the outsiders (those who refuse Jesus' message). Rereading the text of Isaiah 6:9-10, Mark states that God's plan of salvation embraces the rejection by the outsiders. Next Mark introduces the explanation of the parable of the sower that serves as the key for understanding all the parables. The explanation is an allegory or extended metaphor that decodes the original parable. The seed is really the word that fails in the first three cases because of Satan's intervention, the inability to persevere during temptation, and the overpowering allure of wealth and the like. On the other hand, those on good soil hear the word, accept it, and bear fruit thirty, sixty, and a hundredfold.

Reflection. God has the capacity to surprise. In the original parable Jesus discusses the natural inevitability of failure and success in sowing and hence the application of the law of decline and growth in the kingdom. The parable confirms the human experience that people can explain failure much better than success. While Jesus develops the cases of failure, he says relatively little about the success of the seed on good ground. It simply seems to happen. This is the God of surprises working in their lives. Though they search for timetables, cause and effect, effort expended, and results obtained, God overrides their craving for solutions. This is the God of surprises who challenges believers to continue to hope even in the face of imminent failure.

Thursday: Mark 4:21-25   This passage consists of five sayings arranged in two pairs (vv. 21-22, vv. 24-25) with verse 23 serving as the connecting link to the parable of the sower (4:9). In the first pair, just as a lamp is intended to provide light, so the parables are meant to enlighten. The mystery of the kingdom is hidden for the time being but eventually it will be revealed, namely, after the resurrection of Jesus. Jesus the lamp has arrived on the scene, is hidden, but will not remain so. The disciples, in turn, receive the task of making the mystery known. In the second pair the disciples must listen carefully so that their attention to Jesus' teaching will be the measure or advantage they derive from it. In the concluding proverb the disciples are assured that God will deepen their perception of Jesus' teaching. In turn, indifference to that teaching will result in the loss of whatever one initially possesses.

Reflection. This passage presents disciples, not as impassive, reluctant bystanders, but as active participants in the role of making known the mystery of the kingdom. In other words, God chooses to need human beings/disciples to continue the mission of Jesus. Modern disciples are rightly reminded of the sacrament of confirmation they have received. As a result of this sacrament, they are considered Christian adults who must play their part in realizing God's plan for the kingdom. Against the background of this passage, they must lock arms with the early disciples and make the Good News contagious to a weary, forlorn world. Integrity of life, compassion, the pursuit of truth, etc., are but a few of the ways in which today's disciples reveal the mystery of the kingdom to their contemporaries. In fulfillment of this charge they will discover even greater meaning in the parabolic teaching of Jesus.

Friday: Mark 4:26-34   The parable of the seed growing of itself (vv. 26-29) is unique to Mark. Here the contrast is between the relative inactivity of the farmer and the certainty of the harvest. This growth cannot be thwarted. Only at harvesttime does the farmer reappear. The harvest is the time of the last judgment (see Rev 14:14-20). The parable of the mustard seed (vv. 30-32) is an appeal for patience, given the relatively small beginnings of the kingdom. Verse 31 emphasizes the smallness of the venture. Verse 32 stresses the incontestable growth. God can effect such growth even though the initial stages are rather inconspicuous. The kingdom will eventually reach such proportions—in the meantime patience is required. In verses 33-34 Mark offers his view of Jesus' parables. Jesus uses only parables when addressing the crowds. When alone with his disciples, however, he offers a special explanation. For Mark, therefore, since the parables are by their nature obscure, their proper understanding calls for a special revelation.

Reflection. Believers must permit God to be a giver of gifts. Since they are programmed to determine success, believers find it hard to let God have a free hand. They are built to measure success. Consequently they find it difficult to allow God a different manner of calculation. For Jesus, the kingdom does not develop according to human laws of growth. It is like the seed growing of itself. Believers have to allow God a measure of space. The kingdom is like a mustard seed. Disciples, therefore, must make room for God's law of evolution. They must learn to "hurry up slowly."

Saturday: Mark 4:35-41 As a miracle story, this episode assumes the Old Testament understanding of the sea as a force hostile to God and humans but one that God can nevertheless control (see Ps 107:23-32). In this account the disciples experience great awe at Jesus' enormous power. At the same time Mark relates this miracle story to the needs of his postresurrectional community. They sense the absence of the risen Lord and are tempted to lose confidence in the daily struggle of Christian life. Hence the Master appears to be sleeping and thus removed from their world of concern. Verse 40 assures the community that lack of faith is not the proper response. The miracle story teaches that ongoing faith in the Lord at all times and in all situations alone suffices. Hence Jesus is not really asleep.

Reflection. Maturity means mystery. Believers may tend to identify maturity with control—they mature because they are more in control of themselves and their situations. They may also equate growth with manipulation—they grow because they can better handle themselves and, more important, others. Hence they are not unlike the disciples in this episode. They recognize that Jesus is performing the work of God. Their question as to who Jesus is, however, implies that there is a dimension of Jesus that eludes their comprehension. For Mark, maturity consists in probing this question to its final answer in the account of the death and resurrection of Jesus. This miracle story thereby becomes for Mark's audience and later disciples a building block in the unfolding of the mystery of Jesus that is ultimately the mystery of the cross and the empty tomb. Maturity means mystery.

The Fourth Week of the Year

Monday: Mark 5:1-20   Although Mark earlier related an account of an exorcism (1:23-27), in this scene he offers a more compelling story of Jesus' authority over the demonic world. Thus Jesus controls not only the turbulent sea (4:35-41) but also the raging of a possessed man named Legion. Here Mark has imposed a clear structure on this unique story: (1) a description of the possessed man (vv. 1-5); (2) Jesus' meeting with the demons (vv. 6-13); (3) the reaction of the witnesses (vv. 14-17); and (4) a final statement about the former demoniac (vv. 18-20).

For Mark, geography plays a crucial role here. Jesus' presence in Gentile territory reveals the dire state of the pagan world and the effort demanded to free it of evil. Mark develops the picture of a quiet, controlled presence of Jesus (he does not speak until verse 9). Mark emphasizes the enormous strength of the man to direct attention to Jesus' superior power (1:7: the more powerful one). Mark contrasts the scene of the two thousand swine plunging headlong into the sea with the calm demeanor of the man (v. 15: "clothed and in his right mind"). Mark also observes that Jesus actually commissions the man to spread the good news of his cure, thereby making him a model for the postresurrectional community to do likewise among the Gentiles.

Reflection. The extraordinary nature of this exorcism can easily symbolize those violent forces in today's world that incarcerate human beings. Modern believers face a society overwhelmed by drug and alcohol addiction, sexual depravity, violence inflicted on the marginalized, unjust business practices that lead to the impoverishment of all too many human beings, etc. In the face of such evil Mark seems to suggest that Jesus' quiet, controlled, but decisive presence should become the modus operandi for disciples. Ultimately it means adopting Paul's policy: "Do not be overcome by evil, but overcome evil with good" (Rom 12:21). Strength in the face of injustice, compassion in the face of ruthlessness, and hope in the face of despair—to name only a few venues—make the story of the Gerasene demoniac come alive in today's world.

Tuesday: Mark 5:21-43 In this passage Mark has brought together two stories (the daughter of Jairus and the hemorrhaging woman) to show Jesus' lordship but also to have the stories comment on each other. In both cases Jesus helps females who are in difficult situations (hemorrhaging and sickness that leads to death). In both cases the number twelve is prominent (the time of the woman's illness and the age of the little girl). The action of Jesus is to restore wholeness and life. He welcomes the woman ("daughter") and restores a future to a distraught father. By referring to faith in both stories (vv. 34, 36), Mark establishes the bond between healing and association with Jesus. Jesus thus appears as a miracle worker who by God's power sustains a fragile world. Here Mark is preparing for that moment when God's power will also sustain a fragile world in a unique way, namely, at the resurrection. For Mark and his audience, Jesus is anticipating the power of that resurrection experience.

Reflection. This episode challenges believers to follow Jesus' lead in making humanity whole again. Disciples may reasonably object that the healing and the raising to life in these two stories surpass their power and capabilities. In reply, they may observe that making humanity whole again assumes a wide variety of scenarios. For example, overcoming ignorance, offering hope to the despondent and despairing, and comforting the sorrowing provide different venues for restoring humanity. The power of the resurrection of Jesus in baptism must motivate believers to follow the example of Jesus in this wholeness enterprise. To make whole the humanity of only one person is nothing less than a colossal achievement.

Wednesday: Mark 6:1-6 Here Mark offers a startling contrast. In 4:35–5:43 he demonstrates Jesus' power and his acceptance. Now the opposite is true. The people from his hometown have rejected him. According to them there is a glaring disproportion between his human credentials (they know his family) and the recent fame arising from his teaching and miracles. Hence they inquire about the origin and nature of such gifts. Jesus' reaction is one of astonishment since faith seems to be the obvious response. It is only too fitting to have Jesus quote the proverb that a prophet is accepted everywhere except at home. For Mark's audience, this episode helps to explain that, while the Gentiles are accepting the Good News, Israel rejects it. Israel is expecting another type of Messiah and Jesus does not meet that description. The treatment of Jesus recalls the rejection of Israel's prophets.

Reflection. Too often believers feel that they lack the proper credentials and conclude that they cannot speak for God. They acknowledge their failings and maintain that they cannot reflect their God. They admit their weakness and reason that they cannot proclaim their God. Nonetheless, this scene of Jesus' discouragement and failure is calculated to sustain disciples in their ministry. For Mark as well as for later generations of believers, the cross announces that weakness points beyond itself, namely, to the power of the resurrection. Paradoxically, modern disciples must view themselves as sharing in that power by reason of their weaknesses.

Thursday: Mark 6:7-13   This mission charge in Mark envisions future missionary work outside of Palestine. Such work is an extension of Jesus' own teaching mission. Just as Mark earlier linked rejection of Jesus with the call of the Twelve, so he now connects the rejection at Nazareth with the mission of the Twelve (see 3:6, 13-19; 6:1-6). There is a clear note of urgency in this charge. The Twelve are to rely on God for their needs. A missionary who provides for every possible emergency can hardly preach the nearness of the kingdom—hence they are not to seek the best accommodations. Their sole proclamation is total conversion, a complete and radical reorientation (repentance). The expelling of demons continues Jesus' victory over Satan; therefore, Jesus' mission continues in them. With a note of realism, Mark mentions the act to be followed when they are rejected, namely, shaking off the dust from their feet, the removal of the last vestige of contact with a heathen environment.

Reflection. For one reason or another disciples of Jesus too often think that missionaries are special people chosen by God to preach the Good News in foreign lands. While some followers of Jesus receive such a vocation, *all* disciples are by definition missionaries. Whether the mission field involves home, school, workplace, or social setting, the mandate remains the same, namely, to proclaim repentance and thus a complete and radical reorientation of lifestyle. While such missionaries do not need to wear sandals or carry a staff, they still must experience the urgency of their mandate. They must see themselves as evangelizers in their limited but challenging worlds. In this way they advance the message of the kingdom.

Friday: Mark 6:14-29   In his introduction (vv. 14-16) Mark closely connects the fates of the Baptist and Jesus, foreshadowing belief in the resurrection of Jesus. In verses 17-20 Mark provides background for John's arrest and in verses 21-29 relates the account of court politics and regal weakness that culminates in the Baptist's death. Concluding with the burial of the righteous prophet, it anticipates Jesus' own death and burial. Mark has "sandwiched" this episode between the accounts of Jesus' sending of the Twelve on mission (6:6-13) and their return (6:30-32). By this technique Mark seems to remind his audience that contemporary Christian leaders can expect nothing less than harassment and suffering, perhaps even death, at the hands of those rulers who "lord it over them" (10:42). Such rulers obviously prefer their good name and status to justice and truth.

Reflection. Believers can certainly admire John the Baptist but can they also imitate him? While the threat of imprisonment and subsequent execution may be remote in most quarters, harassment and ridicule continue to hound today's disciples. To stand up for the truth, whether in the marketplace or golf club, is hardly a rare occurrence. At such times the story of the Baptist's courage in the face of royal weakness may inspire followers to persevere in their Christian commitment. While the trappings of the insidious royal court may appear utterly strange and unlikely, the temptation to infidelity still abounds in daily living. In these circumstances the prophetic resistance of the Baptist may motivate believers to decide in favor of truth and justice, not complacency and popular acceptance.

Saturday: Mark 6:30-34   This passage is a Markan prelude to the account of the feeding of the five thousand (6:35-44). The missionaries have returned and offer an account of their activities. Jesus then judges that they need a rest after this period of ministry. With this, Mark is preparing for the shepherd motif in verse 34. In Ezekiel 34:15 and Psalm 23:2 the shepherd provides rest for his sheep. Mark then goes on to paint a vivid picture of the converging crowds who travel on foot to meet Jesus. Then he portrays Jesus' reaction as one of great compassion for the people. His description of sheep without a shepherd may stem from such texts as 1 Kings 22:17 and Ezekiel 34:5. To offer proper direction and subsequent hope, Jesus undertakes the pastoral role of teaching.

Reflection. In this scene Mark presents Jesus as a shepherd who grasps the meaning of leadership. When he sees the vast crowd, he immediately identifies them as sheep without a shepherd. As leader, he then asks the proper questions: What's in it for the sheep? What can I do for them? As leaders, today's disciples must also ask leading questions. In view of service to others they must ask: what's in it for them? In view of meeting their needs they must inquire: how can I help them? While Jesus responds in this scene by teaching, modern disciples may react by encouragement, hope, generosity, etc. In the final analysis, leadership means asking leading questions.

The Fifth Week of the Year

Monday: Mark 6:53-56   This passage, one of the longer transitional summaries of Jesus' great feats, reveals an ever expanding picture of Jesus' ministry. Mark adds vivid color to the summary with his mention of mats, begging, and touching the fringe of Jesus' cloak. Mark also envisions the missionary travels of early Christians with his notice of boat, people rushing about, and carrying the sick. Such followers of Jesus are to retrace his journey in other villages, cities, and farmland. The marketplace assumes the position, not simply of commerce and politics, but also of the continuation of Jesus' healing ministry.

Reflection. This continuation of Jesus' healing ministry must resonate with today's disciples. While Mark concentrates on the cure of physical illnesses, believers know that healing today encompasses many other forms of disorder. Followers of Jesus must reach out to those who, for one reason or another, feel alienated from the church. They must seek to heal family members and friends who no longer speak to each other.

They must embrace the discouraged and despairing who have lost the capacity to hope. Briefly stated, they must energize all those who seek to approach Jesus but have nobody to transport them. Today's followers must reestablish all these lines of communication.

Tuesday: Mark 7:1-13 In verses 1-8 Mark discusses the problem of ritual purity involving the washing of hands and the distinction between clean and unclean foods. What is at stake is not the value of law but the interpretation of law. The larger question, however, is the concern for the Gentile mission, i.e., Gentiles do not have to become Jews before becoming Christians. In verse 6 Jesus challenges his opponents by citing the text of Isaiah 29:13. The Pharisees have placed purely human traditions on a higher level than the will of God. Hence they prefer to disregard that will in order to cling to their own machinations. In verses 7-13 Jesus continues his opposition to purely human traditions that subvert God's will by reference to the custom of *korban* (literally an "offering"). By declaring an offering *korban*, one directs money to the temple treasury that should be used in support of one's parents. Such a human tradition violates the Fourth Commandment, thus "nullify[ing] the word of God" (v. 13).

Reflection. For disciples, observing human laws must entail preserving human values. They are told to obey traffic laws but may not reflect enough on the values contained therein. They are obliged to pay taxes but may not question sufficiently the ways in which they are used. Too often they may be programmed to obey because commanded. In this passage Mark has Jesus speak to this quandary. Believers must ferret out the human values inherent in human laws. The good that God ultimately wills for humans must take precedence over any and all legislation that subverts that good. In the end, it is unreasonable and inhuman to obey merely because it is commanded.

Wednesday: Mark 7:14-23 This passage is greatly disputed. To achieve some balance, one must distinguish between the attitude of the historical Jesus and the conditions at the time of Mark's composition (ca. AD 70). Placed on the lips of the historical Jesus, the saying in verse 15 about what causes defilement would indicate his abrogation of Jewish ritual practices for his disciples. One must note that problems about food continued among the early Christian communities (see Acts 10:9-16). Hence it is most difficult to see the historical Jesus pronouncing all foods clean (v. 19).

The historical Jesus upholds the authority of the law but criticizes the potential misuse of ritual laws without abrogating them. At the time of the composition of Mark, however, a significantly different stage in the understanding of ritual laws occurs. In this period (around the time of the destruction of Jerusalem), Christians react against Jewish groups and their self-definition. In such circumstances they attribute to Jesus certain sayings that accommodate their attitude to Jewish law as the communities reach out more and more to the Gentiles.

Reflection. The entire episode raises the thorny question of the attitude of believers toward tradition. While disciples rightly preserve a healthy respect for tradition, they must constantly reassess traditional practices and customs. Their aim must not be moral laxity but a conscious effort to judge everything in the light of the church's developing awareness of what is purely human tradition and what is not. The biblical vision remains an enormous challenge in this difficult enterprise.

Thursday: Mark 7:24-30   Continuing to pursue Jesus' attitude toward the Gentiles, Mark sets this scene in the region of Tyre that includes Upper Galilee. Jesus' desire for privacy indicates the great notoriety he has gained. Prostrating herself before Jesus, a woman asks him to exorcise an unclean spirit from her little daughter. Mark describes her as a Greek, a Syrophoenician by birth—hence clearly a Gentile. This suppliant suffers from a double marginality: (1) a Gentile and (2) a woman.

Jesus responds to her request by insisting that the children (the Jews) are to be fed first. He further argues that it is not proper to take the food of the children and throw it to the dogs (the Gentiles). Jesus' reply acknowledges that his ministry encompasses only the Jews, not the Gentiles. Not to be outdone, the woman wittily responds that after the feeding of the children the dogs hope to receive a few crumbs. Jesus graciously accepts the woman's insight, assuring her that her little daughter has been healed. This healing from a distance suggests to Mark's audience the expectation that the proclamation of the Good News will be fruitful in the Gentile world.

Reflection. The remarkable feature in this episode is the woman's ability to get Jesus to change his mind. In other words, she enables Jesus to look at the whole situation with a different perspective. Hence she ministers to Jesus by getting him to extend his ministry to non-Jews. Such a unique passage must impact today's disciples. Too often there is the tendency to judge people and situations with prejudiced eyes. In so doing, one reacts according to the standard operating procedure. Believers may also need new spectacles to see past their prejudices and discover the truth. To achieve this, they must imitate the Syrophoenician woman. They must jar their foregone conclusions and attempt to see with the eyes of faith.

Friday: Mark 7:31-37   Mark employs this episode to depict his attitude toward the Gentiles. The geographical notice, namely, through the Gentile region of the Decapolis, serves to indicate his intent. The Gentiles who at one time were deaf and speech-impaired are now able to hear God and do him obeisance. This story of the cure of the deaf man with the speech impediment is different from Mark's usual miracle stories. Jesus' actions (putting fingers into the ears, spitting, and touching the tongue) are sacramental gestures, symbolizing the opening of the ears and the loosening of the tongue. By the use of the unique word for speech impediment (v. 32) Mark is clearly citing Isaiah 35:6. Hence the messianic age has arrived in Jesus. Two other features are noteworthy: (1) Jesus' groaning indicating great compassion for the sufferer and (2) the unusual reaction of the people—their amazement is unbounded.

Reflection. Today's disciples should be discriminating by preferring the underprivileged. They naturally tend to prefer the company of the elegant and the powerful—it is hard to identify with the disenfranchised. They may like to associate with those who can reimburse them—it is almost demeaning to be aligned with those who have no means of reimbursement. In today's passage, while the cure of the deaf man with the speech impediment serves a symbolic purpose in Mark, it is also another instance of concern for the underprivileged. Though Jesus dined at some exclusive eating places, he identified more easily with the underprivileged. For Mark's audience as well as for today's believers, the principle is this: be discriminating—prefer the underprivileged.

Saturday: Mark 8:1-10   This account of the feeding of the four thousand shares many similarities with that of the feeding of the five thousand (6:30-44). Such similarities include the people's lack of access to food, the disciples' questioning of Jesus' command to feed them, the references to the Old Testament (e.g., mention of the desert in verse 4), and the actions of giving thanks, breaking, etc. But this feeding occurs after two miracles in Gentile territory (7:24-30, 31-37)—hence an emphasis on the Gentile mission. Omitting mention of Jesus' teaching and his compassion for sheep without a shepherd, this account focuses on the compassion of Jesus for people who have stayed with him for three days and may collapse on the way home without sufficient food. Thinking of his own audience, Mark highlights a Jewish Jesus who reflects concern for Gentiles and Jews.

Reflection. While both feeding accounts underline the centrality of the Eucharist, this account accentuates to a greater degree the actual hunger of the people. This pressing need for physical nourishment must appeal to modern disciples. With an ever burgeoning world population the need for greater supplies of food has become all too paramount. Disciples, therefore, must join the ranks of those who operate food pantries, feed the homeless, and devise more efficient agricultural methods of increasing the world food supply. Disciples will do well to heed the Matthean Jesus: "I was hungry and you gave me food" (25:35).

The Sixth Week of the Year

Monday: Mark 8:11-13   Mark presents the Pharisees as Jesus' opponents in this rather secluded scene, quite different from the huge crowds that have previously mobbed him. They are seeking a sign from Jesus that will ratify the authority he has demonstrated and the power he has displayed. Their seeking clearly reveals hostile intent—they are testing him. Jesus' deep sigh captures the pain he is experiencing in this challenge and foreshadows his reply. After questioning their desire for an authenticating sign, Jesus flatly denies his willingness to accommodate them and dismisses them abruptly. Jesus has evidently emerged as the victor since his enemies do not appear again and have nothing to say in the discussion.

Reflection. This episode underlines the absolute need for faith on the part of modern followers. Mark introduced Jesus as insisting on the central role of faith: "repent, and believe in the good news" (1:15). In this scene he implicitly reiterates that demand. Of themselves miracles do not produce faith. Disciples must discover in Jesus' mighty works the person himself. Once disciples have accepted Jesus by believing him and believing in him, they are prepared to accept his message. The Revealer comes first and only then the revelation.

Tuesday: Mark 8:14-21 In this episode Mark reaches a climax in the theme of the failure of the Twelve to perceive some hidden meaning in what Jesus says or does. In this instance they do not grasp the meaning of the loaves. Jesus' seven questions capture his great disappointment at their slowness. Although the Twelve actively participated in Jesus' feeding miracles, they now show concern only for the fact that they are short of bread. They have failed to recognize that Jesus himself is the one loaf for both Jews (6:30-44) and Gentiles (8:1-10).

The leaven of the Pharisees and Herod (v. 15) recalls the Exodus background of the feeding accounts—at Passover and the feast of Unleavened Bread Jews had to get rid of all the old leaven. Jesus warns them to dismiss the obtuseness that prevents genuine recognition of his person. The ill will of the Pharisees and Herod now seems to have affected the Twelve. In the fourth question directed to the Twelve (v. 18) Jesus harshly criticizes them by citing Jeremiah 5:21. They are like Judah in failing to discern God's mighty deeds (see also Isa 6:9-10). Jesus' questions about the two feeding miracles, specifically about the number of baskets of leftovers (twelve = Jews, seven = Gentiles) probably have relevance for Mark's audience. Some Jewish Christians probably had difficulty celebrating the Eucharist with Gentile Christians. The blindness of the Twelve also foreshadows their misgiving about Jesus' passion and death.

Reflection. The sign of peace plays a significant role in the celebration of the Eucharist. In wishing the other participants peace, modern disciples implicitly pledge themselves to dismantle all those obstacles that make genuine communication impossible. Those obstacles no longer involve the acceptance of Gentile Christians by Jewish Christians. Rather, they may include disputes over wealth, status, power, and the like. By yielding to such prejudice and discrimination, today's followers of Jesus contribute to the destruction of genuine community. Like the Twelve, they fail to recognize that Jesus is indeed the one loaf that unites all the disparate factions in community. To celebrate Eucharist in a truly genuine way is to commit oneself to that unity demonstrated in the sign of peace.

Wednesday: Mark 8:22-26   Like the story of the deaf and speech-impaired man in 7:31-37, this account is also unique to Mark. One must note another feature, i.e., that Jesus is not immediately successful in healing the blind man. Only gradually does Jesus effect the gift of complete sight. Following the theme of the hardness of heart and blindness of the Twelve in the preceding episode, this scene possesses great symbolic value. It looks to the profession of faith that will occur in the next scene at Caesarea Philippi (8:27-29). Both scenes take place in secluded areas and demand two stages before sight is completely restored. Both accounts revolve around the theme of coming to faith. Like the blind man, the disciples will initially see people looking like trees walking. Only at a later stage will they see clearly. As Jesus and the Twelve begin the journey to Jerusalem, the revelation of the cross will command center stage. But the disciples will grasp this revelation only after Jesus' death and resurrection.

Reflection. Modern believers can feel right at home with the gradual recovery of sight by the blind man and the gradual insight of Jesus' followers. Faith very often commences with a blurry vision that attains greater clarity only in later stages. Not infrequently they must shrug their shoulders and complain that they do not fully understand. They experience the breakup of relationships, increasingly poor health, financial mishaps, the death of loved ones, etc. Such disastrous events may strike them as a huge maze in which they do not know which way to turn. Their vision is thus severely limited. In these moments the account of the blind man may offer some solace. Only gradually does he attain complete sight. Their progress is often the same. They are urged to trust the Healer who had similar experiences. The empty tomb lies in the shadow of the cross.

Thursday: Mark 8:27-33 This scene is both a beginning and an end. It is an end because it answers the question already suggested in so many passages of Mark: is Jesus the Messiah? It is also a beginning since it starts to qualify the type of Messiah, namely, a suffering Messiah. As the scene unfolds, Jesus asks what the outsiders think about his identity. The possible identifications include John the Baptist, Elijah, and one of the prophets. After these suggestions the insiders are invited to voice their opinion. Once Peter labels him the Messiah, Jesus issues a strict command not to tell anyone about him. At this point Jesus offers his own interpretation of Peter's perception. He will be nothing less than a suffering Son of Man (pain, rejection, and death) who will be vindicated after three days. Peter reacts by functioning as a prosecuting attorney (Satan) whose legal maneuverings stem from humans, not God. For Mark, one recognizes Jesus as Messiah only against the background of the cross and the resurrection. Anything else is simply a caricature.

Reflection. Will the real "me" please stand up? This scene in Mark addresses modern disciples in a most profound way. Like Jesus, they too are involved in the search for their true identity. They are naturally tempted to discover that identity by extrapolating models from the commercial, entertainment, and sports worlds. They thus like to see themselves as powerful, self-serving successes who command the highest respect for their achievements. This scene, however, urges them to find their models, not on Wall Street, in Hollywood, or at sports complexes, but on Calvary. The saying on the cross now reads: accept no substitutes—only Jesus will do.

Friday: Mark 8:34–9:1 In this first of Jesus' three passion predictions Mark reveals a threefold structure: (1) a statement by Jesus that he will suffer, die, etc.; (2) a misunderstanding by the disciples (here Peter's objection in 8:33); and (3) a clarification by Jesus. By such clarifications Mark has Jesus develop the notion of discipleship.

In this first clarification Jesus challenges disciples to follow him even to the cross, to deny themselves, and to save themselves by losing themselves on his account and that of the Gospel. For Mark, Jesus and the Gospel cannot be separated since they undergird the basis for the abandonment of the disciples' self-interest. Paradoxically one becomes one's true self only by giving up oneself. Even if following Jesus to the cross entails death, that death means eternal life so that death is ultimately profit, not loss. On the other hand, to gain the whole world and forfeit eternal life is loss, not profit. To be ashamed of Jesus and his message in this present life is to invite shame from Jesus when he appears in his glory at the end. (The passage concludes with Jesus' promise that some of his contemporaries will experience the kingdom of God with power before their death.)

Reflection. Genuine discipleship means nothing less than the demise of ego. Disciples find themselves only by losing themselves for others. The ultimate norm for all human behavior is the cross in that it captures the value and worth of service to others. In other words, the cross translates the Gospel message into the relentless command to find profit and gain in loss. The buck stops at Golgotha.

Saturday: Mark 9:2-13   The transfiguration of Jesus is an epiphany, i.e., a manifestation in which a divine figure or figures suddenly and unexpectedly appear and communicate something (in this case the command to listen to Jesus). Jesus himself becomes a heavenly figure (see the dazzling clothes in v. 3) in the company of Moses and Elijah who already belong to the heavenly realm. According to 2 Kings 2:11 Elijah ascended into heaven in a whirlwind. Although according to Deuteronomy 34:7 Moses died on Mount Nebo, in first-century AD tradition he just disappeared and returned to God.

While Moses and Elijah attained heavenly glory without the experience of death, Jesus will experience such glory only after suffering death at the hands of his own people. Coming as it does after the first passion prediction, this event assures Jesus that his Father will exonerate him. During the descent from the mountain Jesus commands silence about the event until his resurrection—a point that leads the three disciples to inquire about the return of Elijah. Jesus responds that Elijah has already returned in the person of John the Baptist, his precursor who suffered death for his prophetic role. Similarly the Son of Man will suffer much and be treated with contempt.

Reflection. It is historically likely that Jesus believed that his enemies would probably bring about his death and thus he would not complete his mission. In the transfiguration, however, he learned that he would achieve his mission precisely through his death. Like the Suffering

Servant (see Isa 52:13–53:12), Jesus realized that his death would benefit humanity and that his Father would intervene on his behalf. This episode offers modern disciples the courage to endure suffering, pain, and even death. These experiences are not unpleasant realities that must be avoided. Rather, they are the raw material that ultimately leads to glory. In turn, today's followers must have the courage to share this insight with their contemporaries. Glory and exoneration after pain and suffering are indeed a light at the end of the tunnel but it is a light flooding the world from the empty tomb.

The Seventh Week of the Year

Monday: Mark 9:14-29   In Jesus' journey to Jerusalem this is the only miracle story, specifically an exorcism. Despite manifestation of Jesus' glory in the transfiguration, the power of evil still persists and the faith of the disciples remains insufficient. In this episode Mark highlights the powerlessness of the disciples. While the boy evidently suffers from epilepsy, that culture traces all the symptoms back to demonic possession. Given Jesus' record of victory over the evil spirits, his berating of the disciples and the boy's father is hardly surprising.

After questioning the father about his son's "medical history," Jesus responds to his request (v. 22: "if you can do anything") by observing that faith sets no limits on God's power. The father then frankly admits that his faith is inadequate and, therefore, implores Jesus to intervene. At this point Jesus sternly commands the demon never to enter the boy again. As the demon violently departs, the boy is like a corpse. Jesus' action, however, of lifting the boy up so that he can stand reminds Mark's audience of Jesus' own resurrection. When alone with Jesus, the disciples inquire about their inability to exorcise the boy. Jesus replies that exorcisms are intrinsically linked to prayer since the exorcist cannot depend on his own power but only on that of God.

Reflection. Mark obviously employs this scene to address the pastoral needs of his community. For Mark, disciples must realize that without Jesus they cannot accomplish anything. If they are to share in Jesus' saving mission, they must join him through prayer. Prayer, therefore, is not merely one option among many for the success of the ministry of today's followers. Rather, prayer is an absolutely indispensable condition. Among other things, prayer assures modern disciples that they collaborate with Jesus in the ongoing proclamation of the Gospel. This union with him in prayer makes them ever aware of his abiding presence that empowers and energizes them. Prayer and ministry go hand in hand.

Tuesday: Mark 9:30-37   This scene is Mark's second passion prediction. He follows the same threefold structure as in 8:32-38: (1) statement by Jesus about his passion, death, etc. (v. 31); (2) the disciples' misunderstanding (vv. 32-34); and (3) Jesus' clarification about the true nature of discipleship (vv. 35-37). Jesus' example of the little child provides a fitting commentary on the nature of discipleship. In the Jewish and Greco-Roman worlds the child is not the object of contemporary American endearment. Being a child is rather precarious since it is totally subject to the authority of the head of the household. Hence the child symbolizes powerlessness and total dependence on others. Jesus points out that the stance of disciples should be the same. They should welcome the powerless and disenfranchised. This interprets first place in the kingdom, namely, being last of all and servant of all.

Reflection. The church presents the preferential option for the poor as the ideal object of ministry. Mark depicts Jesus as supporting such ministry by embracing a little child. Such a person lacks all power, prestige, and privilege. Thus the little child embodies the ideal outreach of modern disciples. In Mark, Jesus assures his disciples that to welcome such a child is, in the final analysis, to welcome his Father. Disciples, therefore, are bidden to discover in the powerless and disenfranchised the special object of the Father's loving care. To minister to them is to be rooted in the reciprocal love of the Father and the Son.

Wednesday: Mark 9:38-40   Mark uses this incident about a supposedly "nonrelated" exorcist to complement the second passion prediction. Here Jesus resists all "in-group" arrogance. God's power is not limited to the Jesus clientele. An outsider's performance of a miracle in Jesus' name is not an attack on Jesus. In effect, the outsider is really an insider since one remains a member of Jesus' community provided one does not separate oneself from Jesus.

Reflection. Dare to acknowledge the good no matter its venue. For some reason believers feel a certain reluctance in going outside the "club." They choose to find virtue and goodness only within the ranks of their select group. This episode in Mark, however, recommends that they eradicate such elitism. Whenever and wherever the Gospel becomes manifest in the goodness of others, modern disciples should join in the chorus of applause. Jesus' statement ("whoever is not against us is for us") applies to all venues across the board even when his name is not explicitly invoked.

Thursday: Mark 9:41-50 In this section Mark continues his "catchword" composition (linking sayings together by means of a key word or phrase). Thus the phrase "in my name" in 9:37 is linked to "in my name" in 9:39 and "you belong to Christ" in 9:41. In this last passage anyone who offers merely a drink of water will not be forgotten. No one has any right to despise a person who takes Jesus seriously. In verse 42 Jesus returns to the little child theme (see 9:30-37). The great millstone is a powerful image for expressing the heinousness of leading astray those who totally depend on God.

In another cluster of sayings Jesus uses the image of mutilation to emphasize that obedience to God and sharing community with him take priority over everything else. Hell or "Gehenna" derives from the Hebrew "Valley of Worthlessness"—a valley just south of Jerusalem where human sacrifice was once offered (see Jer 32:35). It later became the city dump for Jerusalem—hence the reference to perpetual fire. Verse 48 comes from Isaiah 66:24 that speaks of Gehenna's filth and smoldering fires. In verse 49 Mark employs the catchword "fire" (see 9:48). Though the meaning is obscure, it may refer to a holocaust victim that is salted prior to being consumed in flames and thus a possible allusion to the Christian's purification by the salt and fire of persecution. Finally Mark speaks of salt as a quality of the disciple that leads to communal peace, not quarrels.

Reflection. The battle of the individual versus the common good continues to rage for modern followers. In the saying about the parts of the body (head, foot, and eye) that may lead disciples into sin, Mark may be using metaphors that view the body as a community. If so, Mark may have in mind those people who hurt the community. In other words, all sin is essentially social. By personal sins they hurt the community that is the Body of Christ (to use Paul's phrase). Disciples are reminded that, while they derive their identity from the community, they must also contribute positively to that body. To overcome temptations symbolized by hand, foot, and eye is to advance the common good.

Friday: Mark 10:1-12   In this dispute concerning divorce the Pharisees cite Deuteronomy 24:1-4 according to which, in their view, Moses gives permission for a man to divorce his wife. In reply Jesus observes that Moses gave that commandment because the people failed to acknowledge the high demands of Genesis. According to those demands, marriage is a covenantal relationship in which loyalty is essential. Consequently the will of the Creator takes precedence over the permissive rule of Moses. For Jesus, the question is not: what is allowed or permitted? But: what does God intend? For Jesus, the married couple is God's handiwork and, therefore, not even Moses' authority can be invoked to annul it. The questioning scene back in the house shows that Mark is dealing with a Gentile audience since in Roman law, not Jewish law, a woman could initiate divorce proceedings against her husband. These concluding verses reinforce what Jesus has already said in his dispute with the Pharisees. Marriage after divorce is really adultery since the first marriage is still in effect.

Reflection. According to Jesus in Mark, marriage must reflect the covenant bond between husband and wife as seen in Genesis. In Genesis 2:23 the formula of flesh and bone is one of abiding loyalty, i.e., being faithful to each other through thick ("bone") and thin ("flesh"). In Genesis 2:24 a husband "clings" to his wife, i.e., he is committed to and supportive of his wife. Jesus seems to presuppose that covenantal loyalty embraces one's whole life and one's whole being. Marriage implies not abandonment but the ongoing pursuit of a love that includes forgiveness. The Creator's handiwork looks to unending mutual concern and mutual dedication. Married love and covenantal loyalty belong together.

Saturday: Mark 10:13-16   Mark paints a simple but moving scene in this passage. The mothers are most anxious to present their children to this famous teacher and miracle worker. The disciples, however, adopt an air of officiousness by urging the mothers not to bother their Master. Jesus then countermands their orders, takes the children into his arms, lays his hands on them, and blesses them. In this episode, therefore, Mark presents Jesus' attitude toward children. For Jesus, children have the right attitude about entering the kingdom since they are willing to accept what is freely given. In order to share in that kingdom, disciples must display that same simplicity and accept the kingdom as a gift freely bestowed. The use of the verb "to hinder" (v. 14) may suggest that this passage plays some part in the discussion of infant baptism (see Acts 8:37; 10:47).

Reflection. As the Giver of gifts par excellence, God offers the kingdom as nothing less than pure grace. The kingdom is a reality that transcends human capacity to manufacture or attain by dint of strenuous efforts. Modern followers must receive the gift of the kingdom like children. Well known for their simplicity and honesty (parents always worry about what their children will blurt out in public), children do not enjoy power or independence. Their attitude of awe and amazement captures the proper outlook for all would-be recipients of the kingdom. They are Jesus' model for all those invited to see that kingdom as the highpoint of God's gift giving.

The Eighth Week of the Year

Monday: Mark 10:17-27   Mark shows Jesus as a recognized rabbi who can provide answers in religious matters. Obviously the rich man is seeking more than the observance of the commandments. Everlasting life for him means getting rid of anything that keeps him from following Jesus, in this case his wealth. But such a demand is simply too great. Jesus reacts to the difficulty of the rich to enter the kingdom. Wealth is no indicator of God's good pleasure. In this case it is an obstacle—like a camel trying to pass through the eye of a needle. Jesus finally resolves the disciples' astonishment by noting that purely human efforts cannot attain salvation. On the other hand, everything is possible with God (see Gen 18:14).

Reflection. The wise are able to let go. In this episode the rich man is searching for wisdom, specifically everlasting life. Jesus, as the wisdom teacher, focuses on the ultimate reality, namely, letting go and following him. The rich man, however, opts to keep his wealth and thereby refuses to let go. This scene must impact modern followers in their search for wisdom. While wealth creates the great obstacle for the rich man, modern disciples may encounter other barriers. For example, excessive pride in one's accomplishments, the lust for ever increasing dominance over others, spending exorbitant amounts of time on purely personal pleasure, etc., all too easily distract disciples from gaining true wisdom. Today's episode challenges disciples to let go, focus time and energy on the one thing lacking, and thus attain the elusive gift of wisdom.

Tuesday: Mark 10:28-31   Mark connects this scene with the previous episode. Unlike the rich man, the disciples have left everything. Peter is implicitly asking what they can expect from such renunciation. In his reply Jesus employs three categories: home, relatives, and property. In Mark Jesus is relating these forms of renunciation not only to himself but also to the Gospel. For such generosity these disciples will receive rewards in the present as well as in the future (eternal life). Among the rewards in this life Jesus promises a new family and new possessions. Significantly this new family does not depend on actual kinship relationships but on divine power. Mark also remarks that this new family will also experience persecutions. Such a sobering observation reminds Mark's audience of the all too real world in which they live.

Reflection. Jesus invites modern followers to realize that they belong to an extended family. Christian community means that they are not isolated individuals who do not enjoy a sense of belonging. Rather, they are sisters and brothers who can claim support, understanding, and compassion from this community. While disciples can thus anticipate such care and attention, they must also contribute to the community by sharing their gifts and talents. Family honor demands such generosity. The celebration of the Eucharist, in particular, should strengthen the bonds that promote this family unity.

Wednesday: Mark 10:32-45   In this third passion prediction Mark follows the same structure as before: (1) statement by Jesus about his passion, death , etc. (vv. 33-34; here the details are greatly expanded);

(2) the disciples' misunderstanding (vv. 35-41); and (3) Jesus' clarification about the true nature of discipleship (vv. 42-45). James and John have obviously failed to comprehend the mystery of the cross by their request for prestigious positions in the kingdom. Mark has Jesus respond by implicitly linking the cup to his ordeal in the garden where he asks his Father to remove the cup (14:36). Sitting at Jesus' right and left anticipates Calvary where Jesus will be crucified with bandits, one on his right and one on his left (15:27). In his clarification Jesus points out that Gentile rulers lord it over their subjects and their great ones make their authority felt. Among Jesus' disciples, however, real honor consists in serving and becoming the slave of all. Jesus summarizes this theology in verse 45: to serve and not to be served and, like the Suffering Servant, to give one's life as a ransom for all (see Isa 53:12).

Reflection. Titles are tools for interpreting service. In 10:45 Jesus interprets the Son of Man title in terms of serving, not being served. He then expands that title by joining it to the Suffering Servant theme of giving his life for the ransom of all. The passage is calculated to challenge modern followers to do the same, i.e., to interpret their titles in terms of service to others. For example, bosses should see their titles not as a means of demanding recognition but as an endless series of opportunities to serve their employees. Similarly teachers should view their titles as the occasion for promoting the good of their pupils, especially the less talented. Married couples should look at their title of "Mr. and Mrs." as a pledge of ongoing mutual support and concern. Ultimately all disciples must become interpreters who translate their titles into courses of action that will benefit others. The cross on Calvary serves as the most riveting symbol of the challenge to serve, not to be served.

Thursday: Mark 10:46-52 This scene climaxes Jesus' ministry of healing and teaching and provides the transition to his ministry in Jerusalem. In the other direction, it is a decided contrast to the request of James and John (10:37) and shows that the blind man Bartimaeus understands the nature of Jesus' messiahship. The story has great symbolic value. Only those who experience Jesus' exaltation through suffering can have their eyes opened to his significance. This demands great perseverance. Hence the blind man must overcome great odds in communicating his request and then in following Jesus down the road of discipleship. For Mark, the accent falls on the man's faith, not on the miracle. This is the type of faith that the true follower of Jesus should possess.

Reflection. The great discovery is to find values in others. Modern followers of Jesus are tempted to retreat into the sanctuary and arsenal of their own person when they find it hard to uncover values in others. They are often shocked by the inhumanity of people and resolve to remain insensitive to any possible values in them. In this scene from Mark, however, Jesus discovers the value of true recognition in Bartimaeus and promptly heals him. The discovery process of Jesus must become the discovery process of today's followers. They are urged to look beyond externals and uncover the good qualities of family and friends but also of competitors and even opponents. Shakespeare lamented that the good performed by others is "oft interred with their bones." Believers are asked to reverse the process by discovering the person of Jesus in the character of others and the values that lie hidden there.

Friday: Mark 11:11-26   Here Mark once again follows his practice of beginning a story, interrupting it with a second story, and then resuming the original story ("sandwiching"). Accordingly Mark has: (1) the cursing of the fig tree (vv. 12-14); (2) the cleansing of the temple (vv. 15-19); and (3) the withered fig tree (vv. 20-21) followed by an instruction of faith and prayer (vv. 22-26). The symbolic actions of cursing the fig tree so that it withers and cleansing the temple interpret each other. The withered fig tree may possibly represent Israel's failure as a whole to accept Jesus as God's envoy and his message about the kingdom. The cleansing of the temple may possibly symbolize Jesus' critique of the extreme commercialization conducted there so that it too will suffer the fate of the fig tree. In verses 22-26 Jesus provides an instruction on faith and prayer. Since the withering of the fig tree demonstrates God's power at work in Jesus, this instruction is probably intended to show that disciples can also participate in this power through faith and prayer.

Reflection. Not a few modern disciples are hard-pressed to take Jesus' instruction on faith and prayer to heart. To have faith so as to transport a mountain into the sea and to pray with the assurance that the petition will certainly be granted strike such followers as simply too overwhelming. But why doubt the enormous power of faith and prayer? In a world of ceaseless technological breakthroughs, faith and prayer have assumed a distant second place. Nevertheless, Jesus in Mark more than suggests that confident prayer based on faith can achieve unfathomable results. In this episode faith and prayer outstrip the temple cult as the path to God. In modern life faith and prayer deserve their proper place in the journey to God.

Saturday: Mark 11:27-33   This scene is the first of five controversy stories in this section of Mark (11:27–12:37). Here the chief priests, scribes, and elders approach Jesus in the temple area and question him about the source of his authority. Instead of responding directly, Jesus chooses to pose a counterquestion about the authority behind John's baptism. His opponents soon realize that they are caught on the horns of a dilemma. If they acknowledge that John's baptism comes from God, then Jesus will ask why they did not accept it. If they admit that it is merely a human creation, then they will find themselves in danger of losing popular support. Their admission of ignorance reveals Jesus' clever strategy. It is worth noting that the controversy involves a more important issue. The chief priests, scribes, and elders represent the central role of the Jerusalem temple while John and Jesus stand for the proclamation of the kingdom of God.

Reflection. The source of authority remains a key issue for believers. In this scene Mark states unequivocally that the authority of John and Jesus stems from God. In everyday life disciples duly acknowledge that the exercise of genuine authority, whether ecclesiastical, civil, or domestic (e.g., that of parents) must command both respect and obedience. When the bearers of authority abuse their power for purely selfish gain, however, disciples must react. Among other things they must investigate the reasons for laws, decisions, policies, etc. The exercise of authority merits the public scrutiny of disciples so that the common good, not personal aggrandizement, is served.

The Ninth Week of the Year

Monday: Mark 12:1-12   The parable of the vineyard (vv. 1b-9) consists of: (1) the setting (v. 1b); (2) the owner's dispatching of servants and their fate at the hands of the tenant farmers (vv. 2-5); (3) the owner's sending of his own son and his mistreatment (vv. 6-8); and (4) the owner's retaliation against the tenant farmers (v. 9). To this Mark has added an Old Testament fulfillment quote (vv. 10-11) from Psalm 118:22-23 that interprets the parable (the tenant farmers = the builders). Both fail to recognize the significance of the one(s) mistreated. Finally Mark places the parable and the biblical passage in the setting of the rejection of Jesus by the Jerusalem leaders (vv. 1a, 12) so that he figures as the son/stone. The use of the song of the vineyard (Isa 5:1-7) and Israel's history of refusing their prophets' message focus in its final form on Jesus and God's action against the leaders who reject him. At the same time the use of Psalm 118 also anticipates God's dramatic intervention in the resurrection of his beloved Son.

Reflection. The patience of the owner in sending the delegations of servants and finally his own son recalls the long-suffering of Israel's God who waits for a faithful response from his people. The scene speaks today to the ongoing relationship between God and God's people. Modern followers must not construe that relationship as merely meeting obligations and thus receiving the appropriate reward. While such an arrangement has its place, it does not adequately express the response of privileged people to their generous God. Morality must transcend the limits of duties and rewards. It must envision a relationship in which daughters and sons acknowledge the love of their God in free and generous response.

Tuesday: Mark 12:13-17   In this second of the five controversy stories Jesus' opponents (the chief priests, scribes, and elders), having lost out to him in the dispute over John's baptism (11:27-33) and having seen themselves as the target in his parable of the vineyard (12:1-12), now enlist the support of some Pharisees and Herodians. They endeavor to trap Jesus into making controversial statements, such as paying the Roman census tax. Having accepted a Roman coin from them and having asked about its image and inscription, Jesus adroitly answers that one should give to Caesar the things that are Caesar's and to God the things that are God's. Utterly astonished, the Pharisees and Herodians depart in silence. For Mark's audience (probably Roman), this saying of Jesus would probably assure non-Christians that Jesus did not oppose cooperation with the government and its officials.

Reflection. Achieving a healthy balance in life proves to be no easy matter for modern believers. What belongs to Caesar and what belongs to God do not admit of any facile mathematical equation. But perhaps disciples could ask which area (civil or divine) they are more likely to emphasize. In most cases they would probably give the edge to Caesar. This seemingly innocuous episode, therefore, may serve as a powerful reminder that, in determining the proper balance, they should be more prone to favor God over Caesar. The great commandment is still to love God with all one's heart, mind, soul, and strength and to love one's neighbor as oneself (12:30-31).

Wednesday: Mark 12:18-27 This third controversy story focuses on Jesus' debate with the Sadducees about the resurrection. As a sect within Judaism, the Sadducees constitute a rather conservative group, denying not only the afterlife but also the existence of angels and revelation apart from the Torah/Pentateuch. To demonstrate the absurdity of an afterlife, specifically resurrection, the Sadducees appeal to the levirate law in Deuteronomy 25:5-6 whereby a man is obliged to marry his deceased brother's wife if he leaves no son. They propose the case of seven brothers who, in turn, married the same woman without producing a son. At the resurrection, therefore, whose wife will she be since she married all seven brothers?

Jesus responds to his opponents by first accusing them of a twofold ignorance, namely, of the Scriptures and of divine power (v. 24). Jesus then challenges the basic assumption of his interrogators that human relationships prior to death persist in life after death. After denying this, Jesus asserts that the resurrected are like angels in heaven (v. 25). Regarding the Scriptures Jesus refers to the episode of the burning bush in Exodus 3, noting the thrice repeated phrase "the God of Abraham, the God of Isaac, and the God of Jacob" (Exod 3:3, 15, 16). Jesus concludes this citation with the statement that God is not the God of the dead but of the living (v. 27).

Reflection. In this episode Jesus bases hope of the resurrection on faith in the God of the patriarchs who, though dead, are still alive. Jesus further grounds his argument on the character of God as a God of the living, not the dead. This scene must impact how modern followers think of the resurrection. They are challenged to recall those prophetic passages, like Ezekiel 37, that speak of God's power to restore life. They are also urged to return to Genesis 1–2 where God presides as the source of all life. The mention of Abraham, Isaac, and Jacob must evoke for modern disciples the notion of community. Resurrection, therefore, means the regrouping of a family achieved by divine power.

Thursday: Mark 12:28-34   This debate about the great commandment(s) does not constitute any type of controversy or dispute. It resembles more of a conversation between Jesus as teacher and the scribe as pupil. The scribe poses the question about which commandment is the first of all, but Jesus labels it the greatest. Out of the 248 commandments and 365 prohibitions in the Torah, Jesus chooses two that give meaning and validity to all the others, namely, Deuteronomy 6:4-5 and Leviticus 19:18. If there is anything new in Jesus' response, it consists of putting the two commandments together and thus making one commandment out of two. What is significant is that Jesus incorporates this combination into his own lifestyle. He welcomes human beings whom others despise (see 2:16-17; 10:14). He is also obedient to his Father up to the very end (see 14:36). At the end of the scene the scribe's reaction is prophetic. Jesus' great commandment is a sacrificial love that has greater value than the usual sacrificial offerings (see Hos 6:6).

Reflection. This passage continues to speak to the situation of today's disciples. Although Jesus combines love of God and love of neighbor to form one great commandment, modern followers may too often prefer to choose love of God over love of neighbor. Experience teaches that God never gets in their way—only other people do. Jesus, however, realizes that, in order to love his Father, he must also love fellow humans. For Jesus, it can never be *either* love of God *or* love of neighbor. It must be *both* love of God *and* love of neighbor. Modern followers have really no choice. Their love must be *both/and*, not *either/or*.

Friday: Mark 12:35-37 In this scene Jesus has no opponents. He simply raises the biblical question about the Messiah as the Son of David. The whole matter involves Psalm 110:1 that employs the word "lord" twice, i.e., God ("the Lord") speaks to the newly anointed king ("my lord"). Since David is believed to have composed the psalms and since the Messiah is a Son of David (a royal figure), one must conclude that the Messiah has to be more than David and a son of David since David speaks of him as "my lord." While there was no normative notion of a Messiah at the time of Jesus, there was a tradition that anticipated a Davidic Messiah who would crush Israel's enemies and establish a holy people. Obviously Psalm 110:1 easily lent itself to such an expectation. For Mark, although Jesus is properly hailed as the Messiah and the Son of David, he possesses a dignity that far surpasses these titles. He is Lord and, therefore, on a level with the God of Israel.

Reflection. The abundant use of royal language in Mark must force disciples to pause and evaluate such language. While Mark and his community acknowledge Jesus as the Messiah and the Son of David, they must situate the use of these titles in the shadow of the cross. His inscription reads "The King of the Jews" (15:26). But on this royal throne he has two bandits as attendants, one on his right and another on his left. The chief priests and the scribes taunt him, urging "the Messiah, the King of Israel" to come down from the cross so that they may believe (15:32). The centurion, however, observing the manner of his death, acknowledges that he is truly "God's Son" (15:39). Cross and crown are inseparably linked both for Jesus and modern followers.

Saturday: Mark 12:38-44 "Widow" is apparently a catchword that binds the two stories together: (1) the denunciation of the scribes (vv. 38-40); and (2) the poor widow's offering (vv. 41-44). In the first story Mark depicts Jesus' final break with official Judaism (contrast the sheer delight of the people in 12:37). Jesus charges the scribes with (1) ostentation in dress and greeting, (2) the pursuit of places of honor in the synagogues and banquets, (3) long-winded prayers, and (4) exploitation of the helpless (widows).

In the second story the widow's offering demonstrates true Jewish piety—the very opposite of that practice by the scribes. By having Jesus summon his disciples (v. 43), Mark alerts his audience to the significance of the scene. Jesus' analysis is that the widow in effect offers *herself* while the others offer only *something*. By putting in two copper coins, she surrenders herself entirely to God.

Reflection. Modern disciples may find it relatively easy to contribute something to worthwhile causes but much more difficult to contribute themselves. They may find it relatively easy to proffer lip service to social justice but much more difficult to proffer themselves. By contrast, the widow in this episode presents an enormous challenge to today's followers. By putting in two small copper coins, she puts in everything. The wealthy, on the other hand, contribute more but actually give less. They do not commit themselves totally. Only the widow is capable of surrendering everything and thereby surrendering herself. For modern disciples she recommends that they give themselves, not merely something.

The Lenten Season

Ash Wednesday: Matthew 6:1-6, 16-18   In this section of his Sermon on the Mount Matthew considers three forms of Jewish piety: (1) almsgiving (vv. 2-4), (2) prayer (vv. 5-6), and (3) fasting (vv. 16-18). He begins with the general exhortation to avoid Pharisaic ostentation and to focus on the real audience, namely, the heavenly Father (v. 1). The notion of rewards reveals that God regards humans very seriously and takes into account their actions. With regard to almsgiving Jesus excoriates all publicity seeking (blowing a trumpet). Disciples should observe complete secrecy in their almsgiving such that their left hand remains unaware of the actions of the right hand. Concerning prayer Jesus likewise rules out all show and ostentation. Instead, he recommends that disciples look for something like a storeroom and shut themselves in. With regard to fasting, Jesus rejects all external display (disfiguring one's face) that will draw people's attention to their piety. Rather, they should appear quite normal (oil on their head and their faces washed). The Father who sees in secret will not forget to reward them.

Reflection. As Lent begins, many modern disciples take time out to consider what items they will give up, e.g., alcohol, special kinds of food, candy, etc. While such practices are clearly laudable and are traditional, perhaps today's followers could consider other areas of penance and conversion. They may find it profitable and challenging to visit the shut-ins and the homebound. They may also see that seeking out the distraught and discouraged and offering them hope captures the spirit of Lent. They may consider volunteering at food pantries or meals-on-wheels. These Lenten practices shift the focus. Instead of concentrating on personal practices such as prayer and fasting, these suggested practices compel disciples to look beyond themselves to the hurting members of God's extended family. In so doing, they avoid Jesus' criticism in this passage, i.e., neglecting God as one's true audience.

Thursday after Ash Wednesday: Luke 9:22-25   This is Luke's first passion prediction that follows upon Peter's confession of Jesus as the Messiah of God. This scene, moreover, provides a background as Jesus prepares to set out on his journey to Jerusalem where he will endure his prophetic fate. In this passage Luke has three sayings, the first of which (v. 23: self-denial and carrying the cross) sets the tone for the other two (vv. 24, 25). Here Jesus does not hesitate to challenge all who would follow him. For Luke (unlike his source Mark) disciple-ship involves a *daily* share in Jesus' destiny. The way of the Master must be the way of the follower. Like Simon of Cyrene (23:26), disciples must carry the cross *behind* Jesus. In the second saying (a proper assess-ment of one's life in relation to Jesus and his cause) Jesus resembles a field commander urging his troops before battle. In the third saying Jesus demands that his disciples adjust their priorities, i.e., achieving earthly gain and success but losing one's real self. Simply put, journey-ing to Jerusalem behind Jesus is demanding.

Reflection. Unlike his source Mark, Luke stresses the *daily* carrying of the cross in the life of the disciple. While this exhortation applies to the disciple's entire trek with Jesus to Jerusalem, it seems to enjoy a special poignancy during Lent. The modern disciple must view each day of this special season as a summons and challenge to begin anew. The disciple must daily focus on the end of Jesus' journey, namely, Jerusalem and the cross. To carry one's cross each day is to share the company of the Spirit-driven prophet who resolutely sets his face to go to Jerusalem (9:51). During this Lenten season the disciple must relive the determination of Jesus: "Yet today, tomorrow, and the next day I must be on my way, because it is impossible for a prophet to be killed outside of Jerusalem" (13:33).

Friday after Ash Wednesday: Matthew 9:14-15   Unlike his source Mark, Matthew has only the disciples of John the Baptist approach Jesus and ask why his disciples, unlike the disciples of John and the Pharisees, do not fast. (The reference is to private, not public fasts.) In reply, Jesus, equating fasting with mourning, explains that he, the bridegroom, and his disciples, the wedding guests, must join in the joy and happiness of the wedding feast. To fast at such a time is tantamount to mourning and hence out of the question. Jesus does add, however, that his disciples will fast at the appropriate time, namely, after the bridegroom's departure (Jesus' death). For Matthew, in this in-between time, i.e., the time between Jesus' departure and his second coming, fasting is indeed appropriate.

Reflection. The church continues to live in this in-between phase: "Christ has died, Christ is risen, Christ will come again." In this period between the resurrection and the second coming modern disciples must strike a healthy balance. They must derive joy from the fact that the kingdom has come near. But they must also exercise caution from the fact that the kingdom has not fully come. Lent, therefore, provides a special time for helping to promote the coming of the kingdom in various ways. Certainly fasting has its place here. Modern believers are also challenged, however, to discover ever new ways to announce that the kingdom is still in the process of coming. Such ways can include reaching out to the poor, to the unemployed and the underemployed, the elderly, etc. This reaching out implies discovering the image of Jesus in all such people (see Matt 25:31-46). It also implies that, while the kingdom has not yet totally arrived, it is well on its way.

Saturday after Ash Wednesday: Luke 5:27-32   This passage combines two scenes: (1) the call of Levi (vv. 27-28) and (2) Jesus' conflict with the Pharisees and scribes about association with tax collectors and sinners (vv. 29-32). In its present form the account seeks to answer the question in the early Christian community as to why Jesus ate with such unacceptable types (tax collectors and sinners). The answer comes from Jesus' two sayings: (1) only the sick need a doctor (v. 31); and (2) Jesus calls sinners to repentance, not the righteous (v. 32). It is worth noting that Luke sees mere association with Jesus (throwing a banquet) as inadequate. For Luke, one must also follow Jesus as a disciple committed to total conversion. To exemplify this point, Luke observes that Levi leaves everything (v. 28).

Reflection. Lent poses critical questions about discipleship. Is it enough just to know about Jesus, quote some of his sayings, and then do as one pleases? Or is it necessary to follow Jesus on the journey to Jerusalem, abide by his message, and find fulfillment on Calvary? While the first option is more congenial, the second is more demanding and realistic. Disciples must recognize that to know Jesus in their heart and to do nothing else leaves more than a little to be desired. As sinners, believers must respond to Jesus' call to discipleship by attempting to live the Gospel message in daily life. Only this type of association meets all the requirements for following him.

The First Week of Lent

Monday: Matthew 25:31-46   In this segment of his eschatological discourse (24:1–25:46) Matthew reveals the implications of fidelity and vigilance that he already treated earlier in this fifth and last great discourse. Vigilance and fidelity are now reduced to recognizing the Son of Man in those whom the world labels of no account: the hungry, thirsty, strangers, naked, ill, and imprisoned. The standard or basis of judgment is the recognition or nonrecognition of these sisters and brothers of the Son of Man.

Here Jesus appears in all the trappings of regal splendor. As king, he sits upon the royal throne. He also exercises his kingship by his role as shepherd. As a shepherd separates sheep from goats at night, so the Son of Man separates the blessed from the condemned. Fittingly the sheep enjoy the place of honor on the right while the goats are placed on the left. In the dialogue with the two groups, what emerges is a christological criterion. The Son of Man—the king/shepherd—identifies with all those who suffer. The "least ones" are all those who experience any form of need. The christological criterion thereby becomes ecumenical.

Reflection. Disciples must accept a God of disguises. Modern followers naturally prefer to deal with the Son of Man in all his royal trappings. This judgment scene, however, must force them to look elsewhere. Jesus has chosen to disguise himself in the outcasts, the neglected, the unacceptable. Disciples, therefore, must circumvent the externals and look ever deeper into the character of these people. Once they have penetrated the exterior, they will discover the image of the Son of Man. Upon discovering that image, they will hear the reassuring words: "Truly I tell you, just as you did it to one of the least of these who are members of my family, you did it to me" (v. 40).

Tuesday: Matthew 6:7-15   In this section of the Sermon on the Mount, Matthew divides his treatment of prayer into three parts: (1) an exhortation not to follow the pagan practice of babbling (vv. 7-8), (2) the Our Father (vv. 9-13), and (3) a saying on forgiveness (vv. 14-15). After rejecting pagan loquaciousness as a form of prayer, Jesus presents the Our Father as the proper model. It begins with addressing God as their heavenly Father, an opening that captures the family dimension of Matthew's community. Then there follow three "thou" petitions: (1) that God's name be sanctified, (2) that his kingdom come, and (3) that his will be done perfectly on earth. Next come three "we" petitions: (1) that they receive daily sustenance, (2) that their sins be forgiven, and (3) that God protect them from the evil one in the final testing. The final petition on forgiveness (vv. 14-15) enhances the request for forgiveness in the Our Father. Thus disciples who mutually forgive receive the Father's forgiveness; those who do not mutually forgive cannot receive the Father's forgiveness.

Reflection. While this entire section provides a treasure trove for prayer and subsequent action, the demand for mutual forgiveness calls for greater attention. One reason for such attention is that the passage highlights mutual forgiveness twice, namely, in the Our Father and in the final saying. Modern followers, like followers of all ages, experience hurt and pain when others, not infrequently friends and family members, offend them. They naturally react like this: "Hell will freeze over before I forgive you!" At such times Jesus' admonition to forgive each other must enjoy a conspicuous place in the lives of believers. They must realize that, in forgiving each other, they are imitating the forgiveness of their heavenly Father. "Father" captures the right aspect since, in forgiving, disciples recognize and act upon their membership in God's extended family.

Wednesday: Luke 11:29-32   As Jesus makes his way to his destiny in Jerusalem, Luke employs this sign of Jonah to answer those critics who earlier demanded a sign of credibility from him (see 11:16). Jesus responds that he will be a sign to this generation as Jonah was to the people of Nineveh. Luke accentuates not only the person of the prophet but also his preaching that resulted in Nineveh's total conversion. Like Jonah, Jesus is a prophet but also something greater than Jonah. Jesus then introduces the account of the queen of Sheba (see 1 Kgs 10:1-29) who came from the ends of the earth to hear the wisdom of Solomon. But Jesus, the wisdom teacher par excellence, is greater than Solomon. At the judgment the Ninevites and the queen of Sheba (all pagans) will rise to accuse all who challenged the One greater than both Jonah and Solomon.

Reflection. Disciples should be slow to criticize those who challenged Jesus by demanding a sign of credibility. They too are tempted to require something more spectacular than the Gospel message to authenticate Jesus' teaching. Private revelations would seem to satisfy their requirement. Today's passage, however, must compel modern followers to reassess the preaching of Jesus. In reviewing the Gospel message, will they recognize the One greater than Jonah and Solomon? Will they find a form of wisdom there that needs no further authentication? In this passage Luke responds that the message of the Spirit-driven prophet from Nazareth who journeys to the city of destiny finds all its authentication and credibility in the cross. Nothing further is required.

Thursday: Matthew 7:7-12   This passage consists of two components: (1) the admonition to pray (vv. 7-11) and (2) the Golden Rule (v. 12). The commands to ask, search, and knock betray a strong sense of urgency. The reactions of God in giving, making available, and opening, however, reveal a complementary sense of assurance. Disciples should display all possible confidence in making these petitions since they are family members addressing their Father. If human fathers who are sinful take pleasure in meeting the requests of their children, how much more will their heavenly Father attend to their needs? At the end of the passage Jesus quotes the Golden Rule. Although this popular moral teaching is not original with Jesus, Matthew presents Jesus as calling it "the law and the prophets" (v. 12). Here popular wisdom and the message of Jesus are not strange bedfellows.

Reflection. Persevering prayer troubles disciples of all times and ages. They pray and pray for a particular need or problem but nothing seems to happen. Discouragement, abandonment, and frustration soon set in. They want to throw up their arms and walk away, shaking their heads as they do so. At this point Jesus' exhortation in this section of the Sermon on the Mount may lift their sagging spirits. They are urged to continue asking, searching, and knocking. They are assured that their God will respond. Ultimately such prayer is grounded in family relationships. They address God as their Father and Jesus as their Brother. If less than perfect parents provide for their children, will their Father and their Brother do less?

Friday: Matthew 5:20-26 This passage establishes the relationship of the Mosaic Law to Jesus. For Matthew, Jesus stands at the very center of religion. Righteousness, namely, the moral living out of God's will, demands that disciples go beyond the legalistic attitude of the Pharisees. It must be a matter of their total self-giving to God and neighbor.

Matthew 5:21-48 is a series of six antitheses that exemplify the principle propounded in verse 20. The section contrasts what God once said with what Jesus now says. The first antithesis (vv. 21-26) radicalizes the Mosaic prohibition against murder. Anger toward one's neighbor is as detestable as murder, since the neighbor's dignity must be respected. To emphasize this point, Matthew has Jesus articulate the crime and its appropriate punishment: (1) anger—judgment or local court; (2) insult—council or Sanhedrin; and (3) calling one a fool—hell. Committing any of these things falls under the legal category of murder. In verses 23-26 Jesus discusses the obligation of reconciliation. To be reconciled with God, one must first be reconciled with one's sister or brother. Here Jesus appeals to liturgy and the final judgment. Offering a gift to God without being first reconciled to sister or brother prevents reconciliation with God. Before a plaintiff introduces legal proceedings, i.e., while one is still living, the accused must settle accounts or be condemned to eternal punishment.

Reflection. In this passage Jesus demands such profound respect for a person's dignity that anger is tantamount to murder. Modern believers must take this radical demand to heart. Instead of avoiding disparaging remarks about a person, however, disciples can accentuate the positive. Such an approach requires disciples to search out the good in a person's character and publicize it. This may demand at times some searching on the part of disciples but it is a positive way to follow Jesus' radical demand. In the end, disciples must resort to the opening chapter of Genesis where God creates humans in his image and likeness. To announce the positive qualities of a person is to join in the chorus of "It is good, very good."

Saturday: Matthew 5:43-48   In this sixth and final antithesis Jesus does not reject Leviticus 19:18 (the Torah did not command hatred of one's neighbor). Here Jesus addresses those who believe that the enemy of the just person or the enemy of Israel thereby becomes God's enemy and should be handled appropriately. Rejecting this view, Jesus simply eliminates all limitations on love because this is how the Father acts. Hence disciples must love their enemies and pray for their persecutors. Jesus also observes that the Father provides for everyone because he refuses to exclude anyone from his love. The you-scratch-my-back-and-I'll-scratch-yours attitude of the pagans and the tax collectors is declared to be unworthy of Jesus' disciples. The manner of the Father ("perfect") must be the manner of the disciple.

Reflection. Disciples continue to face the problem of dealing with full-fledged enemies as well as with those who denigrate or belittle them. In handling these situations, they naturally search for a moral guide or compass. Their first reaction may be to disregard all such people or at least avoid all possible contact with them. Keeping them at arm's length seems an all too viable strategy. But this final antithesis in the Sermon on the Mount suggests an alternative strategy: love your enemies and pray for your persecutors. Labeling this command unrealistic or utopian simply will not do. In the final analysis the style of the Father must become the style of the disciple. The Father sets no limitations on love: "he makes his sun rise on the bad and the good, and causes rain to fall on the just and the unjust" (v. 45).

The Second Week of Lent

Monday: Luke 6:36-38 In this passage from Luke's Sermon on the Plain (6:17-49) that is comparable to Matthew's Sermon on the Mount (5:1–7:29), Jesus addresses love of one's enemies (v. 36) and love among disciples themselves (vv. 37-38). With regard to love of enemies Jesus commands that disciples imitate one specific quality of the Father, namely, mercy. Such imitation functions as a transition to the next topic, namely, the issue of judging that also demands the application of God's mercy.

In this set of norms Luke has: (1) not judging/not condemning (v. 37a); (2) forgiving (v. 37b); and (3) giving/good measure (v. 38a). In verse 38b Luke provides the motivation: "the measure with which you measure will in return be measured out to you." Judging has to do with finding fault or criticizing other followers, not a judicial process. In turn, mercy in judging should lead to mercy in giving. Forgiveness of other disciples will also lead to God's forgiveness. The full or good measure captures the disciple's way of acting, implying a merciful measure in judging, forgiving, and giving. Such generosity will result in a superabundant harvest of divine rewards.

Reflection. Believers can readily distinguish constructive and destructive criticism. In this passage the accent falls on the latter. Disciples are urged not to spend their time in finding fault with others. Perhaps disciples would do well to emphasize the positive dimension, namely, finding good in others. For some reason there is a blatant tendency to overlook the enormous amount of good in others in order to concentrate on the minimal amount of evil. One cannot see the forest for the trees. In this passage Jesus commands a love of fellow disciples that can be translated into the search for the good. While the bad qualities of others always come to the surface, the good ones unfortunately often lie submerged. Jesus demands that disciples reverse the process.

Tuesday: Matthew 23:1-12 Matthew 23 is the author's condemnation of Pharisaic Judaism. His audience is twofold: (1) the crowds and (2) Jewish Christians excommunicated from the synagogue as heretics. The object of the various sayings is the scribes and Pharisees, i.e., the

Jewish leadership opposing the Christian community. By their interpretation of the law, these forces of opposition create more burdens for the people but provide them with no help in bearing them.

They are also guilty of ostentation: (1) widening their phylacteries (the little boxes containing parts of the Torah and worn on the forearm and forehead during prayer); (2) lengthening their tassels; (3) searching out places of honor at banquets and in synagogues; and (4) longing for marks of respect in public and being hailed as "rabbi" (literally, "my great one"). Jesus, however, urges avoiding the titles of rabbi and teacher since only he is *the* rabbi and teacher. Second, he calls for avoidance of the title "Father" since there is only one common father, namely, the heavenly Father. This inveighing against titles suggests that in Matthew's community the notion of service is being neglected. By contrast, in verses 11-12 Matthew proposes the Christian manner of leadership: (1) service and (2) exaltation/humbling at the last judgment.

Reflection. People like to attain positions of importance but seek to make their importance felt. They acquire new titles but see them only as the springboard for personal gain. In today's passage such tendencies are all too evident. For Matthew, the flaunting of titles and the search for positions of prestige run counter to the Jesus tradition. Hence Matthew teaches that the greatest in the community are really those who serve the community. Moreover, at the final judgment there will be a leveling: those humbling themselves will be exalted but those exalting themselves will be humbled. For Matthew's audience as well as for today's followers, service is still the only paradigm.

Wednesday: Matthew 20:17-28   This third passion prediction in Matthew follows the structure found in his source Mark: (1) statement by Jesus about his arrest, death, etc. (vv. 17-19); (2) disciples' misunderstanding (vv. 20-24); and (3) Jesus' clarification (vv. 25-28). In Jesus' statement Matthew introduces the role of the Gentiles in his death. He also changes Mark's "after three days he will rise again" (10:34) to "he will be raised on the third day" (v. 19), i.e., the Father will be the agent of Jesus' resurrection. Whereas Mark 10:35 presents James and John making their request about prestigious positions in the kingdom, Matthew has their mother make the petition (vv. 20-21). Bypassing the mother, Jesus addresses the two sons directly, asking them if they are prepared to suffer, i.e., to drink the cup of suffering. While Jesus can certainly grant suffering, only his Father can assign positions in the kingdom.

The angry reaction of the others prompts Jesus to resolve the mis-understanding. Instead of extrapolating models of leadership from the secular world in which those in charge make their authority felt, disciples should find the paradigm for leadership in the cross. Reversing the secular value system, Jesus offers two models: (1) the servant who freely follows orders and (2) the slave who enjoys no rights at all. The embodi-ment of such forms of leadership is Jesus himself who comes to serve, not to be served. As Suffering Servant, he will lay down his life to free ("ransom") all humans from the enormous power of evil.

Reflection. The cross serves as the traditional Christian symbol. All too often, however, it has become trite or bland, losing some of its powerful symbolism. In such an impasse this passage compels all followers to rethink its symbolism and reassess their lives accordingly. The cross will regain its scandalous and foolish (see 1 Cor 1:23) dynamism as disciples put themselves at the service of others. By becoming servants and slaves, they will shock the world that puts its stock in power and prestige. While disciples may legitimately aspire to attain leadership positions, this pas-sage sternly commands them to translate such positions into myriad forms of service to others. In this way, the cross will regain its shock value.

Thursday: Luke 16:19-31   In this parable Luke gives the beggar a proper name. (Lazarus is Greek for Eleazar, meaning "God helps.") On the other hand, the rich man has no real identity because he has chosen to isolate himself from others in a world of nonconcern. While the rich man has "proper company," Lazarus has only the dogs.

Death, however, reveals Lazarus as a person and the rich man as a nonentity—wealth and security are obviously no guarantee of God's favor. Even in hell the rich man remains in character. He orders Abraham to order Lazarus to perform services for him. At this point such com-munication is impossible. After all, the rich man erected the chasm while still alive. The conclusion of the parable is a violent reaction to Jesus' audience that demands signs as proof. Luke implies that, although the apostles preach the resurrection of Jesus by appealing to Moses and the prophets, the response of Israel as a whole is quite paltry. To receive the Scriptures that witness to Jesus, one must first be open in faith. In turn, this presupposes that one senses a need. Lazarus perceives such a need, but the rich man does not.

Reflection. In today's world of dollar inflation and spiraling costs, believers may close in upon themselves to eke out a form of security. Such myopic vision can focus only on their own concerns so that they seek security in isolation. By acting in this way, they resemble the rich man in the parable. He dares to call Abraham his father (v. 24), but shows no interest in Abraham's family. In meeting only his own needs, he erects a wall between humanity and himself. To become involved in Lazarus's plight, i.e., to share in his misery, means to bolt over the security wall into the real world of Lazarus's insecurity. This unique parable from Luke challenges believers to accept and live the dictum that only concern for others brings security.

Friday: Matthew 21:33-43, 45-46   Jesus' original parable probably dealt with the account of a landowner who did not receive the proper share of the harvest from his tenant farmers. Taking advantage of the son's (the third emissary) status, they killed him. Christian tradition added the reference to the Isaian song of the vineyard (vv. 33, 40, see Isa 5:1-7), interpreted the son as Jesus, and spoke of his exaltation by quoting Psalm 118:22-23.

In Matthew's hands the parable becomes a judgment on the people of Israel, not only its leaders. Unlike his source, Mark 12:1-12, Matthew speaks of two groups of servants, not two individuals. This may reflect Israel's prophets before and after the exile (see Matt 23:37). Jesus, however, is the Father's last spokesperson. Reflecting the historical situation of the crucifixion, Matthew has the tenants drag the son outside the vineyard and only then kill him. After referring to the resurrection (v. 42), Matthew has Jesus say that the kingdom will be taken away from Israel and given to others. This kingdom will be the church composed of both Jews and Gentiles. At the end of the passage Matthew observes that the chief priests and the Pharisees realize that Jesus is speaking about them and, though anxious to arrest him, fear his popularity with the people as a prophet.

Reflection. Disciples naturally glory in belonging to the Christian community but must admit that at times they do not produce for that community. In baptism they receive a priestly calling but must profess that their lives are not always priestly service. They are not unlike the tenant farmers in today's passage who do not produce for the landowner, representing Israel of old that rejected the prophets. Matthew observes that God will take away their kingdom and give it "to a people that will produce [the kingdom's] fruit" (v. 43). The parable speaks to today's followers who must realize that, to belong to the kingdom, they must produce for the kingdom. Succinctly put, to belong is to produce.

Saturday: Luke 15:1-3, 11-32 Luke's introduction to the parable (vv. 1-2) shows that in his community some are demanding stringent entrance requirements for sinners. It also reveals that in Jesus' audience some are offended by his table companions. In this parable, Jesus is not concerned primarily with the proclamation of the Good News. Rather, he is vindicating the right not to place limits on God's goodness.

The parable has two components: (1) the departure and return of the younger son (vv. 11-24) and (2) the protest of the elder son (vv. 25-32). Both sections end with the same saying ("dead . . . come to life . . . lost . . . found"). In the first section, the kiss is the sign of forgiveness. Moreover, the father's orders (vv. 22-23) reinforce the forgiveness. To be feted is to be welcomed home. On the other hand, the elder son refuses to join in the festivities. He refers to his younger brother as "your son" (v. 30) in contrast to the father who calls the elder brother "son" (v. 31) and the younger son "your brother" (v. 27). For Luke, the father and the younger son reveal what God is like while the elder son reveals what his critics are like.

Reflection. This unique Lukan parable poses a troubling question for modern followers: with whom can they identify? Most would readily claim that the younger son is the easiest to identify with since everyone makes mistakes and sins. It is more difficult to identify with the prodigal father since compassion for the wayward has obvious limitations. Believers must concede, however, that too often they can identify with the elder son. They tend to see their God as the Celestial Administrator or the Heavenly CPA who rewards for services rendered and punishes for poor performance. They can identify with the elder son because they have chosen to place limitations on their God's capacity to give (in this case compassion). Today's disciples must move beyond the administrator or CPA models, proceed inside to join the party, and celebrate unlimited divine goodness.

The Third Week of Lent

Optional Mass: John 4:5-42   (This Mass may be used on any day of this third week, especially in Years B and C when the gospel of the Samaritan woman is not used on the Third Sunday of Lent.) In this passage, the first scene (vv. 4-26), the dialogue with the woman, contains two parts: (1) the discussion about living water (vv. 6-15) and (2) the true worship of the Father (vv. 16-26). The woman moves from a crass material understanding of water to a more spiritual one. Passages like Proverbs 13:14 and Sirach 24:21, 23-29 suggest that living water is Jesus' revelation or teaching. Ezekiel 36:25-26 and John 7:37-39 imply that the living water is the Spirit communicated by Jesus. The discussion of true worship results in a worship "in Spirit and truth" (v. 24). The Spirit elevates the believer above the earthly level to worship God properly. For John, the Spirit is the Spirit of Jesus and the Spirit of truth (see John 14:17; 15:26).

The second scene (vv. 27-38) is the dialogue with the disciples. In the discussion about food, the disciples operate on a material level, whereas Jesus speaks on the level of mission. Jesus then explains the two proverbs by referring to the joy of reaping the harvest, indeed a harvest that they did not see. The conclusion (vv. 39-42) is the conversion of the townspeople. They accept the word of the woman, then the word of Jesus, and finally they confess Jesus to be the savior of the world. These foreigners are a contrast to the Jews and their limited acceptance of Jesus in John 2:23-25.

Reflection. Faith means a higher level. People behold human events but do not realize that they are bound up with God. They notice the ordinary cycle and routine of life but fail to associate it with God's plan. They are so much like the characters in today's passage. The Samaritan woman seeks water on the natural level. She wants it flowing from a well but Jesus wants to give her living water, namely, his self-revelation and teaching. The disciples are also on the material level. They want to give Jesus something to eat but Jesus chooses to talk about the food that is his mission with the Father. The townspeople hear the word of the woman but with the word of Jesus they arrive at a new level. Similarly believers are challenged to discover in the ordinary events of everyday life the raw material of faith. They are bidden to see in their work life and social life more than the chance to earn money and be entertained. They are asked to find the opportunity to grow in faith and thus seek a higher level.

Monday: Luke 4:24-30 In this passage the conclusion of the synagogue service anticipates the incredulity of the Jews and the mission to the Gentiles. Jesus announces the arrival of a new age by applying to himself the texts of Isaiah about anointing by the Spirit and the mission to the captives, blind, and oppressed. The synagogue speech is in effect his inaugural address. Following the initial response of amazement by his hearers, Jesus reacts by presenting himself as a prophet rejected by the hometown people. He then illustrates the universalist thrust of his mission by citing the miracles of Elijah (1 Kgs 17:7-24) and Elisha (2 Kgs 5:1-27)—in fact, Luke is the only evangelist who mentions these miracles. Their relevance is that they benefited pagans. The Good News rejected by the Jews will be preached to the Gentiles (see Acts 13:46-50). The initial admiration of the audience now turns to indignation. Since Jesus' hour has not yet arrived, he simply walks through their midst. As used elsewhere, the verb "to walk, go" implies Jesus' trek to death and consequently to glory. Thus the Spirit-filled prophet who proclaims the new era must go down the path that leads through hostility and death to exoneration. The scene is truly programmatic.

Reflection. God supports his prophets. Through baptism believers share in Jesus' prophetic mission. But they suffer pain and wonder whether they can survive. They have their failures and inquire whether they can still have successes. To some extent they resemble Jesus in this passage. His audience does not want to hear that God is inaugurating a new age with his prophetic message. For some it is bad news that Jesus' message is for both Jew and Gentile, so that Jesus must eventually suffer physically and psychologically. Nonetheless God sustains his Son.

He does not permit the opposition to destroy Jesus at this point. The Father helps the Son through this crisis at Nazareth and later on the Mount of Olives and Calvary. This same God through his Son and his Spirit will support all those who seek to carry out their prophetic mission. At times of discouragement and even failure God supports his prophets.

Tuesday: Matthew 18:21-35　In this scene from Jesus' sermon to a divided community Peter's question is wrong because it seeks to establish limits, although somewhat generous limits. Jesus' answer (that probably refers to the unbridled vengeance of Gen 4:23-24) refuses to establish any boundaries at all. Boundless forgiveness is the way of the kingdom. In the parable the first official owes a boundless debt (ten thousand talents). His prostration and entreaty, however, move the king to boundless mercy. After all, it is utterly impossible for him to pay the debt. Unfortunately the first official does not experience any change at all. When the second official pleads in the same position and in practically the same words, the first official shows no mercy, although the debt of one hundred denarii is payable. The first official finally falls from grace because he refuses to share grace. In Matthew's community to be forgiven means to forgive others. Yet it cannot be something purely mechanical—it must come from the heart. Such is the way of the kingdom.

Reflection. To forgive is to be free. People hurt believers by slander and gossip, so they react by refusing to forgive them. People wound their feelings by not giving them a chance to show their talents and succeed, so they reciprocate by excluding them from their world of pardon. They wallow and fester in their ego. They adamantly refuse to liberate others and to be liberated by offering forgiveness. In this scenario they imitate the first official whose experience is not liberating. Although his debt is cancelled, he does not learn to cancel the debt of the second official. For Matthew, to refuse to forgive is to condemn oneself to a hell of isolationism and severance from the community where repeated forgiveness is the lifestyle. Especially in this season of Lent believers are urged to break free of the incrustations of their ego by reaching out in reconciliation. To forgive is to be free.

Wednesday: Matthew 5:17-19   In this segment of the Sermon on the Mount Matthew establishes the relationship between the Mosaic Law and Jesus. In fulfilling the Law and the Prophets, Jesus exercises a prophetic office. The Mosaic Law anticipated the Messiah so that now the center of gravity is no longer the Law but Jesus. Hence Jesus' teaching will now become the ultimate norm or criterion. Nothing in the Law, not even the slightest commandment, will be abolished until the proper time. For Matthew, that time will coincide with the death and resurrection of Jesus. Until then, Jesus remains within the parameters of Jewish institutions. Human teachers, therefore, should have a proper respect for the Mosaic Law. Breaking the smallest commandment and teaching others to do likewise will result in the lowest place in the kingdom. But doing the least of these commandments and teaching others to do likewise will result in a higher place in the kingdom.

Reflection. In life believers constantly receive guidelines that dictate how they should conduct themselves. In addition to ecclesiastical and civil legislation, they have rules for membership in clubs and a variety of associations. In this maze of legal obligations they must pose the question: what is the ultimate norm or criterion for acting? In today's passage Matthew answers this question simply and directly. The ultimate norm or criterion is the teaching of Jesus. They are reminded of the final scene in Matthew where Jesus instructs the Eleven to teach future disciples to obey everything he has commanded (28:20). When conflicts arise from these various forms of legislation, Jesus and his teaching must remain the ultimate norm or criterion. Jesus is the center of gravity in all laws.

Thursday: Luke 11:14-23   As Jesus continues his journey to Jerusalem, he exorcises a demon from a speech-impaired person and thus provokes the reaction of some people that he is in league with Beelzebul or Satan. In response to this reaction, Jesus employs two images: (1) the divided kingdom and (2) the fallen house. These images connote dissension and anarchy since Jesus' exorcism represents a frontal assault on the power of evil. Jesus then strengthens his argument by appealing to the practice of their own exorcists, i.e., they would have to be in league with Beelzebul or Satan too. Using an Old Testament figure of speech ("the finger of God"; see Exod 8:19), Jesus relates his own activity to God's former agents and announces that the kingdom of God has arrived in their midst. In verses 21-22, while Beelzebul or Satan may be viewed as "a strong man," Jesus is "one stronger than he" who has come to defeat him. In the final verse the phrases "with/against me" and "gather/scatter" unequivocally state that one cannot remain neutral in reacting to Jesus' battle with the demonic forces.

Reflection. At times believers like other people like to sit on the fence and remain perfectly neutral. They really don't want to take sides and thus offend one or the other party. The fence thus serves as a bastion of security. In today's passage, Luke presents Jesus taking the opposite stance with regard to his exorcism and possible association with Beelzebul or Satan. His response is quite blunt: "Whoever is not with me is against me, and whoever does not gather with me scatters" (v. 23). In everyday life disciples make decisions for or against Jesus. While such decisions do not focus on the origin of Jesus' exorcisms, they often touch on issues like justice, compassion, charity, and the like. Reread in such situations, this passage compels them to get off the fence, dismiss all neutrality, and opt for Jesus' position. While the Good News is frequently consoling, it is also equally demanding.

Friday: Mark 12:28-34   See Thursday of the Ninth Week of the Year.

Saturday: Luke 18:9-14   The background of Luke's parable is the proper spirit of prayer that should characterize all kingdom seekers. In the parable both the Pharisee and the hated tax collector adopt the same liturgical position (standing) and invoke the same God. They also employ accepted liturgical prayer forms: a thanksgiving for the Pharisee (see, e.g., Ps 17:1-5) and a lament for the tax collector (see, e.g., Ps 51:1-17). The Pharisee's prayer soon becomes a catalog of his own achievements, a litany of his own praises. His prayer stresses not that he is less than God but that he is more than others, especially the tax collector. His prayer has degenerated into the accolades of his world; it has not penetrated the reality of God's world. The tax collector's prayer, however, is a humble recital of faults and an inventory of his sins. His prayer obviously states that he is less than God. But there is no purpose in further comparison for him. By such a prayer he is in contact with God's (and hence humankind's) real world—a world where honesty undoes sin. Jesus judges that the tax collector went home right with God. In the kingdom only those right with God, not with themselves, make it.

Reflection. Honesty presents problems at times. Like other people, believers also belong to the faker generation. They like to pass themselves off as wealthier, smarter, and even holier than others. They revolve around their own self-imposed world of ego and resist every effort to break free from its gravitational pull. They can thus identify with the Pharisee who would not cease revolving around his self-insulated world. The Pharisee cannot envision a world where his feigned righteousness would be not only obsolete but also totally unacceptable. This parable must force disciples to consider the tax collector. He looks reality straight in the eye by not raising his eyes to heaven. His honest appraisal of himself is a liberating experience. He breaks free of the sinful world by acknowledging God's world of mercy. He tells all believers in no uncertain terms that in the kingdom honesty is the only policy.

The Fourth Week of Lent

Optional Mass: John 9:1-41 (This Mass may be used on any day of this fourth week, especially in Years B and C when the gospel of the man born blind is not used on the Fourth Sunday of Lent.) This passage may be outlined as follows: (1) setting (vv. 1-5); (2) miracle (vv. 6-7); (3) various interrogations (vv. 8-34); and (4) attainment of spiritual sight, namely, faith (vv. 35-41). The case of the man born blind is the triumph of light over darkness; hence Jesus clearly establishes that he is the light of the world (v. 5). While the man advances from darkness to light, the Pharisees/Jews retrograde from halting acceptance to outright rejection of Jesus. The man first speaks of Jesus as a man (v. 11), calls him a prophet (v. 17), attests that he comes from God (v. 33), and finally acknowledges him as the Son of Man (v. 37). On the other hand, the Pharisees/Jews initially seem to accept the healing (v. 16), but then doubt the blindness from birth (v. 18), reject Jesus' heavenly origins (v. 29), vilify the man (v. 34), and are finally judged to be spiritually blind

(vv. 39, 41). The man born blind ends up seeing (faith), but the seeing Pharisees/Jews end up blind (lack of faith).

Reflection. Disciples often sense the need for greater perception and enlightenment. For example, they see people but assess them merely on the basis of externals. They behold the gifts and talents of others but restrain themselves from making them known. They require a movement from purely external judgment to deeply internal acceptance—they need to emulate the man born blind. He begins by calling Jesus a man and then a prophet. Later he insists that he comes from God. Finally he acknowledges Jesus to be the Son of Man. Each step is an ever-widening introduction into the reality of Jesus. The man born blind is touched by the Light of the world. As a result, he begins to see on a completely new level. The man born blind must become disciples' paradigm for assessing and judging others. He challenges them to move from the exterior to the interior. He is their guide down the path of greater perception and enlightenment.

Monday: John 4:43-54   Verses 43-46 introduce the principal characters and the details that will figure in the cure of the royal official's son: (1) Jesus (vv. 43, 46), (2) the royal official (v. 46), (3) reason for Jesus' going to Galilee (v. 44), (4) Jesus' welcome (v. 45), (5) his presence in Cana (vv. 45-46), and (6) the time of his presence (vv. 43, 46). First, the miracle story emphasizes the theme of faith. Whereas many of the Galileans have an inadequate faith in Jesus' signs (v. 45), the royal official and his household come to faith on the basis of Jesus' word and sign. Similar to the wedding feast in Cana, this story shows a pattern of request, apparent rejection of the request, persistence of the petitioner, granting of the request, and coming to faith by another group, namely, the household.

Second, the miracle story underlines the theme of life. Jesus states that the son will live (v. 50). The slaves inform the official that his son is alive (v. 51). Finally the official repeats Jesus' statement that his son will live (v. 53). For John, the boy's life, i.e., his restoration to health, points to the eternal life that Jesus will bestow after his resurrection. It is worth noting that John will pursue the theme of life in the bread of life (6:48), the living water (7:37-39), and the light of life (8:12) discourses.

Reflection. John has linked the themes of faith and life. The royal official believes in Jesus' life-giving word. During this time of Lent it is good to pause and think about the interplay of faith and life in the lives of disciples. Through faith they open themselves up to the acceptance of the person of Jesus. Given that acceptance, they are prepared to receive his message. Life means much more than physical life, although such life provides an image of a deeper level. The life that Jesus experiences in and through his resurrection is the life that he promises to all believers. Introduced to that life in baptism and nourished by the bread of life in Eucharist, believers look forward to its culmination in eternal life. Easter permits them to glimpse that culmination.

Tuesday: John 5:1-16   After setting this scene at the pool of Bethesda in Jerusalem on the occasion of a Jewish festival, John introduces a sick man and Jesus. Jesus speaks with the man and learns his predicament, namely, he has no one to put him into the pool when the water is stirred up. Jesus then simply commands the man to get up, take his mat, and walk. The man immediately begins to walk and Jesus disappears into the crowd. The author strikes an ominous note when he notes the day of the cure, namely, the Sabbath. At this point the Jews question the man about his carrying the mat—a violation of the holiness of the Sabbath in their view. Later Jesus finds the man in the temple. Connecting sin with sickness and suffering, Jesus orders the man to sin no more. Once the man departs, he informs the Jews about Jesus. The passage closes with the notice that the Jews begin to persecute Jesus because of this violation of the Sabbath.

Reflection. "Who is the man who told you, 'Take it up and walk'?" The controversy that ensues ultimately concerns Jesus' identity. The purpose of the Sabbath healing is to begin to unlock Jesus' identity. As the Gospel of John continues, the different episodes will demonstrate that Jesus is much more than a Sabbath healer. This lingering question of Jesus' identity is one that disciples must constantly address. Who is Jesus for them? The question never seems to go away.

Lent offers a special time for reflecting on this question. Is this Jesus a man with utopian dreams, a mesmerizing speaker, a miracle worker, a crusader who provokes the ire of his opponents, a well-intentioned man who gets into trouble with the authorities? And the list of possible identifications goes on and on. According to John, Jesus is the Son of Man who has descended from heaven to tell people who God is. All those who believe in him and his message about the Father will enjoy eternal life. This Father so loves the world that he gives his only Son (see John 3:13-16).

Wednesday: John 5:17-30   This discourse on Jesus' Sabbath work consists of three components: (1) defense of his Sabbath work (vv. 17-18), (2) giving life and judging (vv. 19-25), and (3) another version of giving life and judging (vv. 26-30). In his defense of Sabbath work Jesus observes that his Father continues to work on the Sabbath. In attributing to himself the right to work on the Sabbath, however, Jesus is, in effect, claiming a divine prerogative. Moreover, in calling God his Father, Jesus is placing himself on a level with God. In developing his relationship with the Father, Jesus points out that he is wholly dependent on the Father, doing nothing on his own.

Jesus indicates two works that the Father does perform on the Sabbath: giving life (v. 21) and judging (vv. 22-23). As Son, Jesus possesses the power to give life to all those in the realm of death, i.e., sin. As judge, Jesus has the power to vindicate the righteous. As a result, those who hear Jesus' word and believe in him have already passed from death to life. In another version of this theme, Jesus, as the Son of Man, presides over the final judgment. Those already in their tombs will hear his voice and come out to the resurrection of life (those who have done good) or the resurrection of condemnation (those who have done evil).

Reflection. This passage presents a certain tension. On the one hand, believers have already passed from life to death (v. 24). On the other hand, at a future date they will rise from their tombs for the resurrection (v. 29). Ironically, those who possess eternal life must deal with the grim reality of death on a daily basis as they anticipate the summons to leave their tombs for the resurrection of life. Given this situation, believers must show their fortitude in seeing beyond physical death and accepting a future that relies on Jesus' word. This is the dilemma of "already" but "not yet." Eternal life has already started but its experience in the resurrection has not yet occurred.

Thursday: John 5:31-47   In this passage Jesus continues the discourse on his Sabbath work. It consists of two sections: (1) the list of witnesses who support Jesus' claim (vv. 31-40) and (2) Jesus' direct attack on the disbelief of his opponents (vv. 41-47). In the first section, Jesus enumerates the witnesses who can testify to his claim that the Father sent him to give life and to judge. These witnesses are: (1) John the Baptist (vv. 33-35), (2) Jesus' miracles (v. 36), (3) the Father himself (vv. 37-38), and (4) the Scriptures (v. 39). Unfortunately Jesus' opponents are not prepared to believe in him. In the second section, Jesus directly attacks such disbelief. While his opponents freely countenance self-proclaimed messiahs, they announce their pride in rejecting the glory that ultimately comes from God. Hence to reject Jesus is to reject God since Jesus has come in the Father's name. Finally Moses, the supposedly staunch supporter and ally of the opponents, will accuse them for their failure to believe.

Reflection. This passage presents challenges to modern believers. Since Jesus has gone home to the Father, who will represent him on earth by witnessing to his message? To be sure, witnessing to Jesus' Good News is a daunting task. If that message is to be kept alive like "a burning and shining lamp" (v. 35), however, believers must assume the task. Such witnessing does not require a bully pulpit or street corner haranguing. It takes place in the routine of daily life. The ongoing love of married couples; the devotion of parents to their children; the dedication of priests, deacons, and religious; support of human life from conception to natural death; compassion for "the unacceptable"; etc., keep the message of Jesus alive and well.

Friday: John 7:1-2, 10, 25-30   The opening verses place Jesus in Galilee because of the hostility of the Jews in Judea. They also mention the nearness of the feast of Tabernacles or Booths, a feast commemorating the sojourn of the Israelites in the desert. After the departure of his brothers for the feast, Jesus also goes but in secret.

Verses 25-30 focus on Jesus' origins during the discourse in the middle of the feast. The questions about Jesus' person and his claims continue to mount and provoke the hostility of his enemies. Jesus' origin in Nazareth precludes him from being the so-called hidden Messiah, i.e., one who, after being hidden, would suddenly be revealed to the people (v. 27). Ironically, the people know but they don't know. They know that he comes from Nazareth but they don't know that he comes from heaven and his Father. Jesus further asserts that he possesses a special and intimate knowledge of the Father: "I know him, because I am from him, and he sent me" (v. 29). This statement about his closeness to the Father gives way to an attempt to arrest him. But Jesus' hour prevents all such action.

Reflection. The notion of Jesus' intimacy with the Father must have a profound effect on believers. Jesus states that he sees what the Father does and imitates him (5:19). In today's passage he announces that he knows the Father because he is from the Father (7:29). Elsewhere Jesus solemnly attests that the Father and he are one (10:30). Believers become privy to such intimacy through baptism. They become God's adopted daughters and sons. While the relationship between Father and Son remains unique, believers nonetheless share in their mutual love. As members of God's extended family, disciples fittingly call God "Father" and Jesus "Brother." As disciples, they assume the task of upholding the family honor. By their moral lives they announce who they are and where they come from. Life is all about relationships and their consequences.

Saturday: John 7:40-53   This passage recounts the reactions to Jesus' statement on the last day of the feast of Tabernacles that he is the source of living water. Some think that he is the Prophet like Moses (see Deut 18:15-18). Others identify him as the Messiah. Some find such a claim impossible, however, since Jesus hails from Galilee whereas the Messiah must come from Bethlehem. The rest of the passage reveals the frustration of the Jewish authorities in dealing with Jesus. Clearly Jesus enjoys a reputation among the people. Even the temple police are impressed. The authorities, however, scoff at the crowd's opinion of Jesus, denigrating them as utterly ignorant of the law. At this point Nicodemus reminds the authorities that a person is not to be judged without a hearing. In reply, the authorities ridicule Jesus' Galilean origins, maintaining that the Prophet like Moses does not stem from Galilee.

Reflection. For John, the Pharisees are blind because they adamantly refuse to see. When confronted with the testimony of the crowd, the temple police, and Nicodemus, they can only ridicule and scoff. Jesus simply cannot be the type of person that these witnesses acknowledge. Perhaps believers should not be so hard on the Pharisees since they also may choose at times to be blind when judging other people. These may be people with impeccable credentials who are recognized as deeply committed and self-giving. They may be well known for their compassion and philanthropy. Somehow or other disciples may elect to dismiss all the evidence and even denigrate them. They thus become like the rabble in today's passage that does not know the law. This scene may serve as a warning to adopt different criteria in assessing people. One such criterion is that goodness in whatever form ultimately comes from God. To acknowledge the goodness of others is to proclaim that God is good.

The Fifth Week of Lent

Optional Mass: John 11:1-45   (This Mass may be used on any day of this fifth week, especially in Years B and C when the gospel of the raising of Lazarus is not used on the Fifth Sunday of Lent.) Just as the healing of the man born blind shows that Jesus is the light (see John 9:5), so the raising of Lazarus demonstrates that Jesus is the life (v. 25). The account may be outlined as follows: (1) setting (vv. 1-6); (2) questions about the journey (vv. 7-16); (3) Martha and Jesus (vv. 17-27); (4) Mary and Jesus (vv. 28-33); and (5) the raising of Lazarus (vv. 34-44). (Verse 45 is the start of the next section.)

Martha's character is in keeping with Luke's description (see Luke 10:38-42). She sees Jesus as an extraordinary mediator between God and her plight. When Jesus informs her that Lazarus will rise, she limits her vision to the resurrection on the last day. Jesus then states categorically that he is the resurrection and the life and that believers who have physically died will live in him and never die. Hearing this, Martha confesses that Jesus is the Messiah, the Son of God. For John, belief in Jesus is the gift of eternal life. The raising of Lazarus demonstrates this. As a whole, this account points to the interconnection of faith and glory. To accept Jesus is to open oneself to that transforming experience wherein the Father glorifies the Son in his passion, death, and exaltation. That glory forms the basis for eternal life.

Reflection. Accepting Jesus as the resurrection and the life does not mean denying the reality of physical death. Believers are bidden not to downplay or reject it. Rather, believers must view physical death as a stage in the eternal life to be conferred by Jesus: "whoever believes in me, even if he dies, will live" (v. 25). The model for all believers must be Jesus himself in his passage from death to life. For John, the cross becomes Jesus' throne, the moment of his glorification as Son: "And I, when I am lifted up from the earth, will draw all people to myself" (12:32). Jesus' death, therefore, is birth into glory. Whereas Lazarus can expect to die again, Jesus has conquered death—he has been transformed. This is the hope of all believers.

Monday: John 8:1-11   Although never an original part of the Gospel of John, this story of the adulterous woman eventually found its way into the Fourth Gospel. No matter what its origin, it is a priceless account that demonstrates both Jesus' forgiveness and wisdom.

It is likely that the situation in the story places Jesus in a dilemma. On the one hand, the Jewish court has found the woman guilty and sentenced her to death. On the other hand, the Romans have reserved to themselves the use of the death penalty. If Jesus approves the sentence, he flies in the face of Roman law. If he disapproves the sentence, he flies in the face of Jewish law. In the story, however, Jesus refuses to answer the question because it is wrong. The writing on the ground may have been Jesus' doodling to distract the audience. In any event, without condoning adultery, Jesus shows that the proper question is: what is the extent of mercy? Obviously the accusers have no interest in the purpose of the law—they are there only to test Jesus. The outcome is the disappearance of the accusers and a new orientation: "and from now on do not sin any more" (v. 11).

Reflection. Depression can take a terrible toll on people. They experience the depth of their sinfulness and reason that they cannot begin again. They realize the heinousness of their actions and infer that they must simply live with the burden of their guilt. They forget that their God is a forgiving God and that forgiveness provides a new orientation. This story of the adulterous woman may offer some help in dealing with such cases of depression. Here Jesus, in effect, believes the right question to be: what is the extent of mercy? In forgiving the woman, Jesus absolutely refuses to set limits on God's forgiveness. In this story Jesus embodies the love of his Father by revealing his boundless compassion for weak human beings. By recalling such compassion and generosity, disciples can defeat depression and begin life on a new level. The Father of Jesus is a God of surprises.

Monday: John 8:12-20 (In Year C when John 8:1-11 is read on the previous Sunday, John 8:12-20 is used.) Continuing his discourse on the feast of Tabernacles, Jesus declares that he is the light of the world. Perhaps against the background of the flaming pillar during the Exodus, Jesus uses the imagery of light to declare his revelatory message. Contrasting light with its polar opposite (darkness), Jesus assures his audience that his followers will never walk in darkness but will enjoy the light of life. To the Pharisees' objection that his testimony is invalid, Jesus responds that it is verifiable because his Father backs him up.

Concerning his role as judge, Jesus remarks that he passes judgment on no one. His Father, however, will acknowledge whatever judgment he provokes among the people. Jesus then refers to the statement in the law that requires the testimony of two witnesses for validity (see Deut 19:15). Both his Father and he constitute the two witnesses in question. The Pharisees' question about the whereabouts of his Father assumes that they know. Actually they fail to ask the right question, namely, who is your Father? Unfortunately his opponents are completely ignorant of who Jesus is and who his Father is. Jesus points out to them that to know him is to know the Father. The scene closes with the observation that his hour prevents any arrest at this moment.

Reflection. John states unabashedly that Jesus is the light of the world. The Matthean Jesus, however, in speaking to his disciples in the Sermon on the Mount, announces: "You are the light of the world" (5:14). There is no real contradiction here since disciples reflect the light that is Jesus. In a world without electricity the image of light must have had a powerful impact. Light makes it possible for people to see and recognize each other as well as to communicate. Modern disciples must illuminate their world with the Good News that is Jesus. In respecting others, in showing compassion, in fighting for justice, in defending the helpless, etc., they light up the world with the message of Jesus. Rather than curse the darkness, they choose to share Jesus the light.

Tuesday: John 8:21-30   Continuing his discourse on the feast of Tabernacles, Jesus strikes a note of urgency. His audience has but a short time to see Jesus, to search for him, and to find him. Failing to find him, they will die in their sins by rejecting Jesus and thus refusing life itself. Once Jesus departs, they have no further chance for deliverance from sin. Contrasting himself and his audience, Jesus remarks that, while he is from above and thus able to bring them up to God's level, they are from below. While Jesus does not belong to this world, they do. If they opt not to die in their sins, believers must recognize that Jesus bears the divine name of "I AM" (v. 24; see Isa 45:18). An editor comments in verse 27 that Jesus is talking about his Father. Following that, his being lifted up and exalted in his death, resurrection, and ascension will reveal that God sent him and is always with him. The scene closes with the statement that many come to believe in Jesus.

Reflection. Three times John speaks about Jesus' being lifted up (see 3:14; 8:28; 12:32). This image conjures up two meanings: (1) being lifted up on the cross and (2) being exalted or glorified. John presents the reader with a paradox, namely, that death is the condition for glory. Thus Jesus in his crucifixion mounts a throne that leads to his exaltation in his resurrection and ascension. Perhaps this theology may prove useful when disciples attempt to cope with pain, suffering, and ultimately death. While some would see these experiences as totally negative, John would reply that they are the stuff of life, the raw material for exaltation. While the reality of pain and frustration does not disappear, believers acknowledge that, like Jesus, they are also being lifted up in a twofold way. For Jesus as well as for believers, Good Friday means life, not death. Calvary marks the transition to the empty tomb.

Wednesday: John 8:31-42   Despite the note in verse 30, Jesus addresses these remarks on the feast of Tabernacles to some kind of disbelievers. The truth that will set the audience free is Jesus' revelation. In this discourse Jesus is countering the false notion that his audience, as children of Abraham, automatically enjoys a privileged position. In Jesus' view, however, a true disciple is one who abides in his word. That word or message is a liberating one, i.e., one that goes well beyond any purely nationalistic or political understanding. For Jesus, genuine freedom is freedom from sin, a freedom that constitutes a person a true descendant of Abraham. His audience, however, does not consist of such descendants since they are seeking to kill Jesus. What his audience must do is to follow Jesus' message that comes from the Father. As children of Abraham, they should do what Abraham did. The audience's claim to legitimacy may be a veiled attack on the legitimacy of Jesus' birth.

Reflection. Pedigree or performance. In today's passage Jesus' opponents take refuge in their pedigree of being descendants of Abraham. However, according to Jesus, they do not perform as Abraham did. Today's believers face a similar problem. They readily bask in the glory of being a Christian. They duly note that their baptism has made them members of God's extended family. They thus enjoy a remarkable pedigree. But how do they perform? Do they live up to the obligations of such a pedigree by moral living? Do they equate pedigree with performance? Perhaps one may rephrase Jesus' comment in verse 39 this way: "If you are God's children and the sisters and brothers of Jesus, you must do what Jesus did, namely, honor God through genuine performance, not lip service."

Thursday: John 8:51-59   In this final scene in the temple on the feast of Tabernacles, Jesus states emphatically that the person keeping his word will never experience spiritual death. Misunderstanding this death as physical death, the Jews accuse Jesus of having a demon and cite the instance of the deaths of Abraham and the prophets. Trying to probe his identity, they ask if Jesus is greater than Abraham and the prophets. Jesus responds that it is his Father who glorifies him, i.e., the Father whom they acknowledge as God. Once more Jesus affirms categorically that he knows the Father. Were Jesus to say that he does not know the Father, he would be a liar like his opponents. For Jesus, Abraham anticipated his coming, finding joy in this great event. Referring to Jesus' age as less than fifty, the Jews wonder how he could possibly have seen Abraham. With his "I AM" response (v. 58), Jesus lays claim to divinity. Realizing the implications of his statement, the opponents attempt to stone Jesus but he hides and slips away.

Reflection. Once again the issue of Jesus' identity emerges. Time and again his opponents seek to pin him down but constantly misunderstand his words. During Lent disciples can perhaps focus on the Johannine depiction of Jesus' identity by contrasting it with that of the Synoptics (Matthew, Mark, and Luke). For the Synoptics, Jesus proclaims the kingdom of God. He announces that the time has been fulfilled and that the kingdom has come near. He challenges his audiences to total conversion and acceptance in faith of the Good News. In John, however, Jesus exists with the Father from the beginning. At a certain point he descends from above to below. His charge is to tell people who God is. He shares with them the bond of intimacy that exists between the Father and himself. As he says repeatedly in this chapter, he knows the Father and the Father, in turn, testifies on his behalf. Whereas the Synoptics have Jesus proclaim the kingdom, John has Jesus share knowledge of his relationship with the Father. During the time of Lent the liturgy underlines the Johannine perception.

Friday: John 10:31-42   On the occasion of the feast of Dedication or Hanukkah Jesus finds himself once again in the temple. Because of the previous statement that the Father and he are one (v. 30), the Jews prepare to stone him. Jesus reacts to this murderous intent by asking which of his good works prompts such hostility. His opponents retort that Jesus' blasphemy, not a specific good work, motivates their action— although only a human being, he has made himself God. In reply, Jesus refers to Psalm 82:6 where God calls the judges, the members of his heavenly council, "gods" and "children of the Most High." Jesus argues, in effect, that judges can be called gods because they communicate the word of God. With all the more reason Jesus deserves the title of God because the Father has consecrated him and sent him into the world.

Jesus goes on to claim that God stands behind the work he performs as his envoy. If he is not doing the works of his Father, however, his opponents should not believe him. But if he is doing the works of his Father, they should believe those works, even though they do not believe him. Through such works they will grasp that the Father is in Jesus and Jesus in the Father. After this explanation of the unity between the Father and the Son, his opponents attempt to arrest him but he slips away across the Jordan. In this area many people come to believe in Jesus, acknowledging the Baptist's testimony about him to be true.

Reflection. The theme of faith plays a conspicuous role in this passage. The verb "to believe" appears no less than four times (vv. 37, 38 [2x], 42). Whereas Jesus' opponents do not believe him but may believe his works, the people across the Jordan believe *in* Jesus. The faith or lack of faith of Jesus' opponents has to do with believing or not believing someone (Jesus) or something (Jesus' works). To believe *in* Jesus, however, implies a deeper commitment, an acceptance of Jesus and his claims, and a willingness to respond to God's word as presented by Jesus. It is such a faith that the people across the Jordan exhibit. Especially in the setting of Lent disciples are encouraged to emulate this type of faith that involves commitment, acceptance of the person of Jesus, and a willingness to respond to his message. To believe in or not to believe in, that is the question!

Saturday: John 11:45-56 John links the session of the Sanhedrin or council to Jesus' raising of Lazarus, an event that prompts some to inform the authorities. The whole account is organized to highlight Caiaphas' statement: "it is better for you that one man should die instead of the people, so that the whole nation may not perish" (v. 50). While Caiaphas intends to provide a commonsense solution to the Jesus problem, he unwittingly prophesies the salvific aspect of his death, namely, to die for the people and save the nation. Caiaphas does not suspect that Jesus will die on behalf of the true Israel. He thinks he will be executed in place of Israel. In verse 52 John notes that Jesus will die not only on behalf of the true Israel but for the Gentiles as well ("the dispersed children of God"). Hence the true Israel and the Gentiles will form one body. John also observes that Jesus leaves for a town called Ephraim and remains there with his disciples. The passage concludes with the notice of the approach of Passover and the question of Jesus' attendance at this festival. The chief priests and the Pharisees now seek information about Jesus' whereabouts in order to arrest him.

Reflection. It is all a matter of interpretation. For Caiaphas, Jesus' execution is seen as the way to spare Israel and avoid problems with the Romans. For John's audience, Jesus' death is perceived as a death for the people (the true Israel) and the Gentiles. Jesus' death, therefore, will be a saving event, not just a political ploy. This matter of interpretation affects all believers. For example, how do they interpret their everyday existence? For some, it is a matter of working in order to pay bills and also afford some leisure time. It is also a question of staying healthy to pursue life to the fullest. For believers, the interpretation takes a different turn without denying the validity of the claims already mentioned. Believers interpret life as a series of faith opportunities to witness the goodness of others, to cultivate mutual love and understanding, and to accept each day as a gift from the Creator. Outwardly the lives of both groups may appear the same. Inwardly, however, it is not quite the same. Interpretation makes everything different.

Holy Week

Monday: John 12:1-11   In this Johannine account of the anointing woman (contrast Matt 26:6-13; Mark 14:3-9; Luke 7:36-38), the author begins with the setting, namely, a dinner in honor of Jesus at which Martha serves and Lazarus is in attendance. Next Mary, the sister of Martha and Lazarus, approaches Jesus with a costly perfume and anoints Jesus' feet, wiping them with her hair. This extraordinary gesture provokes outrage on the part of Judas. He announces that the perfume could command a handsome price that would benefit the poor. At this point John delves deeper into Judas' motives, portraying him as a thief with no real interest in the poor. Jesus then intervenes on Mary's behalf, seeing her gesture as anticipation of his burial and observing the multiple opportunities for helping the poor. The passage concludes with mention of the large crowd that comes out to see not only Jesus but also Lazarus. Regarding Lazarus John notes that the chief priests intend to kill him as well because many Jews are believing in Jesus on his account.

Reflection. In his presentation of Mary John offers a profound analysis of discipleship. In his account Mary anoints Jesus' feet and dries them with her hair. This act evokes the scene in John 13 where Jesus washes the feet of his disciples and dries them with a towel attached to his waist. This footwashing is the act that Jesus commands his disciples to perform for each other (13:14). Against this background Mary's gesture for Jesus clearly depicts her as a disciple. This scene speaks volumes about the modern practice of discipleship. It implies that discipleship consists of at least two elements: (1) perceiving a need and (2) addressing it. Here Mary first perceives that Jesus has a need, namely, proper burial procedure. Second, she addresses that need by anointing Jesus' feet. Mary's gesture, therefore, complements Jesus' footwashing. Briefly put, disciples must perceive each other's needs and address them.

Tuesday: John 13:21-33, 36-38   In this passage John has Jesus predict his betrayal (vv. 21-30) and introduce the last discourse (vv. 31-33, 36-38). Jesus' troubled state reflects the presence of evil, especially in the context of Judas' betrayal. At Jesus' acknowledgement of the betrayal the disciples wonder who the betrayer may be. Simon Peter motions to the Beloved Disciple who is reclining next to Jesus to ascertain the identity of the betrayer. As Jesus' intimate, the Beloved Disciple poses the question and receives the answer that the betrayer is the one to whom Jesus gives a morsel of bread dipped in the dish. After receiving the morsel, Judas experiences the presence of Satan within himself. Jesus then instructs Judas to complete his diabolical mission, although the others remain ignorant of the scope of Jesus' command (buying food for the festival or giving alms to the poor). With the command, however, John emphasizes Jesus' control of his destiny. As Judas departs to accomplish his mission, John remarks that it is night—a fitting image for Satan who now plays a key role in the drama.

After Judas' exit, Jesus speaks of his glorification, i.e., the total process running from the passion to the ascension. The outcome of this process is the glory that Jesus will enjoy in the Father's presence. "My children" (v. 33) is a term of affection that suits the last testament or farewell discourse in which a father or leader takes leave of his family or community (see Gen 49:1-28; Deut 33:1-29). Jesus warns his disciples, as he warned the Jews, not to look for him. With the disciples, however, the warning takes on a note of joy since after the departure the Father and Jesus will come to them. After learning that he cannot follow Jesus now, Simon Peter protests that he is willing to lay down his life for Jesus. Such an avowal of fidelity provokes Jesus' prediction that Simon Peter will deny him three times before the cock crows.

Reflection. With whom can believers identify? John develops the special connection of three disciples in this scene and challenges modern believers to an identity contest. First, the Beloved Disciple in John is the model disciple, probably the principal source for the traditions in the Fourth Gospel. In this scene John develops his intimacy with Jesus by noting his position next to him. Moreover, he is the faithful disciple who will reappear on Calvary and become a member of Jesus' family (see John 19:26-27). To be sure, identifying with such a disciple poses a formidable challenge. Second, Simon Peter perhaps presents less of a challenge. He is both loving and impetuous, even to the point of pro-testing his fidelity by laying down his life for Jesus. However, this loving, impetuous Simon Peter is also weak since he will deny Jesus no less than three times. But he will repent and be rehabilitated (see John 21:15-19). Third, there is Judas the betrayer. Satan enters into him so that under demonic influence he carries out his plan to initiate the action that will seal Jesus' death. He will be the one to lead the arresting contingent to the Garden of Olives (see John 18:1-11). To identify with Judas seems all too shocking. Nonetheless, his role in Jesus' death must continue to challenge identity seekers.

Wednesday: Matthew 26:14-25   In this passage Matthew describes three scenes: (1) Judas' proposal to betray Jesus (vv. 14-16); (2) Jesus' command to prepare the Passover (vv. 17-19); and (3) Jesus' prediction of his betrayal (vv. 20-25). In the first scene, Matthew, unlike his source Mark, offers a motive for Judas' action, namely, greed. Among the evangelists only Matthew mentions the exact amount of money (thirty pieces of silver), a quotation from Zechariah 11:12 where the rejected shepherd receives this trifling amount. Using the same Greek verb, Matthew draws a contrast: while Jesus is handed over by his Father for humanity's salvation, Judas will hand Jesus over for a sum of money.

In the second scene, Matthew emphasizes Jesus' command and the disciples' prompt obedience in executing it. Jesus' statement that the time is near (v. 18) makes him all too aware of the destiny awaiting him.

In the third scene, Jesus continues this awareness by solemnly an-nouncing his betrayal—a declaration that stuns the Twelve and leads to their individual interrogations. Jesus responds that the person in ques-tion has dipped his hand into the bowl with him. At this point Matthew narrates the paradox of the betrayal. The Scriptures (v. 24: "as it is writ-ten of him") predict his death as God's will. Nonetheless the perpetrator sins grievously by carrying out the divine plan. Matters would be far different if that man had not been born. In asking Jesus about the culprit, Judas addresses him as "Rabbi," a title used only by unbelievers in Matthew. Jesus replies that he did not say so, Judas did.

Reflection. God has the capacity to take what is evil and change it into what is good. Judas' betrayal is clearly evil, a heinous crime that sets in motion the chain of events culminating in Jesus' death. But Calvary is not the last stop—the empty tomb is. God transforms death by raising Jesus to glory and offering the same transformation process to others. Against this background, the evil that people suffer (e.g., malicious gossip, injustice, slander, ridicule) can become the raw material for radical change. While all these experiences remain painful, they can also enable believers to see them as a springboard for growth. Through perseverance and ongoing loving service to the authors of such wickedness, followers of Jesus can see evil converted into good. Jesus, therefore, stands as the parade example of this whole process, especially during Holy Week.

The Easter Season

The Octave of Easter

Monday: Matthew 28:8-15   In this passage Matthew presents two scenes: (1) the mission of the women and the encounter with Jesus (vv. 8-10), and (2) the account of the guards at the tomb (vv. 11-15). In the first scene, at the command of an angel of the Lord the women become the first heralds of the resurrection. With a mixture of joy and fear the believing women leave to seek out the as yet unbelieving disciples. Jesus' greeting, however, leads to an act of homage and reverence. Although Jesus' message seems to repeat the words of the angel, there are significant emphases to suggest it is not mere repetition. Thus the body of Jesus is a real body. Moreover, by using the expression "my brothers" (v. 10), Jesus communicates forgiveness to the sinful disciples. Finally the purpose of Jesus is not to renew old friendships but to initiate the mission of the church.

In the second scene, Matthew continues the story of the guards at the tomb whose presence he previously noted in 27:62-68. With the appearance of an angel at the tomb they are extremely frightened and act like dead men (28:4). As the women leave, the guards announce the embarrassment of the empty tomb to the Jewish authorities who then concoct a story to counter the message of the women. The authorities propose to bribe the guards who must then spread the report of the disciples' nocturnal visit to the tomb and the subsequent theft of Jesus' body. Matthew presents this story as utterly preposterous since the guards are supposedly asleep during the theft, although they were purposely posted there to avoid such a possibility (see 27:64). The authorities then assure the guards that they will handle things with Pilate. As the scene concludes, Matthew observes that this story is still circulating among the Jews of his own time.

Reflection. The charge given to the women, namely, to announce the resurrection of Jesus, continues to endure. This scene must energize disciples to carry out this same mission. In a world filled with news of depression, greed, war, injustice, etc., the antidote is the startling news that Jesus has been raised. While some may choose to proclaim this message in the public square, others may elect to let the authenticity of their lives communicate the impact of the resurrection. Marital fidelity and mutual support, compassion for the less than beautiful people, defense of human life from conception to natural birth, help for the unemployed and underemployed, etc., powerfully demonstrate that he has been raised. Such moral authenticity announces that the empty tomb must mean a full life for others.

Tuesday: John 20:11-18   Mary Magdalene functions as a primary witness to the resurrection of Jesus in the gospels. In this present account John has her lingering at the tomb as Simon Peter and the Beloved Disciple leave. As she weeps, she looks into the empty tomb and discovers two angels sitting where Jesus' body had been. Noticing her distraught state, they ask about its cause. She replies that people have removed Jesus' body to an undisclosed place. At this point, as the two angels disappear from the scene, Jesus takes center stage. Though it is the same Jesus, he has undergone a change so that Mary does not immediately recognize him. Like the two angels, Jesus seeks the reason for her weeping and the object of her search. Taking him to be the gardener, she states that she will personally take away the body of Jesus, if the gardener is responsible for the transfer. When Jesus calls her by name, she immediately recognizes him, addressing him as "teacher."

Mary's recognition of Jesus by his voice establishes her as a disciple. In John 10:3 the sheep hear the voice of the Good Shepherd who calls them by name and leads them out. After this recognition Jesus instructs Mary not to cling to him since he has not yet ascended to the Father. Jesus is implying that his permanent presence will take place through the gift of the Spirit. Hence he must first ascend to the Father and then bestow the Spirit (see John 20:22). Jesus then commissions her as an apostle who must share the news of his resurrection and imminent ascension with his disciples. The scene closes with Mary carrying out her apostolic commission.

Reflection. Mary Magdalene has admittedly had bad press. In this passage, however, Jesus counters such erroneous press with his affirmation of her twofold status as disciple and apostle. She remains faithful to Jesus as witnessed by her presence on Calvary. She also brings the Good News about Jesus to the other disciples. In Western Christian tradition she is known as *apostola apostolorum*, i.e., the female apostle to the male apostles. Such an exalted position must compel today's believers to appreciate the leadership roles of women in the modern church. Together with Simon Peter she is a primary witness to the resurrection. In this scene John breaks through all gender bias in presenting her as both disciple and apostle. Today's church must heed her status in any discussion of women's roles.

Wednesday: Luke 24:13-35   The Emmaus story has the following structure: (1) introduction involving the journey and encounter with Jesus (vv. 13-15); (2) body (vv. 16-31) moving from nonrecognition (v. 16) to recognition (v. 31); and (3) conclusion containing the reaction of the two disciples and their return to Jerusalem (vv. 32-35).

In the body of the text there are two elements: (1) a dialogue narrative (vv. 17-27) and (2) a meal narrative (vv. 28-30). The dialogue first notes the acceptance of Jesus but an acceptance that ended in tragedy. Next the two disciples give expression to their personal hopes. Finally they mention the report of the women at the tomb. Jesus then responds by expounding the Scriptures, especially the nexus between tragedy and glory. In the meal narrative the guest performs the tasks of the host. The language of blessing, breaking, and distributing has eucharistic overtones. For Luke's audience, Jesus is both guest and host at the Christian meal. Luke also suggests that those who share with others can rediscover the risen Lord and thus regain hope.

In the conclusion the disciples acknowledge the impact of Jesus' interpretation. In turn, they are moved to communicate it to others. They repeat the recognition theme, namely, the breaking of the bread reveals the person of the risen Lord.

Reflection. The theme of God's plan plays a key role in Luke-Acts. (See Acts 2:23-24: "this man, handed over to you according to the definite plan and foreknowledge of God, you crucified . . . But God raised him up.") Humans do not always see the nexus between events. In this passage the two disciples fail to discover the plan of God. Even if the women's report is true, how does it all fit together? To resolve this dilemma, Luke has Jesus show God's plan in the Scriptures whereby the Messiah must suffer in order to enter into his glory (v. 26).

Modern followers can resonate with the two travelers because they too sometimes fail to grasp the connection between events. For example, a relationship breaks up, someone loses a job, a person contracts a serious disease, or a loved one suddenly dies. Followers naturally feel perplexed, wondering if there is any rhyme or reason in these and other tragic events. In this quandary Luke would respond that there is a plan and that Providence plays a part in all this. Ultimately this scene challenges believers to trust in a God who writes straight with crooked lines. The God who saw through his plan for his Son will do no less for his Son's sisters and brothers.

Thursday: Luke 24:35-48   In this appearance of Jesus to the apostolic circle Luke presents two scenes: (1) Jesus' appearance (vv. 36-43) and (2) his instruction (vv. 44-48). In the appearance scene, Jesus is the prototype of the Christian missionary. The peace greeting and the acceptance of food from the community are, for Luke, part of the itinerant missionary's life. While "it is I myself" (v. 39) announces the identity of the risen Lord with the earthly Jesus, Luke nonetheless postpones the disciples' recognition of Jesus until the ascension scene (24:53). For Luke, presence must be coupled with the revealing word.

In the instruction scene, Luke has Jesus once again unravel the meaning of the Scriptures. Luke's emphasis on the divine necessity covers: (1) passion and glory (v. 46) and (2) universal preaching (v. 47). The missionary preaches "in his name" and is a witness. For the evangelist these terms envision more than being a guarantor of the events. They connote reenacting Jesus' journey and sharing in his prophetic status. Facts are simply not enough. The meaning of the facts must be exemplified in the missionary.

Reflection. While the Lukan Jesus speaks of the divine necessity covering suffering and glory, he also refers to the divine necessity covering repentance and forgiveness of sins. Disciples, therefore, are under divine compulsion to preach in his name, so that all the nations may adopt a new way of thinking and acting (repentance) and thereby receive the forgiveness of their sins. Luke, therefore, implies that all disciples must become missionaries. All too often people think that missionaries are limited to those sent to foreign lands to proclaim the Good News. Luke, however, adopts a different stance, namely, that all followers of Jesus must assume this obligation. The missionary work thus envisioned occurs in the workplace, in school, at home, at recreation, etc. In such venues the lifestyle of disciples can promote repentance and thus lead to forgiveness of sins. Missionaries move in very diverse settings. Nonetheless, the constant factor is the message rooted in the authentic lives of believers.

Friday: John 21:1-14 This chapter is an epilogue, the work of a redactor who wanted to preserve certain traditions for the Johannine community. This passage consists of the following: (1) a fishing scene by the Sea of Tiberias (vv. 1-8), (2) a meal on land (vv. 9-13), and (3) an observation (v. 14). The catch of fish and the meal on land were originally two different accounts. In the first, Jesus appears to be without fish (v. 5), yet when the disciples arrive, he has already prepared a fish (v. 9). Peter and the Beloved Disciple recognize Jesus because of the large catch (v. 7), but later there is some dispute about Jesus' identity (v. 12). It is possible that this passage combines two appearances of Jesus: (1) to Peter and (2) to the Eleven on another occasion. Nonetheless, in this joint account there is ample symbolism. The catch of fish is no longer the clue to Jesus' identity. It symbolizes their apostolic mission, for they are now fishers of humans. Jesus' action at the meal points to the Eucharist: "took the bread and gave it to them, and in like manner the fish" (v. 13) closely resembles Jesus' action at the multiplication of loaves and fish (John 6:11). For the audience, this establishes a link between the Eucharist and the presence of the risen Jesus in the community.

Reflection. Most believers enjoy the Easter music but a few see it as involving only Jesus. Most believers thrill at Jesus' victory over death but some at least do not consider themselves caught up in that victory.

To that extent they fail to realize that Easter Sunday is their catalyst for ministry, one of the themes of today's passage. The primitive story in this chapter associates the mission of the disciples with the appearance of the risen Lord. Their huge haul of fish symbolizes their mission as haulers of people. The appearance of the risen Lord, therefore, provides the energy and the zeal for believers to continue to be haulers of people. Jesus' presence offers the strength and the wisdom for their mission. Easter Sunday has become Mission Sunday.

Saturday: Mark 16:9-15   Mark 16:9-20 is the so-called longer ending of that gospel. Vocabulary and stylistic differences indicate that it is not the work of the author of Mark, although it is canonical. It is a summary of the postresurrectional appearances of Jesus and reflects traditions common to Luke 24 and John 20. A common theme running throughout the longer ending is the disbelief of the Eleven. Thus Jesus appears to Mary Magdalene who communicates the news of the resurrection to the disciples. Still mourning and weeping, they refuse to believe. Similarly Jesus reveals himself to the two travelers who, in turn, report this appearance to the disciples. Once again they dismiss the news in disbelief. Finally Jesus himself appears to the Eleven at table and upbraids them for their lack of faith and their stubbornness. Such disbelief notwithstanding, Jesus commissions them to proclaim the Good News to all creation or every creature.

Reflection. Modern disciples may think that the proclamation of the Good News is limited only to the Eleven. Actually all baptized believers receive this commission. Admittedly some, e.g., ordained clergy and vowed religious, fulfill this mandate in special ways. Nevertheless it is incumbent on all believers to share the Good News in whatever situation they find themselves. For example, by consoling mourners, they announce that Jesus has conquered death in his resurrection. By comforting the sick and the dying, they proclaim that pain and death prepare them to experience their Lord who through his own suffering and death is exalted in the presence of the Father. Ultimately the Good News is not a private message for believers alone. Rather, it is a contagious legacy to be shared with all the world. The mission of the Eleven lives on in all those who take their baptism seriously.

The Second Week of Easter

Monday: John 3:1-8   John begins this passage by introducing Nicodemus as a Pharisee and most likely a member of the Sanhedrin, the Jewish ruling party. His meeting with Jesus at night projects the image of evil, although later in this discourse (3:19-21) Nicodemus comes into the light. He belongs to that group of Jews who acknowledge Jesus as a teacher sent from God because of his signs (the Johannine term for miracles). Nicodemus approaches Jesus in faith with an ardent desire to enter the kingdom. Jesus then informs him that entrance into the kingdom of God requires birth from above. The Greek word for "from above" can also mean "again." Using the device of misunderstanding, John shows Nicodemus thinking in terms of being born again and thus reentering the mother's womb. Jesus is obviously speaking on a higher level, pointing out that entrance into the kingdom of God hinges on the eternal life bestowed by the Father through the Son.

Jesus then links eternal life with the role of the Spirit. (The Greek word for "Spirit" has to do with breath/breathing, the principle of life.) The addition of water suggests the Christian sacrament of baptism. John also has Jesus mention another contrast, namely, flesh and spirit. This dualism contrasts a person as a mortal human ("flesh") with a person as a daughter/son of God. Jesus goes on to tell Nicodemus not to be surprised at this birth from above. Here a dimension of mystery is clearly present, comparable to the phenomenon of the wind. (The Greek word in question means both "wind" and "Spirit.") The mystery, however, does not detract from the reality of the Spirit's role.

Reflection. The dimension of mystery in this passage may prove to be somewhat unsettling in the science-oriented society of the twenty-first century. Many demand a clear account involving cause and effect. The interaction of the Father, Jesus, and the Spirit, however, does not meet the criteria for such an account. To that extent, mystery prevails. But, on another level, believers can see a certain cause and effect. Wherever goodness is found in whatever form, the Spirit is present. Those who see their lives as service to others experience the role of the Spirit. Goodness, the Spirit, and Spirit-filled people are linked together. To that extent, the veil of mystery is lifted.

Tuesday: John 3:7b-15   In this passage Nicodemus exits the scene after having failed to understand Jesus. In turn, the failure prompts Jesus to provide a more detailed version of his revelation. Actually Nicodemus' incredulity indicates a wider reluctance to receive Jesus' testimony. Although Nicodemus did not grasp entering the kingdom of God through the analogies of birth and wind (v. 12: "earthly things"), Jesus will now speak of the heavenly origins of the birthing process through the Spirit. To be sure, Jesus has the credentials to discuss this matter. Such credentials are the fact that only he has been in heaven since he descended from there, notwithstanding Enoch (see Gen 5:24) and some others. Jesus elaborates that this begetting through the Spirit depends on Jesus' crucifixion, resurrection, and ascension. The comparison with Moses' bronze serpent shows that "to be lifted up" refers to the crucifixion (see John 12:33). But, for John, this is only the beginning of Jesus' return to the Father that reaches fulfillment in exaltation (see John 8:28; 12:32). "Being lifted up" ultimately brings life to all believers (see John 7:37-39).

Reflection. Some believers at least may be put off by John's version of Jesus' death. Good Friday for them must be a somber day with all the paraphernalia of mourning and sorrow. The traditional practice of the three-hour agony of Jesus on the cross has a conspicuous place in such circles. John, however, plays on the verb "to be lifted up." While this certainly includes Jesus' crucifixion and subsequent death, it also means Jesus' glorification that embraces his resurrection and ascension. On Good Friday the Johannine Jesus bestows the Spirit on the community of believers (see 19:30). Thus death gives way to new life. In today's passage John expresses it this way: "so must the Son of Man be lifted up, so that everyone who believes in him may have eternal life" (vv. 14-15). For John, Calvary should ring with hallelujahs, not lamentations.

Wednesday: John 3:16-21   The opening verse of this passage emphasizes the role of the Father. Like Abraham, he gives his *only* Son, whom he loves, for the benefit of all nations of the earth (see Gen 22:2, 12, 18). Verse 16 parallels verse 17. In verse 16 the Father's giving of the Son brings eternal life to believers. In verse 17 the Father's sending of the Son brings salvation to the world. The presence of Jesus is calculated to force a decision. Whoever does not accept Jesus in faith is already condemned. In verses 19-21 John employs the imagery of light and darkness. Humans must make a decision between light and darkness. Their way of life influences the choice: evildoers opt for darkness while those acting in truth opt for light. Jesus himself is the one who provokes this choice. Those hardened in radical evil reject the light. Those accustomed to doing good bathe in the light.

Reflection. When you care enough to send the very best! Experience teaches that service is the barometer of caring, i.e., people provide services for others in proportion to their caring. The vocabulary in today's passage substantiates this claim: the Father loves, gives, and sends (vv. 16-17). The symbolism of Abraham's sacrifice heightens the element of caring—it is the Father's *only* Son. At the same time the Father's action envisions all humanity. It is designed to lead to eternal life, not death; to salvation, not condemnation. The cross as the symbol of the Father's caring must prompt believers to do likewise. It must challenge married couples to care to the point of sacrifice and perseverance. It likewise challenges children to care to the point of family loyalty and self-giving. In the final analysis, the cross captures the most profound aspect of caring.

Thursday: John 3:31-36 Perhaps once an isolated discourse of Jesus, this passage is now attached to this chapter with its scenes of Nicodemus and John the Baptist. Jesus states that the purely natural cannot elevate itself without the aid of the one coming from above, namely, Jesus himself. Although Jesus has his origins from above and knows whereof he speaks, some at least do not accept his testimony. Those who have accepted that testimony, however, can acknowledge the bond between Jesus' testimony and the Father's truth. This bond is reinforced when Jesus, God's envoy, communicates his words. In addition, Jesus bestows the Spirit without measure. The Father's love for the Son becomes evident in the former's handing over all things (e.g., judgment, glory, followers) to the latter. The discourse concludes with a twofold reaction to Jesus. Those who accept Jesus in faith possess eternal life. Those who disobey Jesus experience God's wrath, not life.

Reflection. Salvation too often seems to be reduced to keeping impersonal commandments. One fulfills the commandments and thus qualifies for salvation status. John takes an entirely different approach by speaking of "believing *in* the Son" (v. 36; emphasis added). Such belief involves the acceptance of the person of the revealing Jesus and consequently the readiness to carry out his will—a far cry from a purely impersonal execution of a divine will. Obeying commandments is relevant because of the bond between Jesus and the believer. On the other hand, "whoever disobeys the Son will not see life, but the wrath of God remains upon him" (v. 36). To disobey, therefore, is to reject the person of Jesus. Faith and obedience thus go hand in hand. Christian maturity always implies looking beyond *what* is commanded to the one *who* is commanding.

Friday: John 6:1-15   While the Synoptics (Matthew, Mark, and Luke) and John reflect eucharistic symbolism in the story of the multiplication of the loaves, it is John alone who exploits this scene for its special "sign" potential. In John, where signs are perceived only as miracles, they do not lead to faith. To lead to faith, the sign must provoke God's presence as revealed in Jesus.

The scene, as a whole, is tied up with Moses. Just as Moses goes up the mountain (Sinai), so Jesus goes up a mountain. Philip's question reechoes Moses' question to God about providing food (see Num 11:13). Philip's answer also reechoes Moses' question (Num 11:22: "Are there enough flocks and herds to slaughter for them?"). Similarly, the Prophet coming into the world is expected to be a new Moses who would found a new Israel. The miracle makes the audience conclude that Jesus is such a figure. At this point John adds a historical note missing in the Synoptics, namely, the people's attempt to make Jesus their king because of the miracle. For John, therefore, the sign does not lead them to recognize the true nature of Jesus. It is "just" a miracle.

Reflection. John presents Jesus as one who works "signs," i.e., miracles that should lead one to acknowledge God's presence in Jesus. For John, however, Jesus is also the sign of the Father's love and concern. The task of Jesus is to reflect the mystery of the Father and to make humans aware of his person. By this feeding of the five thousand, Jesus attests to his Father's presence, although the people remain merely on the level of miracle. For John, therefore, Jesus' whole existence is to be a sign.

This passage urges believers to work signs. Such signs need not fall into the theological category of miracles but they are signs nonetheless. Thus husbands and wives who develop their mutual love over the years choose to be signs of God's love over the centuries. Those who generously provide for the needs of the lonely and distraught elect to be signs of God's loving concern for all. Workers who opt to meet their obligations choose to be signs of God's justice. These and similar people function as signs of Jesus' love and concern. They can provoke both believers and unbelievers to discover in these signs the presence of a provident God. As such, these signs point beyond seemingly mundane events to God's involvement with humanity—a reality that shares in Jesus' mission as sign and worker of signs.

Saturday: John 6:16-21   After the feeding of the five thousand John narrates the account of Jesus walking on the Sea of Galilee. Here John directs his attention to the manifestation of the divine in Jesus, specifically in the phrase "It is I" (v. 20). (This is a form of the divine name [see Isa 45:18] that Jesus uses to identify himself.) This manifestation contrasts with the five thousand who recognize Jesus solely as the prophet or king. John may also be hinting at the Passover symbolism in the walking on the water. (See 6:4 that states that the Passover is near.) One synagogue service for the Passover uses Isaiah 51:6-16 that speaks of the redeemed passing through the sea (v. 10), the Lord stirring up the water (v. 15), and his saying "I, I am he" (v. 12). All of this suggests linking Jesus walking on the water with the crossing of the sea during the Exodus and Israel's God creating a path through the waters.

Reflection. The manifestation of the divine continues to attract people. They search for specific locales where Jesus is supposed to have appeared. In this account, however, John appears to take a subtler approach. He suggests that the walking on the water may recall God's great liberation of the people in the Exodus experience, an experience reenacted in the feast of Passover. If so, this manifestation of the divine is not designed to satisfy curiosity seekers. Rather, it underlines God's will to save his people. It is interesting to note that John places the death of Jesus on the eve of Passover, i.e., at a time when the Passover lambs are being slaughtered in the temple. Against this background John depicts Jesus' manifestation of God's will to save. Calvary thus becomes the place to visit to understand the Christian celebration of Passover.

The Third Week of Easter

Monday: John 6:22-29   The first three verses serve as an introduction to the Bread of Life discourse (vv. 25-59). "[T]he crowd that remained across the sea" (v. 22) and those who "had eaten the bread when the Lord gave thanks" (v. 23) realize that Jesus and the disciples are separated. A certain confusion arises since Jesus and the disciples are not with them. The participants in the feeding sign hail boats from Tiberias and set out for Capernaum.

The mention of "gave thanks" (v. 23) suggests that the Bread of Life discourse will deepen the eucharistic aspect of the feeding scene. The question about the time of Jesus' arrival (v. 25) implies a more profound interest about Jesus' (the bread from heaven) origins. Jesus responds to this question by noting their lack of deeper insight into the sign as opposed to satisfying their hunger with the loaves. Jesus then contrasts food that perishes with food that endures for eternal life. The latter food is a gift of the Son of Man whom the Father has consecrated. The crowd, still thinking on a material level, asks about works that they can do. In reply, Jesus urges the role of faith in submitting to what God has done in him.

Reflection. Families are always concerned about putting enough food on the table. Some become so absorbed in making money for this and other goals that they lose sight of other values in life. To that extent, they resemble the crowd that places satisfying their hunger on a higher level than penetrating the meaning of Jesus' sign. Believers can derive profit from Jesus' distinction between perishable food and food that endures for eternal life. Without disparaging the need to feed their families, modern disciples are urged to focus on the food that endures for eternal life. As this discourse develops, such food is nothing less than Jesus' revelation. This passage, therefore, proposes a healthy balance in which nourishing the body does not neglect abiding by Jesus' word. It accentuates Jesus as the Bread of Life, not the loaves the crowd ate the previous day.

Tuesday: John 6:30-35 Jesus' mention of faith disturbs the crowd to the point where they ask Jesus to perform a sign that will prompt them to believe in him. Such a sign would be a supply of bread comparable to the manna that their ancestors received in their wilderness wandering in Exodus 16 and Numbers 11. Countering their request, Jesus observes that it was not Moses who gave them bread from heaven. Rather, it is his Father who gives the true bread. Thus the Father more than meets their expectations since the manna anticipates the real bread from heaven in Jesus' revelation. Jesus, therefore, is the Bread of Heaven that comes down from heaven and provides life for the world. Once again the crowd fails to understand by asking for a continuous supply of material bread. Seeking to get the crowd to a new level of perception, Jesus solemnly announces that he is the Bread of Life. Those who accept Jesus will never experience hunger or thirst for anything other than Jesus' message from the Father.

Reflection. Bread, water, life—how dearly people cherish these realities, especially when put in situations where lack of food and drink threatens life itself. Anyone who has experienced the precariousness of the desert knows and appreciates the incalculable value of such staples. This passage as well as others in John must compel believers to take the value and shock of these material images and elevate them to a higher plane. In verse 35 Jesus proclaims himself to be the Bread of Life. In 7:37 he welcomes all who are thirsty to come to him. In 11:25 he informs a grieving Martha that he himself is the resurrection and the life. Projecting all these basic human wants and needs to a higher level, disciples learn that only Jesus the Revealer is true Bread, true Water, and authentic Life.

Wednesday: John 6:35-40 In this section of the discourse Jesus seeks to raise his audience to a new level of understanding by proclaiming himself to be the Bread of Life. Those who accept him in faith will hunger and thirst only for his revealing word. The verses following these statements articulate the need to believe in Jesus and his Father's plan that human beings derive life from him. Jesus assures his audience that he will not drive away all those who come to him (v. 37), although people may still opt not to believe (v. 36). Jesus goes on to emphasize his purpose in coming down from heaven is to fulfill his Father's will, not his own. Pursuing the intent of the Father's will, Jesus focuses on the final day of judgment when he will raise up those whom the Father has given him. Restating the theme of resurrection on the last day, Jesus underlines the theme that those seeing the Son and believing in him will enjoy eternal life.

Reflection. This passage on resurrection and eternal life causes some to picture heaven as a place "up there" where one moves precariously from cloud to cloud in white garments while playing a harp. For John, however, nothing could be further from the truth. In this scene John emphasizes the personal dimension of "the life of the world to come." The vocabulary of the passage reinforces this accent: (1) believing *in* Jesus (vv. 35, 40), (2) coming to Jesus (vv. 35, 37), and (3) the giving of people by the Father to Jesus (v. 37, 39). Resurrection and eternal life follow upon union *with* Jesus. Being with Jesus in faith on earth and demonstrating that faith in obedience to him culminate in being *with* Jesus forever. Hence the sense of community with Jesus prevails. The One who descended from heaven to earth will lead such intimates from earth to heaven.

Thursday: John 6:44-51   Rejecting the crowd's inquiries about his human origins, Jesus shifts to his heavenly origins, namely, the fact that his Father sent him (v. 44) and that he is from God (v. 46). In turn, to accept Jesus in faith is to have the Father draw them to Jesus. Jesus then quotes Isaiah 54:13 that all will be taught by God. Jesus fulfills this prophecy by presenting himself as the one who provides what is contained in the religious symbol of bread. Since bread maintains life, Jesus will maintain life in all who come to him in faith. For their part, the people must look beyond purely human credentials (Jesus' family origins) and perceive him as the manifestation of the Father.

Returning to the experience of the crowd's ancestors in the wilderness wandering, Jesus points out that their eating of the manna did not prevent their death. The Bread that has come down from heaven, however, does prevent believers from dying. In verses 51-60 bread now functions not as Jesus' teaching or revelation but as the Eucharist. This living bread is now Jesus' own flesh for the life of the world.

Reflection. In this passage Jesus announces that he has come to share the mystery of his Father and his Father's plan with the crowd. At this point the image of bread symbolizes Jesus' teaching or revelation from the Father. Such sharing of bread must impact the lives of modern believers. Most of the time such sharing occurs subtly in the ordinary events of everyday life. Generosity to the poor, compassion for the sick and dying, an encouraging word to the despairing, etc., communicate in different ways Jesus' revelation, namely, that all people are God's children and must provide for each other. This is the daily bread of Jesus' teaching that energizes, nourishes, and offers hope. In living out Jesus' revelation in these and similar ways, believers announce that they too are the bread of life.

Friday: John 6:52-59   Starting in 6:51, this passage passes from the use of bread for symbolizing Jesus' identity as the Father's revelation to its sacramental use. It is now a question of eating the flesh and drinking the blood of Jesus. Thus Jesus has not only become flesh (human; see 1:14) but he has also given up his flesh and blood as the nourishment for believers. It must be noted that flesh and blood are not parts of Jesus. Flesh connotes the whole person as mortal and natural. Blood designates the entire person as living. Together flesh and blood means the living human person. Here John emphasizes more the personal than the communal dimensions of Eucharist. By sharing in Eucharist, believers share in the life of the Father, the Son, and the Spirit (see John 15:26). The result of this sharing is the establishment of an eternal relationship with God. Eucharist is for living now, so that believers can continue to live. By contrast, the manna in the wilderness is only a very weak analogy.

Reflection. Baptism, Eucharist, and eternal life form a unity for believers. While baptism confers the life that the Father and the Son share, Eucharist provides the food that sustains and nourishes that life. Eucharist highlights the self-giving of Jesus that makes eternal life possible: "Just as the living Father sent me, and I have life because of the Father, so also the one who feeds on me will have life because of me" (v. 57). Eucharist energizes believers, not only as individuals, but also as members of a community who even now begin to share ongoing life with God and one another. The Bread of Life strengthens believers for the journey whose destiny is eternal life.

Saturday: John 6:60-69   This passage focuses on the reactions of the disciples to the Bread of Life as Jesus' revelation or teaching, not the Eucharist. These reactions oscillate from murmuring, to unwilling-ness to believe, to complete loyalty. To those finding this teaching on the Bread of Life difficult, Jesus wonders if his ascending to the Father would resolve their hesitation. Jesus goes on to remark that humans left to their own resources (flesh) cannot obtain eternal life. Those who believe Jesus' words, however, will receive the life-giving Spirit. (At this point an editor comments that Jesus knew from the start the unbelievers and the betrayer.) Only those who believe in Jesus are able to come to him. Given this situation, many of the disciples reject Jesus and no longer walk with him. The Twelve, however, serve as a contrast. Speaking for this group, Peter vows their loyalty to Jesus. As the Holy One of God, only he has the words of eternal life.

Reflection. Decisions, decisions! Each day followers of Jesus must decide where their loyalty lies. Ultimately it is a question of faith, namely, to believe in Jesus or not. Temptations do not state this matter of choice in such clear, well-defined terms. Nonetheless all temptations revolve around this ultimate question of loyalty. Today's passage urges disciples to respond after the manner of Peter, namely, to abide with Jesus who alone has the words of eternal life. Only he provides access to this life by the gift of the Spirit. To accept Jesus or not to accept him—that is the ultimate decision.

The Fourth Week of Easter

Monday: John 10:1-10   This passage that follows Jesus' altercation with the Pharisees over the man born blind (9:1-41) consists of: (1) two parables (vv. 1-3a, 3b-5), (2) reaction at the failure to understand (v. 6), and (3) explanation of the parables (vv. 7-8, 9-10). In the first parable, the right way to approach the sheep is by means of the gate opened by the keeper. "[A] thief and a robber" (v. 1) may refer to the Pharisees in the previous chapter who do not approach the sheep properly but merely provide for themselves. In the second parable, "leads them out" (v. 3) may suggest Ezekiel 34:13 where Yahweh the shepherd meets the needs of his sheep. According to Numbers 27:16-17 Joshua ("Jesus" in Greek) guides the community so that they are not like sheep without a shepherd. Sheep will not follow a stranger, not unlike the man born blind who refuses to follow the Pharisees.

In the first explanation, only Jesus is the sheep gate by which the sheep can be approached. "All others who have come" (v. 8) may allude to leaders from Maccabean times on who pastured themselves, not the sheep. In the second explanation, only Jesus is the gate that leads to salvation. It is, however, a gate for the sheep, not the shepherds. Jesus brings life to the sheep; the thief brings death. Jesus identifies in terms of the sheep, the thief in terms of himself.

Reflection. To fleece or not to fleece—that is the question. This passage especially addresses disciples who have leadership positions of one type or another. Too often leaders may consider those being led as a means to promote their own ends. They merely see them as objects to advance their careers. Contrary to these leadership styles, today's passage powerfully challenges all leaders to model themselves on Jesus. He is the shepherd who calls each by name and leads them out. He views his sheep as recipients of life, not as objects of theft, slaughter, or destruction. He demonstrates genuine care for the sheep and consequently they recognize his voice and follow. He knows the proper avenue of approach to the sheep—he is shepherd, not thief or marauder. Fleecing the sheep is not his style.

Monday: John 10:11-18   (In Year A when John 10:1-10 is read on the previous Sunday, John 10:11-18 is used.) This passage also has links to Jesus' dispute with the Pharisees over the man born blind (9:1-41). Here Jesus contrasts himself with these leaders in Israel. "Shepherd" carries all the connotations of authority and responsibility, implying complete dedication to those in one's charge. This passage consists of: (1) first parable of the ideal shepherd (vv. 11-13), (2) second parable of the ideal shepherd (vv. 14-16), and (3) Jesus' laying down of his life (vv. 17-18). In the first parable, Jesus is the ideal shepherd because he does not shrink from laying down his life for his sheep. Given this context, it is likely that the hired hands are the Pharisees. In the second parable, Jesus is the ideal shepherd because he knows the sheep. As in 1 John 3:1, this knowledge implies a deep personal knowledge between shepherd and sheep. According to verse 16, the goal of this knowing is to bring about unity among all of Jesus' followers—hence a reference to the mission to the Gentiles.

Verses 17-18 are outside the parable and perhaps link the Gentile mission with the death-resurrection of Jesus. In John, since the Father and the Son have the same power (see 10:28-30), Jesus' rising from the dead is the same as the Father's raising of Jesus from the dead. Verse 18 shows that the death-resurrection of Jesus is tied to the Father's will. Jesus freely submits himself to taking up his life again.

Reflection. Letting go presents problems. Humans like to exercise control and thus determine their own future. They choose to regulate their own destiny and thus shape their own possibilities. They take care to manipulate the course of events and so ensure their happy outcome. Today's passage, however, provides a contrast with this human reluctance to let go. As the ideal shepherd, Jesus does not shrink from laying down his life for his sheep. This laying down of his life is a free act that fulfills the Father's will. By opening himself up to death, Jesus makes it possible to rise again. To surrender himself to the Father's will, namely, to let go, is to be assured of the Father's love.

Tuesday: John 10:22-30   This passage deals with Jesus' replies to his enemies on the feast of Dedication or Hanukkah. In the first exchange, their question about Jesus' messiahship introduces Jesus' reply that culminates in a declaration of his union with the Father. Jesus' response in term of shepherd/sheep is not surprising since kings in the ancient Near East were often called shepherds and Israel's kings also bore this title (see Ezek 34). Jesus, however, cannot buy the excessive political and nationalistic overtones of much popular messianic thinking. He replies to his adversaries that they remain unconvinced by his works because they are not sheep who hear his voice. On the other hand, those who are his sheep recognize him and follow him. Unlike the hireling, Jesus will not allow wolves to snatch his sheep. Similarly no one can snatch the sheep from his Father's hand. There is, therefore, a union existing between the Father and Jesus. That union is the bond by which Jesus will bind people to himself. Admittedly Jesus is a different type of shepherd.

Reflection. The Word must become enfleshed. Believers enjoy hearing the Word but hesitate at times to be moved by it. They delight in reading their Bibles but are reluctant to let that Word impact them. In contrast, Jesus exemplifies in this passage the extent of letting the Word become enfleshed. He teaches a messiahship based on the bond between the Father and himself. Thus he will be Messiah only in the way the Father designates, i.e., he will enflesh his Father's will or Word. The Word that he will speak is also his Father's (see 17:8). Not even the threat of death will shake his union with his Father and his Word. The Word has not only become flesh (1:14) but he has also enfleshed his Father's Word by submitting himself to his will.

Wednesday: John 12:44-50 In this summation of the first half of the gospel John begins by linking Jesus and the Father in terms of faith and mission. Whoever believes in Jesus believes in the Father who sent him, and whoever sees Jesus likewise sees the Father who sent him. Jesus goes on to state that he has come as light so that believers may not remain in darkness. Jesus then considers those who do not receive his words and thereby reject him. While Jesus does not judge such people, the word that he has spoken will judge them on the last day.

Jesus refers once again to the relationship between the Father and himself. He maintains that he has not spoken on his own. Rather, his Father has commanded him what to say and speak. This command is nothing less than eternal life. One is thus reminded of God's promise of a prophet like Moses: "I will put my words in the mouth of the prophet, who shall speak to them everything that I command. Anyone who does not heed the words that the prophet shall speak in my name, I myself will hold accountable" (Deut 18:18-19).

Reflection. Too often people tend to think of prophets as highly charismatic individuals who predict the future. The biblical reality, however, is quite different. While some prophets make future statements, most prophets concentrate on the here and now. They have a criticizing and/or energizing function. In criticizing, prophets tell it the way it really is by pointing out the evils in community life that must be destroyed. In energizing, prophets tell it the way it can be by projecting a new world and thereby offering hope. By their efforts to stamp out injustice, today's prophets assume the criticizing stance. By their efforts to encourage the distraught, they take on the energizing aspect. Today's passage reminds believers that they must continue to exercise the prophetic office they received in baptism.

Thursday: John 13:16-20   This part of Jesus' discourse provides an interpretation of the washing of the disciples' feet. It opens with Jesus saying that servants are not greater than their master and messengers not greater than their sender. The disciples, therefore, must know their proper place as servants and messengers. They will be truly fortunate, if they know what Jesus has said and done and if they do likewise. Jesus then announces that he knows the moral caliber of those he has chosen, including betrayal and lack of understanding. Paradoxically, however, his choice fulfills the Scriptures. Here Jesus refers specifically to Psalm 41:9. One of those at table with him will lift up his heel against him. When that betrayal takes place, the disciples will believe that Jesus is God's special revelation. Ironically, Jesus has not only selected weak followers but also sends them out as his representatives. Here the chain of command is in operation. To receive the disciple is to receive Jesus and to receive Jesus is to receive the Father.

Reflection. God's love defies human calculations. In this passage Jesus announces that one of his intimates will betray him. He also knows the frailty of the others. Some would argue that Jesus has made some very poor choices. Jesus, however, dismisses such logic by observing that these fragile disciples will also represent him to the world when they are sent out. The footwashing, among other things, demonstrates his boundless love: "Having loved his own who were in the world, he loved them to the end" (13:1). This scene in John must challenge believers to raise questions such as these: What is the limit of my loving? Can I continue to love in the wake of hurt and betrayal? Do I dare to wash the feet of those who have neglected me? The scene on Calvary readily provides Jesus' answers to these upsetting questions.

Friday: John 14:1-6   This scene consists of the following: (1) Jesus' departure and return (vv. 1-4), (2) misunderstanding about "the way" (v. 5), and (3) Jesus as "the way" (v. 6). This farewell discourse is caught up in an atmosphere of imminent departure. The "troubled hearts" describe the subsequent battle between the forces of evil ("the world") and the disciples of Jesus upon the latter's departure. Originally verses 1-3 dealt with Jesus' return after the disciples' death when he would take them to heaven ("my Father's house"). It was later reinterpreted, however, to focus attention on the union between the disciples and Jesus/God. "My Father's house" now refers to the body of Jesus (see John 2:19-22; 8:35). As the way, Jesus is the unique means of salvation. As the truth, he is the revelation of the Father. As the life, he is the communication of the life he shares with the Father.

Reflection. In situations charged with great sorrow and possibly imminent death, believing in God and believing in Jesus pose no little difficulty. Hence believers can rather easily grasp the meaning of troubled hearts as Jesus prepares to leave the disciples. Yet despite the enormous problems involved, Jesus continues to urge them to believe in his Father and himself. Such faith is not reducible to a declaration of the tenets of the creed. Without excluding such tenets, the faith envisioned here is more profound and personal. It embraces the acceptance of the persons of the Father and the Son, an acceptance that anchors believers in the intimacy of their relationship. Having accepted that relationship, believers are prepared to do what the Father and Jesus command. It is the presence of the Father and Jesus that makes troubled hearts grow fonder.

Saturday: John 14:7-14   Verses 7-11 develop the implications of Jesus as the way, the truth, and the life. To know Jesus, i.e., to acknowledge him, is to know and acknowledge the Father. To see Jesus is to see the Father. After the manner of Deuteronomy 18:18, Jesus is the emissary of the Father. His words and deeds point beyond, namely, to the intimate bond between the Father and himself. Jesus goes on to link faith with the present task of the disciple. To believe in Jesus is to be empowered to perform his works. To be united with Jesus and the Father is to share their power. Moreover, Jesus announces that after his departure greater works will continue in the lives of his disciples.

During the time between Jesus' departure and return these disciples must ask in his name. Upon their asking, he will keep on performing the works of his Father in their midst. Hence the absent Jesus will continue to be present, especially when the disciples gather for worship and address their petitions to him. The glory of God, revealed in Jesus' works on earth, will also manifest itself in the works of the worshiping disciples.

Reflection. The absent Jesus is present. The Jesus who has gone home to his Father has not abandoned his disciples. At times, however, today's disciples may sense a certain disadvantage when they compare themselves to the original disciples during Jesus' earthly ministry. After all, Jesus walked and talked with them—something quite impossible now. Today's passage, however, is calculated to counter such a perceived disadvantage. Whenever believers gather for worship, especially for the Eucharist, this same Jesus is present, albeit in a different mode. In fact, there is continuity. The disciples will now perform even greater works than Jesus on the condition that they continue to ask in his name. The absent Jesus is still present.

The Fifth Week of Easter

Monday: John 14:21-26   This section of Jesus' farewell discourse consists of: (1) the keeping of Jesus' commandments (v. 21), (2) Judas' question (v. 22), (3) the coming of the Father to the believer (vv. 23-24), and (4) the mission of the Paraclete (Advocate) to teach (vv. 25-26). Verse 21 makes abundantly clear that love and keeping the commandments are two components of the same way of life. Thus love provides the motive for keeping the commandments and articulates their very essence. In turn, the Father will love them and Jesus will reveal himself to them.

Judas' question prompts Jesus to assure those keeping his word/ commandment that his presence after the resurrection will include the Father's presence. On the other hand, those who refuse to keep Jesus' word/commandment divorce themselves from that life that only Jesus can bring. Once again Jesus takes up the role of the Paraclete (Advocate). Actually Jesus is the first Paraclete. The Holy Spirit is another Paraclete (see 14:16) whom the Father will send in Jesus' name. One function of the Paraclete is to develop the teaching of Jesus. To "remind" is not to recall an event statically but to live the implications of Jesus' word at a later date.

Reflection. Let the Holy Spirit do it! Not infrequently believers eagerly await a new Pentecost but they do not see themselves involved in such an event. They want to see people changed because of the Spirit but do not view themselves as changing those people. Today's passage, however, eliminates the basis for such reluctance. Here Jesus promises his disciples that the Spirit will teach them and remind them of all that he told them. By reminding, John means that the Spirit will provide the full meaning and sense of Jesus' words. Jesus commissions believers, therefore, to mine the riches of his message. Hence believers are empowered to effect a new Pentecost. They are charged to help change the lives of others by communicating in word and deed the meaning of Jesus' message today. Let believers with the Holy Spirit do it!

Tuesday: John 14:27-31a   In this passage, as Jesus prepares to leave the world, he offers his disciples the gift of peace that is the equivalent of eternal life. In this atmosphere of his imminent departure the disciples naturally experience overwhelming fear and trepidation. They project a deep sense of possessiveness. They are not yet ready to let Jesus depart and so complete his mission. The disciples cannot love because they do not believe. Once they come to accept in faith the mission of Jesus and thus his need to depart for the Father who is greater, they will be able to love Jesus. To frustrate the Father's plan is to refuse to love. As the passage winds down, Jesus speaks of the impending struggle with the powers of evil personified as "the ruler of this world" (v. 30). Jesus quickly adds that this ruler enjoys no power over him because he surrenders his life freely—no one takes it from him (10:18). Jesus then states categorically that he loves the Father because he accomplishes the Father's will. Love and obedience go hand in hand.

Reflection. To love is to let go. Letting go poses formidable problems for all disciples. It may be a question of material goods, power over others, desire for greater fame and prestige, etc. Modern believers thus share to some degree the possessiveness of the disciples who do not want Jesus to depart. For them, his presence means security while his absence spells disaster. Jesus, on the other hand, serves as the embodiment of letting go. He has surrendered his will to his Father and, therefore, is prepared to let go by fulfilling his Father's will. For Jesus, letting go and loving are but two aspects of the same reality. Jesus loves the

Father because he acts in accordance with the Father's command. The sign on Jesus' cross may also be read as follows: "This is the extent of letting go."

Wednesday: John 15:1-8   Verses 1-6 are a parable about the vine and the branches that contains certain allegorical elements, e.g., Jesus is the vine; the Father is the vine grower. The passage in John 15:7-17 adapts and develops this imagery within the framework of the farewell discourse. The Old Testament frequently uses the vine as a symbol of God's people (see Ezek 15:1-6). Here John applies the imagery to Jesus but in such a way that the new Israel, the branches, is part of the vine.

Jesus claims to be the real vine, i.e., the one who brings genuine life from the Father. Not to bear fruit is not to share in the genuine life/vine and hence to be dead. But to share in that life/vine is to share it with others (v. 2: "bears more fruit"). In verse 3 Jesus' word in the farewell discourse cleanses the disciples. But the cleansing implies response, namely, living on in Jesus (v. 4). Productivity is also bound up with this intimate, personal union. To be apart from Jesus means to be unproductive (v. 5) and to be unproductive means to suffer final punishment. In verse 7 John applies the parable to the farewell discourse setting. Union with Jesus means a life founded on Jesus' words or revelation. Harmony with that revelation ensures the fulfillment of any and all requests. Verse 8 shows that these requests look to productivity and discipleship. The Father, the vine grower, is glorified in the disciples who continue the mission of the Son (see 12:28).

Reflection. Union means communion. All believers are pleased to share in Jesus' life but some are less pleased to share it with others. Most believers are thrilled to worship God in private but less thrilled to worship that same God in public service for others. John, however, counters such tendencies by presenting Jesus under the image of the vine. While productivity means life in Jesus, it also means life for others: "bears more fruit." To share the life of the vine means to reveal the mystery of Jesus to others. Being a disciple and bearing more fruit go hand in hand. Union means communion.

Thursday: John 15:9-11   Like 15:7-8, this passage adapts and develops the parable of the vine and the branches (15:1-6) within the framework of the farewell discourse. In verse 9 John introduces the theme of love that is connected with abiding in Jesus' love that, in turn, has its origin in the Father's love. "To abide" means to acknowledge Jesus' love by responding and, indeed, by responding to Jesus' commandments. Love and obedience share a mutual relationship. Love originates in obedience and obedience stems from love. The union of the disciple with Jesus will effect joy. Such joy derives from the union of love and obedience that Jesus first experiences by fidelity to the Father.

Reflection. Love, obedience, and joy constitute a trinity of inseparable values according to this passage in John. Ironically, however, disciples are often tempted to discover real joy outside this trinity. They prefer to be "genuinely" happy by "doing their own thing" and thereby dismissing love and obedience. This passage subtly but forcefully reminds them that their true joy derives from keeping this trinity intact. Hence whenever love arises from obedience and obedience from love, the stage is set for abiding joy. In such circumstances Jesus' joy lives on in the disciples and their joy is complete (v. 11).

Friday: John 15:12-17   As John continues to adapt and develop the parable of the vine and the branches (15:1-6), he has Jesus inform the disciples that the fundamental commandment is love. Mutual love flows from Jesus' love of the disciples that, in turn, flows from the Father's love of Jesus. Jesus' death for others is the specific model that John holds up to his audience. Such a love constitutes the circle of Jesus' intimates. These intimates are made privy to the revelation that Jesus has received from the Father. Jesus chose the disciples, not vice versa. Nonetheless, their selection envisions going on mission for others (v. 16: "go and bear fruit"). Enduring productivity assures the disciples that the Father will heed their requests. "Love one another" is the appropriate conclusion of this passage.

Reflection. This passage declares that love is the family tradition. Family members who rejoice in being followers of Jesus sometimes fail to share the Jesus tradition with others. While they are pleased to call God their Father, on occasion they fail to treat others as daughters and sons of this same Father. As a remedy for such inconsistencies, John unabashedly lays down this principle: love one another. He then offers divine love as the model for human love. The Father loves the Son and so shares his word with him. The Son loves the disciples and so shares the Father's word with them. In turn, the disciples are to share that reality by holding fast to Jesus' word/commandment: love one another. In the Fourth Gospel, love is the family tradition.

Saturday: John 15:18-21   As Jesus continues his discourse, he paints a realistic picture of the dangers and problems that lie ahead for the disciples. The hatred of the world that Jesus has experienced will be the lot of his followers. Here Jesus speaks of two different realms: (1) his own and (2) that of the world. The fact that Jesus called and chose his disciples does not remove them physically from the world. Rather, in bearing Jesus' revelation, they will stand in opposition to the world. Jesus further announces that they will fare no better than he. After all, servants are not greater than their master. The persecution of the disciples follows upon the persecution of Jesus himself. Far from being purely coincidental, such persecution is intrinsically linked to Jesus' name, namely, his revelation of God to humanity. To persecute Jesus' disciples, therefore, is to reject this revelation.

Reflection. Family honor is at stake. Modern followers of Jesus at times experience ridicule and verbal abuse. They present a value system at odds with that of the world. They project a different image of what it means to be truly human. In dealing with these put-downs, disciples do well to reflect on today's passage—family honor is at stake. They suffer this type of persecution because of Jesus' name. They profess that Jesus is the Father's revelation to humanity. The disciples' faith is thus rooted in Jesus who communicates the Father's message to the world. In coping with the world's resistance to this revelation, they know that family honor is at stake.

The Sixth Week of Easter

Monday: John 15:26–16:4a   In this passage Jesus begins by developing another aspect of the Paraclete (Advocate), namely, that of witness. In testifying on Jesus' behalf (v. 26), the Holy Spirit acknowledges the success of Jesus' mission and arranges the segments of his life into a meaningful whole. Once the Spirit has strengthened the disciples' faith and assured them of God's plan, however, the disciples must take up their own task of witnessing. They are unique in that they have been with Jesus from the start. Jesus next considers the persecution of his disciples because of their witnessing. He does so to avoid the scandal of having their faith shaken. Thinking of his Christian community at the end of the first century AD, John has Jesus predict their expulsion from the synagogues—a form of persecution that their perpetrators will consider a form of divine service. Lack of knowledge of the Father and Jesus dictates their course of action.

Reflection. For not a few people witnessing has become a reality limited to courtrooms where one swears to tell the truth, the whole truth, and nothing but the truth. Today's passage moves beyond this judicial setting to consider the larger framework of ordinary life. A Christian witness is one who has so absorbed the message of Jesus that she or he lives it out in a variety of nonjudicial circumstances. These witnesses, for example, provide encouragement, vision, and hope for others. They reassert Jesus' priorities and opt for the Gospel message despite contemporary gloom and doom. In so doing, the Holy Spirit and the Christian witness form a team that challenges the world with the modern meaning of Jesus as God's revelation.

Tuesday: John 16:5-11 This passage opens with Jesus' declaration about his going home to the Father. Sorrow has so overwhelmed the disciples that not one of them has dared to ask Jesus about the route. Jesus then notes the advantage that they will derive from his departure, namely, the sending of the Paraclete (Advocate). At this point the Gospel of John presents the Paraclete as a lawyer, specifically a prosecuting attorney. In this capacity, he seeks to reverse the decision of the lower court (v. 8: "convict the world") that condemned Jesus to death. The real sin is the refusal to believe in Jesus as the Messiah and the Son of God (the charges of that first trial). The righteousness or justice involved is Jesus' glorious return to the Father. To be sure, righteousness or justice is on the side of Jesus. Finally the Paraclete exposes the opposing attorney, the devil and ruler of this world, who was the real culprit behind Jesus' betrayal and trial.

Reflection. Modern believers need the legal maneuverings of the Paraclete in daily life. The Paraclete assures them that Jesus has achieved final victory and thus vindicated himself. In the problems besetting the modern church, such believers collaborate with the Paraclete in seeking justice for all. In fighting for the rights of the underprivileged, for example, disciples follow the legal strategy of the Paraclete. The ongoing presence of the Paraclete assures ultimate victory in the wider courtroom setting.

Wednesday John 16:12-15   John addresses the question of the preservation and understanding of Jesus' message by developing the role of the Paraclete as the teacher. What is at stake is a deeper penetration into the mystery of Jesus. The Paraclete functions here after the manner of Lady Wisdom. He guides the disciples along the way of truth. As in Proverbs, it is a question of life, namely, a life in keeping with Jesus' teaching. "[Declaring] to you the things that are coming" (v. 13) looks to the significance of Jesus for each new generation. One cannot simply ask: what did Jesus teach? One must also ask: what does that teaching mean for disciples today? As guide and teacher, the Paraclete resolves the problem of the generation gap. John also develops the roles of the Father, Jesus, and the Paraclete. By revealing the Father, Jesus glorifies the Father. By revealing Jesus, the Paraclete glorifies Jesus. The Paraclete, moreover, announces not only the Son but also the Father since both the Father and the Son possess everything in common.

Reflection. Modern believers stand in need of the Paraclete as teacher and guide. To be sure, the teaching of the Paraclete conforms to the teaching of Jesus but goes beyond it. "[T]he Spirit of truth . . . will guide you to all truth" (v. 13). Believers can no longer be satisfied with what Jesus taught. They must also concern themselves with the meaning of Jesus' message for a new time and situation. Under the guidance of the Paraclete modern followers possess a guide to see the implications of Jesus' message in ever new circumstances and crises. The role of the Paraclete, however, does not dispense with leadership roles in the believing community. Rather, the Paraclete urges the entire people of God to seek the significance of Jesus' revelation in a new setting.

Thursday: John 16:16-20   (In countries where the celebration of the Ascension is transferred to the Seventh Sunday of Easter, this gospel is used on Thursday of the Sixth Week of Easter.) In this passage not seeing Jesus concerns his departure following his death on the cross. During this "little while" he will not be seen. Seeing Jesus, however, seems to capture the joy linked to Christian life after the resurrection. Obviously such an experience involves the Paraclete since he continues Jesus' glorified presence among believers after Jesus has gone home to the Father. Jesus' sayings about the little while and seeing/not seeing as well as going home to the Father have left the disciples confused. Jesus reads their minds and anticipates their questions. In responding indirectly to these questions, Jesus speaks of the privileges or prerogatives they will enjoy after the "little while." The first such privilege or prerogative is enduring joy, a joy opposed to the false joy the world experiences at Jesus' death. Pain and suffering will precede the disciples' joy but that pain and suffering will provide the raw material for this overwhelming joy.

Reflection. It's all about interpretation. Today's passage contrasts the reactions of the disciples and those of the world. At Jesus' death on the cross the world rejoices while the disciples weep and mourn. The world interprets the crucifixion as their defeat of Jesus. For the moment, the disciples interpret this same event as at least a discouraging setback. But the disciples have yet to see the total picture. Jesus' resurrection and the Paraclete's ongoing presence create an entirely different scene and hence a new interpretation grounded in faith. This passage urges modern disciples to continue to hope. Despite human failures and setbacks, the Paraclete continues the presence of the glorified Jesus. His role as consoler implies patience in waiting for a fuller picture and a new interpretation.

Friday: John 16:20-23a   This passage opens with the last verse of yesterday's gospel. For the moment the disciples experience pain and sorrow while the world rejoices at the death of Jesus. Their pain and sorrow, however, will give way to intense joy. Jesus compares this movement from suffering to happiness with a woman's experience of the pangs of childbirth. While this comparison appeals to human childbirth, John may also be suggesting the ordeal of Israel in the Old Testament prior to the coming of salvation (see Isa 26:17-18; 66:7-10). This joy that no one can take away from the disciples is twofold: (1) that linked to Jesus' victory over death in the resurrection and (2) that connected to the abiding presence of the Paraclete. Moreover, besides joy the disciples will enjoy a second privilege or prerogative, namely, an understanding that eliminates the need for further questioning. Obviously the Paraclete plays a vital role in providing such understanding.

Reflection. This dimension of intense joy did not stop after Jesus' postresurrectional appearances. The Paraclete continues to provide such joy in tandem with believers. This collaboration between the Paraclete and believers is designed to make joy a contagious reality for those who experience frustration and anguish in the world. To encourage, to offer hope, to dig deep into one's pockets, etc., are different ways in which this collaboration manifests itself. The Paraclete and believers help to ease the pangs of such childbirth and so create an atmosphere of pervasive joy.

Saturday: John 16:23b-28   This passage promises two more privileges or prerogatives to believers after the "little while": (1) intimacy with the Father that assures the granting of their requests (vv. 23b-24, 26) and (2) perception of Jesus as the Father's revelation (vv. 25, 27-28). Owing to the presence of the Paraclete and hence the presence of Jesus, believers will experience intimacy with the Father. Such intimacy will enable them to make requests of the Father in Jesus' name and be assured of their granting. Jesus' "hour," consisting of his passion, death, resurrection, and bestowal of the Spirit, makes such access to the Father possible.

In verse 25 Jesus promises to speak plainly and not in figures of speech about his entire message, a message that highlights his Father. Indeed Jesus will create so close a bond of love between the Father and believers that he will seem not to be involved. The Father will thus see in believers his own Son. This passage concludes with Jesus' statement about coming into the world and going home to the Father. Having established a profound bonding with humanity, Jesus returns to the Father to renew his total union with him.

Reflection. The intimacy reflected in this passage is simply staggering. Jesus has shared his revelation of the Father with his disciples. Simply put, he has told them who God is. The Father already loves these disciples because they love Jesus and accept in faith that he came from the Father. The bond between the Father and the disciples has become so close that the Father, in seeing the disciples, sees his very own Son. It is presence, not absence, that makes the believer's heart grow fonder. This passage assures modern disciples that despite all the gloom and doom in the world they have special access to the Father through Jesus in the Spirit. Calamities and crises notwithstanding, believers must find consolation in the truth that they share in divine life and love. Their task, therefore, is to continue to nurture and develop that life and love with each passing day. The enjoyment of heaven thus begins on earth.

The Seventh Week of Easter

Monday: John 16:29-33   The disciples acknowledge that Jesus is now speaking plainly and not in figures of speech. With a boastful form of developing faith they now profess that Jesus knows all things and the time for questioning is past. They think that the promise of verse 23a (the end of raising questions) has been fulfilled and confidently affirm that Jesus came from God. After asking them about their faith, Jesus announces that the decisive moment (the hour that comes through suffering and death) is here. At that moment the disciples will be scattered, leaving Jesus quite alone. But Jesus then qualifies his statement by observing that, owing to his Father's presence, he is not alone. Even if his disciples abandon him, his Father will not. He mentions the Father's presence in order to assure the disciples of peace—ironically a peace that coexists with pain and suffering and is grounded in faith in Jesus and community with him. Given Jesus' victory over death, believers must also overcome the world. Courage rooted in faith will enable them to achieve victory.

Reflection. Day in and day out, believers face formidable obstacles in the world. In Jesus' turn of phrase they undergo persecution. A collision of values has been set in motion, namely, the values of Jesus versus those of the world. Nonetheless, believers enjoy a significant precedent in the ongoing struggle. They have inherited Jesus' victory over the world and acknowledge that they too can conquer. To achieve this victory, they must demonstrate limitless courage in the face of the world's value system. Such courage must stem from their unqualified faith in Jesus and ongoing union with him. The believers' "hour," while it involves pain, also boasts of the peace that Jesus shares with them.

Tuesday: John 17:1-11a   In a farewell discourse, the speaker often concludes with a prayer for those left behind. Although Jesus addresses the Father in this passage, the burden of his prayer touches the disciples. (This prayer is commonly known as Jesus' High Priestly Prayer.) Even if the exaltation has not yet taken place, one senses that Jesus has already ascended to the Father and that the disciples are privy to a private exchange. The intimacy of this exchange is heightened by the frequent use of the title "Father." While the glory and divinity of Jesus figure significantly in the prayer, Jesus' dependence on the Father is also marked. The first eight verses focus on Jesus' prayer for his own glorification. "Glory" connotes the external demonstration of majesty by acts of power. Jesus will glorify the Father by giving eternal life that, in turn, will beget new disciples. Significantly Jesus does not pursue his own good on his return to the Father but the good of the disciples.

Verses 4-5 reveal Jesus' petition for glory on the basis of what he has already accomplished. Like Lady Wisdom (see Prov 8:23-30), Jesus requests the glory he shared prior to creation itself. In verse 6 the work that glorified the Father was the communication of God's name ("I AM") to the disciples. As a result of that revelation, the disciples are aware that everything Jesus has—his message—comes from the Father. In verses 9-11 Jesus introduces a new focus by including the disciples in his prayer. It will be through their efforts that God's name, confided to Jesus, will be glorified. Indeed, Jesus has already been glorified in them. The "world" expresses the totality of the forces opposed to Jesus' revelation of the Father. For John, the "world" must cease to be "world" in order to be saved.

Reflection. Two's company but three's a prayer. Some believers have a tendency to regard prayer as solely an intimate dialogue between God and themselves. They usually bring only their own needs to God. Even when they include others, they view them within the framework of their own needs. Today's passage, however, counters such a prayer style. John presents Jesus' prayer as an intimate exchange in which the disciples are both privileged participants and objects. Even when Jesus asks for glory from the Father, it envisions giving eternal life to the disciples. In the very act of returning to God, Jesus looks to the needs of others. In today's world the sick and the dying who include others in their prayer of pain have captured the Christian prayer style. The shut-ins who break through their despair of loneliness by considering others in their prayer life have understood the Christian manner of prayer. The successful who focus their prayer on the needs of the less successful have learned the meaning of Jesus' prayer. Two's company but three's a prayer.

Wednesday: John 17:11b-19   In this part of Jesus' High Priestly Prayer the situation of the disciples is paramount. They do not belong to the "world." Yet Jesus gives them his Father's word and sends them into the "world" to provoke faith in him. Nonetheless the "world" responds with hatred. Jesus, therefore, prays that the Father protect them with his divine name. In the midst of pain and frustration they will experience great joy. By sharing the mission of Jesus, they also share the joy of Jesus. In verses 17-19 John deals with the consecration of Jesus and the disciples. The disciples are to be holy because of their mission. Specifically they are consecrated in the truth, namely, God's word. That word has purified them and sends them forth to provoke faith. With regard to Jesus' self-consecration, John may be thinking of Jesus' voluntary sacrifice of his life. Jesus' self-consecration in death sanctifies the disciples for their mission.

Reflection. Selection means service. On occasion believers, in enjoying their status as believers, content themselves with limiting faith to God and themselves. Other believers proud to be chosen as bosses or supervisors soon become satisfied with promoting only their own good. The Johannine Jesus in today's passage recommends an entirely different approach. Here Jesus states that he chose the disciples, not vice versa. In the High Priestly Prayer John elaborates a theology of service stemming from Jesus' choice.

Disciples receive the Father's word but that word is for others. Jesus sends them forth into the "world" but that sending is for the faith of others. Jesus consecrates them by the Father's word but that consecration is for provoking the acknowledgment of Jesus. In today's world bosses and supervisors who see their positions as a chance to provide for others understand the meaning of selection. Leaders, both civil and ecclesiastical, who use their status for advancing the welfare of others reflect the proper understanding of selection. The talented who use their gifts to bring happiness and joy to others evince the true sense of selection. For these and similar people, selection means service.

Thursday: John 17:20-26   This passage forms the conclusion of Jesus' High Priestly Prayer and also the conclusion of the farewell discourses. Verses 20-23 deal with the unity of those who believe in Jesus, while verses 24-26 are Jesus' wish that such believers be with him. This prayer is admittedly a fitting finale for the farewell discourses. In verses 21-23 the unity of believers that is modeled on the unity between the Father and Jesus will challenge the "world" to accept Jesus' mission, namely, that the Father sent him. This unity of believers is two-dimensional. First of all, it reflects the unity between the Father and the Son. Second, it makes the believers into a community. A community that lacks unity among its members can hardly reflect the unity between the Father and Jesus.

In verses 24-26 Jesus' final wish is that believers should share his company. There is, consequently, a final revelation reserved for these believers in heaven. Indeed it is appropriate that these believers should be finally united with Jesus since they have been his intimates on earth. Verse 26 identifies the Father's love for Jesus with the presence of Jesus himself. Such a presence is clearly dynamic.

Reflection. Forgiveness brings unity to the community. Believers who usually dislike disruption occasionally tend to cut off from their world of concern and affection those who have hurt them. Such believers ordinarily disdain the breakup of a group into factions, yet in refusing to pardon they contribute to the disunity. This segment of Jesus' prayer, however, militates against such breakups. For John, the unity that is the basis of community is the unity between the Father and Jesus. The openness and solidarity between the Father and Jesus are to be reflected in the community of believers in Jesus. In turn, the unity of believers will challenge the world to accept Jesus' message. The failure to communicate forgiveness distorts the Father-Son unity and hence offers no challenge. Only forgiveness brings unity to the community.

Friday: John 21:15-19 This chapter is an epilogue, the work of a redactor who wished to preserve certain traditions for the Johannine community. This section deals with Peter's rehabilitation and fate. Here the author presents Jesus' threefold question and Peter's threefold answer in order to demonstrate that Peter's love is genuine. In the Old Testament, feeding sheep (see Ezek 34:2) and tending sheep (see Ezek 34:10) are the tasks of kings. (The Greek verb translated "to tend" has the connotation "to rule/govern.") Jesus, the model shepherd, gives Peter both responsibility for the flock and authority over it. Verse 18 is probably an independent unit added to link Peter's future with his death. This verse contrasts Peter as a young man and as an older man. As an older man, he will follow Jesus in suffering (see the binding of Jesus in John 18:12, 24).

Reflection. In this rehabilitation scene the author describes Peter's leadership style. In instructing Peter to feed and tend the sheep, the author may be implying the manner of leadership of the Good Shepherd, e.g., such a shepherd lays down his life for the sheep (10:11). More striking, however, this passage points out that the sheep belong to Jesus ("my sheep"). Leadership, as it is known today, takes on a variety of forms: governors and presidents, CEOs, parents, teachers, and the like. (Notice that the person in charge of a parish is commonly called "pastor," i.e., "shepherd.") In all these and similar leadership positions, Jesus' words to Peter are instructive—the sheep belong to Jesus. In dealing with their charges, leaders cannot view them as objects to be manipulated. They belong to Jesus and, as such, possess an inherent dignity. In this scenario leaders must care and provide for the sheep in their care because their model is always the Good Shepherd.

Saturday: John 21:20-25 In the Gospel of John the Beloved Disciple is the model disciple and the source of many of the traditions behind it. It is only natural that the Johannine community is upset by his death since he was not expected to die. Such an expectation was probably based on his advanced age. To Peter's question about the fate of the Beloved Disciple, Jesus responds whether he should not be concerned. Peter's task is simply to follow Jesus. In verse 23 a redactor explains that: (1) Jesus' question gave rise to the belief that the Beloved

Disciple would not die; and (2) Jesus said nothing about his immortality. In the conclusion this redactor identifies the Beloved Disciple as the witness behind the tradition in the Fourth Gospel. This embraces the development of that testimony for future generations.

Reflection. Occasionally believers can suffer from the debilitating effects of the comparative degree. For example, so-and-so has more money than I; therefore, I am unhappy. In today's passage the Johannine community mentions its rich legacy, namely, the prominence of the Beloved Disciple and the significance of his testimony. Such boasting, however, can lead to the creation of a rivalry between him and Peter. In the end, however, such rivalry achieves nothing. Both Peter and the Beloved Disciple are followers of Jesus with different functions in Jesus' community. Greatness is not measured by position or status but by the fulfillment of one's calling, no matter what it is. It is not a question of Peter *versus* the Beloved Disciple but of Peter *and* the Beloved Disciple.

The Tenth to the Thirty-fourth Weeks of the Year

The Tenth Week of the Year

Monday: Matthew 5:1-12   In the Sermon on the Mount (5:1–7:29) Matthew has Jesus set out his plan for the kingdom. To the question about what constitutes the happiness of the kingdom, Jesus responds that a combination of qualities will make his followers truly happy. These are the Beatitudes, a profound expression of such qualities.

The first beatitude looks back to the poor/humble of the land in Zephaniah 2:3. By accepting God's view, such people already possess the kingdom. To those who mourn because of their human condition, God promises consolation on the last day. The meek, i.e., those who do not assert their power, the unassuming like Jesus, enter the kingdom as well. Those hungering for the right covenantal relationship between God and people will be satisfied. The merciful who exclude no one will not find themselves excluded. Those with an undivided heart ("clean of heart"), totally given over to God's outlook, will experience God in paradise. Those who remove the barriers to genuine human living (the peacemakers) will learn on the last day that they are truly God's daughters and sons. Those who continue to suffer by accepting God's view are already worthy of the kingdom. Finally those who suffer harassment because of allegiance to Jesus are in the tradition of the prophets and will have a comparable reward.

Reflection. The Beatitudes pose this question for believers: who are the truly happy people? Assessing their contemporary world, disciples will discover that those who pursue "the good life" as a purely personal quest for pleasure may find pleasure but not happiness. Believers will also learn that those who spend their time and energy amassing fortunes only for themselves may accrue wealth but not happiness. By turning to the Beatitudes, disciples realize that they list the truly happy, enviable people. The pleasure seekers, the wealth cravers, the power hoarders, etc. have no place there. In Jesus' view of the kingdom, those who meet the needs of others are truly happy, enviable. The self-effacing, the merciful, the peacemakers, and the like are proof that only those who live the Beatitudes attain genuine happiness.

Tuesday: Matthew 5:13-16   In the last beatitude (5:11-12), Matthew speaks of the persecuted. By linking two originally separate sayings (salt and light), he paradoxically addresses these persecuted as the hope of the world. Salt was an invaluable commodity for the ancients. The followers of Jesus are to be to the world what salt is to the ancients. The lifestyle of these followers is thus vital for the world's welfare. Should their lifestyle cease to be genuine, then they would become as useless as flat salt. Unfaithful Christians are insipid Christians.

Light also exemplifies the public character of the Christian vocation. In the one-room, windowless house, the light from the lamp was important for all in the household. Similarly believers live for others. Again, they are as public as a city on a hill: their presence cannot be mistaken. In verse 16 Matthew returns to the light image and establishes a system of links for disciples. People in general will notice their lifestyle and, in turn, link that style with their heavenly Father. Thus discipleship that is fundamentally concerned for others is grounded in the glory of God.

Reflection. The one-on-one relationship of believers with God is never a problem. God never gets in their way; only other people do. Somewhere certain disciples learned that, if their relationship with God is right, then it is complete. Today's passage shows that Matthew's community is tempted to identify in terms of one-on-one. To counteract such a temptation, the evangelist suggests two images. They are to be salt, disciples who will season the world by being for others. They are to be light, set apart to illumine the way to the Lord. They are to be as conspicuous as a city on a hill, as needed as a lamp in a one-room, windowless house. They are to be contagious for others. By pointing to the Father's glory, they show that one plus one makes three.

Wednesday: Matthew 5:17-19   See Wednesday of the Third Week of Lent.

Thursday: Matthew 5:20-26   See Friday of the First Week of Lent.

Friday: Matthew 5:27-32   The second antithesis or contrast (vv. 27-30) enlarges the Mosaic prohibition against adultery to include lustful looks and thoughts. For Jesus, the woman is not a sex object—she is a person who is to be accorded her rightful dignity. Verses 29-30 (tearing out one's right eye and cutting off one's right hand) are metaphorical language: the saving of the entire person at the final judgment deserves any and every demand now. The third antithesis or contrast (vv. 31-32) revokes the Mosaic permission regarding divorce. "Unlawful" may refer to incestuous marriages already forbidden by the law (see Lev 18:6-18), hence not a departure from Jesus' strong stand against divorce.

Reflection. This passage challenges believers to adopt the following system of priorities: (1) they must always treat persons as persons; and (2) they must always regard objects as objects. Danger sets in whenever persons are reduced to objects and objects are elevated to persons. In his second antithesis Matthew has Jesus expand the content of the sixth commandment. Adultery now embraces more than the physical act itself—it includes reducing a woman from person to object. In Jesus' view a woman possesses an inherent dignity precisely as a person. The metaphors of cutting off one's right eye and right hand intensify the efforts necessary to avoid degrading a woman. In today's promiscuous world where pornography reduces women to the level of sex objects, believers encounter ceaseless opportunities for following Jesus' system of priorities. To respect a woman as a person with an inherent dignity is ultimately to strike a blow for preserving not only Jesus' priorities but basic human values.

Saturday: Matthew 5:33-37   In this fourth antithesis or contrast Jesus takes up the Jewish practice of swearing oaths. Oaths were part and parcel of Israel's everyday life. For example, a woman suspected of adultery by her husband had to take an oath that she was innocent of such an egregious crime (see Num 5:19). But despite the abundance of occasions for swearing an oath, Jesus prohibits in the most absolute manner any such procedure, whether by heaven, earth, or Jerusalem. Jesus further insists that one must not even swear by one's head since one cannot manage one's graying hair. The reason for such an absolute prohibition is the violation of God's majesty. Oaths, in Jesus' view, seek to control and manipulate God. Hence one should limit oneself to saying yes or no.

Reflection. Believers simply take it for granted that, e.g., in a courtroom setting, they will swear to tell the truth, the whole truth, and nothing but the truth, so help them God. The Matthean Jesus, however, finds something incongruous in this procedure, namely, the attempt by humans to control and manipulate God. This absolute prohibition of oaths may give believers pause to think of other ways in which they may unwittingly seek to limit and control God. While disciples usually value their freedom to a great extent, it is paradoxical that they should try to restrain and manipulate God's exercise of freedom. In adding conditions and restrictions to their prayers of petition, they seem to be infringing on God's freedom and capacity to give. In following Jesus' advice of saying yes or no, they should be content to allow the fulfillment of their requests in accordance with God's will. Such openness is a powerful antidote against human control and manipulation.

The Eleventh Week of the Year

Monday: Matthew 5:38-42   In this fifth antithesis or contrast Jesus revokes the Mosaic command regarding proportionate retaliation (see, e.g., Exod 21:24). Actually this law of talion served a good purpose in that it sought to control limitless fights and feuds. In its place Jesus does not propose a new program, for in him the end of human society has arrived. Human legal systems (e.g., going to court) and human checks and balances (e.g., a slap for a slap) simply must go. The principle advocated by Jesus is to yield one's rights in view of strict claims (e.g., walk the extra mile). The reason underpinning such radical approaches is the reality of Jesus' kingdom in which his followers already live.

Reflection. In their you-scratch-my-back-and-I'll-scratch-yours world, believers learn that mutual rights mean mutual obligations. In their

I-owe-you-one world, disciples find that a service performed implies a title to future compensation. Today's passage, however, rejects such a system, proclaiming instead a much more radical stance. Instead of new and better programs and policies, Jesus solemnly announces the end of such procedures. Instead of retaliation, there is submission. Instead of redress, there is forgiveness. Instead of minimal compliance, there is maximal acquiescence. To be a disciple is to surrender one's rights.

Tuesday: Matthew 5:43-48   See Saturday of the First Week of Lent.

Wednesday: Matthew 6:1-6, 16-18   See Ash Wednesday.

Thursday: Matthew 6:7-15   See Tuesday of the First Week of Lent.

Friday: Matthew 6:19-23   In this section of the Sermon on the Mount Jesus challenges his followers to choose between either terrestrial or celestial wealth. Here heaven functions as the place where disciples store up lasting riches that do not succumb to the ravages of nature (moth and rust) or the danger of thieves. Here Jesus does not envision the enjoyment of such treasures in heaven. Rather, he allows human efforts to capture to some extent the experience of everlasting, not transient, life. In verses 22-23 Jesus presents the parable of the sound and the unsound eye whose interpretation is far from clear since Jesus does not provide any explanation. Against the background of this chapter (the call to focused service on God) the parable suggests the need to concentrate on the light provided by Jesus' teaching. The service demanded of followers must be illuminated by the light of Jesus' kingdom preaching.

Reflection. In today's passage Jesus discusses values: (1) those of the world and (2) his own. He sees the world's pursuit of wealth as dangerously exposed to the ravages of nature and the acts of rapacious humans. He views his own values as not subject to these dangers but safe and secure in the treasure-houses of heaven. At this point he emphasizes the word "treasure": "where your treasure is, there also will your heart be" (v. 21). The disciple's heart and the disciple's treasure/value are thus interconnected. Ultimately the disciple must make a choice between the purely terrestrial and the profoundly celestial treasure/value. In this selection process the disciples will embrace the light of Jesus while the nondisciple will submit to the darkness of the world. Treasure/value and light/darkness go hand in hand.

Saturday: Matthew 6:24-34   This section of the Sermon on the Mount revolves around verse 24, the worship of the true God or the worship of false gods (earthly possessions). The only options are hate and love. What Matthew expects from his audience is an attitude of trust. He does not rule out concern for material needs. Rather, he invites his audience to liberate itself from slavery to the anxieties of daily needs. The only means of liberation is total trust in God as provider. This allows believers to maintain the following priorities: life and body as gift for which food and clothes are merely means. If God feeds the birds and clothes the flowers of the field, with how much more care will he provide for the needs of his people?

Matthew then scolds his audience (v. 30: "you of little faith") for they are asking the wrong questions, questions that smack of the pagans and their worship of this passing world. Without disparaging the quest for physical needs (v. 33: "seek *first*"; emphasis added), Matthew suggests that the right question is: how can I seek God's saving plan ("kingdom") in my circumstances? Using a proverb, Matthew teaches that the future is in God's hands. The only quest should be for today's bread.

Reflection. The image of God as mother may strike some believers as slightly bizarre. Nonetheless, while Matthew speaks of "your heavenly Father" (v. 26), he also refers to those chores that were the lot of the mother and wife, namely, cooking, fetching water, and providing clothing. While Matthew emphasizes the Christian priority ("seek *first*"), he does not omit depicting the concerns of God as mother. Because God is also mother, she knows with maternal feelings her vocation to provide food, water, and clothing (see Exod 16:14-14; 17:1-7 where Mother Yahweh provides food and water). The needs of the community thus become the concern of God.

For believers, to be mother is to image their God. The involved who are moved by other people's misery and are then moved to help image their God. The concerned who recognize the pain and frustration of others and then offer comfort understand God as mother. The interested who feel dehumanized by human derelicts on alcohol and drugs but then show their humanity by caring reflect their maternal God. For such believers, to be mother is to image their God.

The Twelfth Week of the Year

Monday: Matthew 7:1-5   Human beings like to play God the Judge on the last day by passing final condemnation on fellow humans. Matthew observes that those who make such a judgment will receive God's corresponding judgment. The "measure for measure" (v. 2) standard attempts to warn followers not to form such severe judgments. In verses 3-5 Jesus takes up the issue of correction and admonishes his audience to bear two items in mind: (1) the sister or brother status of the person to be corrected and (2) one's own failings. Disciples should begin with their own faults (the log) before presuming to correct the lesser faults (the speck) in their sister or brother. Only an initial self-correction makes subsequent correction of others feasible. Otherwise they can all too easily fall into the category of hypocrites.

Reflection. Believers must face the reality of criticizing. They are readily tempted to ask: what's wrong with this person? Their negative response quickly leads to disparaging and denigrating the person in question. To counter this tendency, disciples must learn to ask first: what's right with this person? Such a shift in interrogation will alert believers to the unsettling truth that there is more good than evil in the world. This approach reverses Shakespeare's dictum that the good that humans do is oft interred with their bones.

Tuesday: Matthew 7:6, 12-14   The opening parable presents interpretive problems. Disciples are advised not to offer sacrificial food (holy food) to dogs lest they attack the providers or to throw pearls to swine lest they trample them. It may mean that inappropriate behavior toward other people will have corresponding results. Such an interpretation dovetails to some degree with the Golden Rule in verse 12. While not significantly Jewish or Christian, this commonsense approach to other people possesses a profound wisdom. Matthew equates it with the Law and the Prophets so that the observance of the Golden Rule ensures fidelity to the Law and the Prophets. In verses 13-14 Matthew discusses the two gates and the two roads—metaphors that capture the consequences of leading a moral or immoral life. By entering the narrow gate and treading the hard road to life, disciples are preparing for eternal life.

Reflection. While the Golden Rule smacks of self-interest, it offers no little wisdom to modern followers of Jesus. "Do to others whatever you would have them do to you" (v. 12) may force believers to think twice before initiating any course of action against others. Thus they may feel compelled to entertain this question: how would I feel if so-and-so did this to me? After posing the question and anticipating their own reactions to the issue at hand, they will probably have to conclude that the action is at least undesirable, if not totally wrong. In this process of discernment, disciples do not focus solely on themselves but engage the other person, entering into his or her frame of mind. While the Golden Rule may not prove to be the highest motive for doing or not doing something, it does promote a high degree of desirable human behavior.

Wednesday: Matthew 7:15-20   The easy road (7:13) forms an easy link with the false prophets in this section. Such prophets love to proclaim a gospel that suits the fancy of their audience by eliminating or watering down the demands of Jesus' message. Aware of ancient Israel's disastrous experience of complacent prophets, the Matthean Jesus offers guidelines for assessing the truth or falsehood of their claims. It is what they do, not what they say or how they look that matters. Borrowing an analogy from the agricultural world, Jesus states unequivocally that his audience can distinguish the true prophets from the false ones by their fruits. A true prophet like a good tree bears good fruit and a false prophet like a bad tree bears bad fruit. It simply cannot be otherwise. Fittingly, Jesus threatens the false prophets with fiery damnation (v. 19).

Reflection. While this passage focuses on the discerning of true and false prophets, it also offers believers insight into the judging of other people: "by their fruits you will know them" (v. 20). To be sure, this passage does not endorse random judging of others. Nonetheless, human experience tells disciples that the evil perpetrated by others always receives full attention. Reacting to such notice, this passage may implicitly seek to rearrange the focus so that disciples search for and make known the good performed by others. Their good fruit (works) must come from a generous and loving heart. Unfortunately the media coverage is saturated with the evil committed in the world. A focus on the good achieved in the world would be more than a welcome change. As Genesis 3 shows, however, the snake gets all the lines. But does not the good deserve equal time as the troublesome serpent?

Thursday: Matthew 7:21-29 In the conclusion of the Sermon on the Mount, Matthew describes two different types of disciples. In verse 21 he begins his attack on the charismatic fakers in the community. At worship they enthusiastically cry out, "Lord, Lord," but in practice they amount to nothing. Like Israel, the church is called upon to do God's will. On the day of judgment, prophecies, exorcisms, and miracles will count for nothing—doing the Father's will is the ultimate criterion. It is not enough to *say*, one must also *do*.

Verses 24-27 are Matthew's parable where the accent is now *hearing/ doing*, not *hearing/not doing*. Hearing/doing is the characteristic of the wise person. Hearing/not doing is the mark of the foolish person. The image is one of a serious rain- and windstorm. The hearers/doers survive because the house is built on a solid rock foundation. The hearers/non-doers do not survive because the house is built on sandy ground. To survive the final judgment, one must be a hearer/doer.

As the Sermon on the Mount concludes, the audience is spellbound at Jesus' teaching. They are amazed, not at *what* he says, but *how* he says it. Unlike the scribes, Jesus does not have to base his authority on tradition—he possesses authority.

Reflection. Disciples believe that they must care for their neighbor, yet their practice does not always match their belief. They profess that they must practice justice for all, yet their actions do not necessarily square with their profession. Today's passage speaks to the situation of such believers. Matthew realized that his community was composed of two types: hearers/doers and hearers/non-doers. It was one thing to proclaim, "Lord, Lord," in ecstatic prayer, but quite another thing to carry out the Father's will in daily living. Shows of power and prestige counted for little, if they were not linked with performance. At the final judgment, actual deeds, not the protestations of good will, are to be the ultimate criterion. In Matthew's community as well as in today's community, believers must be doers.

Friday: Matthew 8:1-4   While the Sermon on the Mount depicts Jesus as powerful in word, chapters 8–9 reveal Jesus as mighty in deed by reason of the miracles he performs. In this passage Matthew shows Jesus healing a leper, a significantly marginalized person in the Jewish community. The leper addresses him as "Lord," a title of respect used by believers in this gospel. His faith is demonstrated by his petition, i.e., everything depends on Jesus' will to heal. Jesus responds to the request with a simple command (v. 3: "Be made clean."). Jesus next instructs the former leper to maintain silence, present himself to the priest, and make the appropriate sacrificial offering (see Lev 14:2-9).

Reflection. The faith of the leper must catch the attention of disciples. He provides evidence of his faith in two ways: (1) he addresses Jesus with the title used by believers ("Lord"), and (2) he phrases his petition with reference to Jesus' capacity to heal. While the passage is rather brief, its message is profound. In their needs disciples must approach Jesus with an attitude of faith, recognizing him as the person who communicates God's love and compassion. At the same time disciples must respect Jesus' capacity to act. Faith requires believers to see Jesus as more than a dispenser of emergency aid. They must also reckon with his at times inscrutable will. Granting Jesus the freedom to act in accord with that will overcomes the human tendency to manipulate and control. The leper stands as an exemplar of the proper manner of petitioning Jesus.

Saturday: Matthew 8:5-17   This passage consists of four components: (1) the cure of the centurion's servant (vv. 5-13), (2) the cure of Peter's mother-in-law (vv. 14-15), (3) the evening exorcisms and healings (v. 16), and (4) a fulfillment statement (v. 17). In the cure of the centurion's servant Jesus reaches out again to an "outsider" (see the leper in the preceding pericope). This time the outsider is a Gentile military officer who seeks a cure for his paralyzed servant from Jesus. Having learned proper military discipline in the Roman army, the officer does not require Jesus' visit to the sick servant—only a word of command is necessary. It is hardly surprising, therefore, that Jesus is astonished at the centurion's faith. It is a faith that Jesus has not found among his own people (the "insiders"). Israel's unbelief prompts Jesus to promise the kingdom (symbolized as a banquet) not only to the centurion but to all Gentiles and to warn Israel of exclusion with images of darkness, weeping, and gnashing of teeth.

Matthew has adapted the cure of Peter's mother-in-law from his source Mark (1:29-31), introducing some significant changes. Thus Jesus takes the initiative by recognizing the woman's malady. After being touched by Jesus, she proceeds to serve him, not the other four men mentioned in Mark. With these modifications, Matthew has turned Mark's healing story into a call story with a healing motif (compare Matt 9:9). The call story acknowledges Jesus' recognition of the right of women to participate in the faith life of the community.

In the evening cures Matthew emphasizes Jesus' immense power. While *many* demoniacs are brought to Jesus, he heals *all* the sick. Fittingly, Matthew cites Isaiah 53:4 to underline Jesus' miraculous healings. While the text reveals Jesus as the Suffering Servant, Matthew employs it to depict Jesus as the one who makes humanity whole (v. 17: "*took away* our *infirmities and bore* our *diseases*"; emphasis added).

Reflection. Today's passage offers a variety of points to ponder. Certainly one of them must be Jesus' call of Peter's mother-in-law to follow him as a disciple. In this scene Jesus first sees the one to be called. He then observes her situation (suffering from a fever). Finally she responds to the call by getting up and serving Jesus. While "serving" obviously includes waiting at table, it also embraces the giving of oneself after the manner of Jesus. As Matthew 20:28 observes, Jesus has not come to be served but to serve. In this scene Jesus invites women to participate in his saving mission. The early church thus recognizes the crossing of gender boundaries. Today's believers must note that in this episode discipleship knows no such boundaries. Peter's mother-in-law is as much a disciple as her famous son-in-law.

The Thirteenth Week of the Year

Monday: Matthew 8:18-22   After a trio of miracles (8:1-17), Matthew introduces sayings of Jesus that hammer home the cost of discipleship. In view of the great crowds, Jesus gives orders to cross over to the other side of the sea. The first candidate for discipleship is a scribe who addresses Jesus as "teacher," a title used by nonbelievers in this gospel. Recognizing Jesus as an itinerant missionary, he promises to follow Jesus wherever he goes. In response, Jesus contrasts the security of foxes with their holes and birds with their nests with his own homelessness and restless ministry. To follow Jesus is to assume a lifestyle that radically departs from one's former mode of living. Jesus may be implying that the cost of discipleship for the scribe is much too high.

The second candidate is already described as a disciple (he uses the title "Lord") who may be renewing his commitment to Jesus. In any case he asks permission of Jesus to bury his father and only then join up with him. While respect for the dead was a highly commended form of piety in Jewish society, the command to follow Jesus here and now takes precedence over all family ties and allegiances. Using hyperbolic language with enormous shock value, Jesus replies that the dead must bury their own dead.

Reflection. Modern disciples must take this passage to heart and ask what obstacles prevent them from fully following Jesus. Such obstacles may include pursuing greater fame and fortune, amassing more power, seeking more exotic pleasures, etc. Needless to say, the list is endless. To counter such temptations, disciples may profitably ask themselves what obligations their station in life imposes on them. In terms of job or employment, they may inquire how much better they can serve others. In terms of spouse and family, they may ask themselves to what extent they meet the expectations of husband or wife or family. In terms of faith development, they may ponder how much time they devote to their prayer life. Discipleship and vocation need not compete with each other. Rather, one's vocation provides the raw material for following Jesus and letting the dead bury their own dead.

Tuesday: Matthew 8:23-27   With this passage Matthew begins his second trio of miracles (8:23–9:8). The boat that is designed to take Jesus to the other side of the lake may represent the church and the dangers it constantly faces. Actually a great earthquake (see Matt 27:51; 28:2), not a great windstorm, functions as an image of the end times that relentlessly threatens the church and seeks to overwhelm it. In such circumstances the church must react like the disciples in this episode.

They must approach the sleeping Jesus and alert him to their grave danger (v. 25: "Lord, save us! We are perishing!"). Jesus responds to their urgent plea by first rebuking the disciples for having little faith and then rebuking the wind. Though they have faith, in times of crisis they go to pieces. Jesus' calm demeanor in the face of such imminent danger, however, prompts the disciples as well as Matthew's community to wonder what sort of man this Jesus really is.

Reflection. All too often modern believers fall apart and panic as the church faces ever new crises and scandals. While these crises and scandals are not to be trivialized, disciples can regain their courage by recalling and acting on today's passage. In the midst of cataclysmic events overwhelming the church, Jesus appears to be asleep, totally oblivious to what is happening in his church. Some may even describe this condition as a comatose state of benign neglect. The reality, however, is that Jesus, far from sleeping, is ever alert to the situation. He follows the order of this passage: (1) he rebukes the disciples for having little faith, and (2) he rebukes the wind or whatever else threatens his community. Crises and scandals can reveal all too readily the little faith of today's disciples. They must learn to be overawed by Jesus' display of power and concern. He is never absent, even when the disciples think otherwise. The earthquake will eventually pass because the seemingly uninvolved Jesus will hear the disciples' petition by his awesome display of involvement.

Wednesday: Matthew 8:28-34   Severely modifying this account from his source Mark, Matthew opts to focus practically all his attention on Jesus so that the two demoniacs play relatively insignificant roles. A menace to travelers, these fierce supernatural beings recognize Jesus as the Son of God. Realizing that it is not appropriate for Jesus to condemn them before the final judgment (v. 29: "before the appointed time"), they petition him to send them into the swine (an indication of a non-Jewish area). With a single word of command Jesus accedes to the demoniacs' wish so that the entire herd rushes into the sea and perishes there. When the herdsmen relate the event in town, the entire citizenry comes out to meet Jesus, requesting that he leave their area. For Matthew's community, this episode provides no little hope. They realize that, as long as they remain faithful to the Son of God, no demonic power will overtake them.

Reflection. This passage presents a variety of characters: (1) the two demoniacs, (2) the herdsmen, (3) the townspeople, and (4) Jesus. While the first three groups play minor roles, Jesus occupies center stage. His commanding presence offers hope in today's evil-infested world symbolized by the demoniacs. Will evil triumph over good? Will vice defeat virtue? Will sin prevail over moral goodness? Matthew responds to all these questions with a resounding no. As long as disciples remain faithful to their commitment, the all-powerful Son of God will protect them from all the insidious attacks of the Evil One. The drowning of the swine in the sea captures Jesus' victory over evil. Hope has become enfleshed in the person of the Son of God.

Thursday: Matthew 9:1-8   This episode is the third of Matthew's second trio of miracles. The scene combines two stories: (1) a miracle story and (2) a dispute story about the forgiveness of sins. Focusing on the dispute story, Matthew depicts Jesus as recognizing the paralytic's spiritual state and offering him forgiveness. Some of the scribes, however, object to Jesus' action and accuse him of blasphemy since forgiveness of sins is a divine prerogative. Reading his opponents' thoughts, Jesus asks which is easier, to forgive sins or to perform a miracle. The implication is that the one who enjoys power over paralysis must also possess power over sins. The sight of the standing and walking former paralytic leaves the crowds awestruck. At the end of the scene, Matthew combines the crowds' praise with their observation that God has given such power to human beings. By doing so, Matthew emphasizes that his community possesses the power to forgive sins, thus linking itself with Jesus.

Reflection. How should today's disciples react to goodness when they see it? What emotions should they express in the presence of wonder? Matthew's description of the crowds points believers in the right direction. The only adequate response to goodness and wonder is praise. Praise involves two stages: (1) the recognition of something praiseworthy and (2) its articulation in word or gesture. Disciples experience no difficulty at all in acknowledging God's goodness and wonders through praise. Their difficulty, however, comes with the feats, successes, and exploits of fellow humans. For some reason a number of disciples forego this ministry of praise until someone's death. In the setting of a wake they lavish praise on the deceased. Unfortunately the deceased gains no profit from this postponement. Today's passage urges disciples to praise the accomplishments of others during their lifetime. This is clearly the only time for exercising this ministry. After all, to praise the cocreators is to praise the Creator.

Friday: Matthew 9:9-13 This pericope in Matthew is a reaction to the healing of the paralytic (9:1-8) that underlines Jesus' mercy and forgiveness of sins. Because the tax collectors worked for the hated Roman IRS and had a reputation for injustice, the call of Matthew is an example to be elevated of the gratuitous nature of the call to discipleship. The Pharisees become upset because Jesus eats with tax collectors and the nonobservant Jews ("sinners"). Significantly, they approach the disciples of Jesus rather than Jesus himself.

Overhearing them, Jesus reacts, first of all, by citing a proverb, namely, the ill, not the healthy, require a physician (and Jesus is one). Second, Jesus quotes Hosea 6:6. In the period after the destruction of the temple (AD 70), the rabbis taught that works of mercy could take the place of sacrifices. By his use of Hosea 6:6, Matthew has Jesus reject all temple sacrifices and give precedence to acts of mercy. Jesus' invitation (v. 13) reveals this precedence. Matthew also implies that, if the so-called righteous reject Jesus' modus vivendi, they may find themselves excluded from the final banquet, namely, the kingdom.

Reflection. Disciples may find it relatively easy to discover God in church, but much more difficult to uncover him in the needs of their neighbors. They may also find it easy to contribute their weekly envelope, but much more difficult to contribute their services to the community. They may find it easy to share the bread and wine at Eucharist, but much more difficult to share themselves in the grief and hurt of others. Today's passage, however, shows Jesus insisting that the temple sacrifices must cede to works of mercy. To acknowledge Jesus as Lord, to offer him due worship and homage means to open oneself up to Jesus' world of concerns, e.g., the hated tax collectors and the nonobservant Jews. The laws of ritual purity have to give way to the demands of human compassion. To heed the call of Jesus as a disciple is to be caught up in the world of others. To acknowledge Jesus as Lord is to acknowledge others as sisters and brothers of this same Lord. For Matthew, worshiping God includes serving one's neighbor.

Saturday: Matthew 9:14-17   Unlike his source Mark, Matthew has only the disciples of John the Baptist approach Jesus and ask why his disciples, unlike the disciples of John and the Pharisees, do not fast. (The reference is to private, not public, fasts.) In reply, Jesus, equating fasting with grieving, explains that he, the bridegroom, and his disciples, the wedding guests, must join in the joy and happiness of the wedding feast. To fast at such a time is tantamount to mourning and hence out of the question. But Jesus does add that his disciples will fast at the appropriate time, namely, after the bridegroom's departure (Jesus' death). For Matthew, in this in-between time, i.e., the time between Jesus' departure and the second coming, fasting is indeed appropriate.

Matthew next introduces two parables: (1) the unshrunk cloth and (2) the new wine. At first glance these parables appear to emphasize the incompatibility of the old (cloak and wineskin) with the new (unshrunk cloth and new wine). Thus the message of Jesus would demand a new form and a new carrier because of the discontinuity between Judaism and Christianity. Matthew, however, does not want to abandon the old, namely, the Jewish-Christian traditions in his community. There must be a balance so that "both are preserved" (v. 17).

Reflection. "Be not the first by whom the new are tried, Nor yet the last to lay the old aside." Alexander Pope's saying provides some food for thought in view of the parables in today's passage. Disciples often face a quandary when confronted by new items or practices that seem to reject their old counterparts. The best approach in this situation seems to be both/and rather than either/or. Believers must seek to preserve old values that now appear in new forms. For example, except for Ash Wednesday and the Fridays of Lent, Catholics are no longer required to abstain from meat on Fridays. The value in the old law of Friday abstinence, however, was the memory of Jesus' self-giving on Good Friday. Nowadays Catholics may retain that value in various ways, e.g., visiting the homebound, making a charitable donation, assisting the marginalized, etc. In this way the old value takes on a new configuration. "And both are preserved."

The Fourteenth Week of the Year

Monday: Matthew 9:18-26   This passage (a combination of two accounts) serves as the first miracle in Matthew's third and last trio. Here Matthew offers a stark contrast between the synagogue leader's status and position as the head of a patriarchal family with the hemorrhaging woman who is marginalized both socially and religiously. Her flow of blood makes her ritually unclean so that she is cut off from participating in worship. Matthew enhances her sense of marginalization by having her approach Jesus from behind and speak to herself. She cannot address Jesus directly while the synagogue leader does precisely this, making an even greater request (the restoration of his dead daughter to life). When Jesus catches sight of the woman, he addresses her as "daughter," even though, unlike the synagogue leader, she has no connections. As in Mark, Matthew has Jesus emphasize her great faith. Unlike Mark, however, Matthew does not have Jesus dismiss the woman and observes that she is cured instantly.

With regard to the synagogue leader's daughter, Matthew has streamlined Mark's account. Jesus commands the dismissal of the flute players and the crowd, announcing that the young girl is sleeping, not dead. After enduring the crowd's ridicule, Jesus takes the girl by the hand and she gets up.

Reflection. Like most human beings, disciples are tempted to label people as insiders or outsiders, those with connections and those without them. In this they are not unlike the Jewish society in today's passage. This society clearly labeled the hemorrhaging woman an outsider. In terms of ritual religion she is perpetually impure. In terms of connections she has none. But in terms of faith she is as stalwart and courageous as any of her male counterparts. Significantly Jesus does not dismiss this daughter in Matthew's account. As in the case of Peter's mother-in-law (8:15), Jesus' touch probably symbolizes the call to discipleship.

Matthew's portrait of this woman should prompt believers to discard the categories of insider/outsider, having connections/not having connections. Instead, they should ponder the faith of this woman and the gifts she brings to the communities of Jesus and Matthew. They should dismantle all those barriers that prevent free access to Jesus and his life-transforming powers. They should envision offering new possibilities to all those who seek to serve, whether women or men.

Tuesday: Matthew 9:32-38   This passage consists of: (1) the healing of the speech-impaired demoniac, including the Pharisees' accusation (vv. 32-34); and (2) discipleship and mission (vv. 35-38). In this third miracle of Matthew's last trio, there are two different reactions to Jesus' healing of the speech-impaired demoniac. First, the crowds are truly amazed and observe that there has been nothing comparable in the history of God's dealings with Israel. Second, the Pharisees accuse Jesus of being in league with the prince of demons. For them, only this diabolical power can explain the cure of the demoniac. Moreover, this accusation anticipates Jesus' forthcoming clash with his enemies and their growing rejection of him.

In the second section dealing with discipleship and mission, Matthew begins with a summary of Jesus' ministry that involves both the proclamation of the Good News and the healing of all ills and diseases. Next Matthew depicts Jesus' compassionate reaction to the crowds. These crowds resemble helpless, exhausted sheep that are deprived of a shepherd (see Num 27:17; 1 Kgs 22:17). Jesus reads the scene in terms of a great harvest in which his disciples will play a key role by bringing the Good News to others. At the same time, given the scarcity of laborers, one must beg the Father, the Lord of the harvest to provide.

Reflection. The torch of discipleship has been passed to a new generation. How will today's disciples respond to Jesus' invitation to sign up as laborers who will bring in the harvest? This invitation is not addressed solely to the hierarchy, priests, deacons, and religious. On the contrary, it is addressed to all baptized Christians. In baptism they assume the role of bringing the Good News to all those who comprise their world. Their basic charge is to reveal the kingdom not only in word but also in deed. They must articulate the compassionate message of this kingdom by reaching out to all who need to hear the Good News but also to see it demonstrated in daily life. To borrow Jesus' pastoral image, they must be shepherds who care for the harassed and helpless sheep.

Wednesday: Matthew 10:1-7   Verses 1-4 comprise the introduction to the mission discourse, Matthew's second great sermon (10:1–11:1). Jesus thus provides an answer to the prayer of 9:38 by summoning the twelve disciples and sharing his mission with them. In verse 1 Jesus empowers them to carry out what he has exemplified in chapters 8–9, namely, exorcisms and healings. Only here (v. 2) does Matthew call the Twelve "apostles." For him, they symbolize all later disciples and, more significantly, the later leaders of the community.

The discourse itself begins in verse 5. The Twelve are to go only to the house of Israel, not the Gentiles (see 28:16-20 where there is mention of a universal mission). The Twelve are to announce the arrival of the kingdom, just as Jesus did. With the exception of teaching, the Twelve carry out the same work as Jesus.

Reflection. Today's disciples may have leadership positions but may be tempted to reserve their benefits only to themselves. They may attain status but perhaps see it as a purely personal acquisition. They may make it to the top but may be prone to regard their rank as the chance for merely personal aggrandizement. In this passage, however, Jesus sees his own powers as enrichment opportunities for the people. As a result, in chapters 4–9 he teaches, heals, exorcizes, etc. He also realizes that his disciples share in the mission, in his Father's harvest. In 10:1 he empowers them to undertake what he has undertaken in chapters 8–9, namely, exorcizing and healing. In 10:8 he will extend their powers to raising the dead and healing the leprous. In both instances the powers conferred by Jesus are for the people. Indeed, their use of such powers is to be like Jesus' use, namely, gratuitous. Powers, position, and rank are for the people.

Thursday: Matthew 10:7-15   As Matthew has Jesus continue his mission discourse, he envisions the missionary activity of his church, not just that of the Twelve. He makes the activity of his church and that of the Twelve mirror what Jesus has done in the previous six chapters. Jesus establishes no price for the conferral of those powers. In turn, the missionaries may not charge any fee for their use. In addition, Jesus announces a demanding regimen in such missionary enterprises: no money to put in their belts, no bag for food and similar necessities, no change of tunics, and no sandals or staff. This regimen depicts an urgent but relatively short missionary campaign in Galilee. The people they serve will provide the necessary food and lodging. Once they find a worthy host, they are to stay put and dismiss any thought of seeking better accommodations.

Upon entering the house of their host, they are to bestow their peace on it. If, however, the house proves to be unworthy, they are to retract their message of peace. If people will not bid them welcome or refuse to listen to their proclamation, they are to shake off the dust from their sandals—a gesture used by Jews upon leaving Gentile territory and returning to Israel. At the final judgment the infamous inhabitants of Sodom and Gomorrah will fare better than those who refuse to welcome or hear them.

Reflection. This passage invites modern disciples to trust more in God's Providence and less in their own capacity to satisfy needs. This poses the following questions for them: (1) do they dare to exercise such confidence in their God's ability to provide? (2) without excluding human procedures to meet reasonable needs, are they willing to trust beyond that? and (3) to what extent do they take the petition of the Our Father for daily bread seriously? Disciples soon learn that there is no absolute norm for distinguishing between trust in God's Providence and taking reasonable human precautions. But will modern disciples lean more on the side of Providence and less on their own ingenuity?

Friday: Matthew 10:16-23   In this passage Matthew paints a vivid picture of the enormous difficulties and problems his missionaries will encounter. Briefly stated, they will share the fate of their Master. Nonetheless they must combine the shrewdness of serpents with the innocence of doves. They will be handed over to the local Jewish courts ("councils") where they will be flogged. They will also be brought before the civil authorities. On all such occasions they will have opportunities for bearing witness to Jesus in the presence of both Jews and Gentiles. But in these trying circumstances they need not worry about what to say because the Holy Spirit, the Spirit of their Father, will speak through them.

The missionaries will also experience domestic crises when the bonds of kinship will count for nothing, even to the point of family members killing family members. In these desperate situations the disciples who persevere to the end will be saved. If persecuted in one town, they should flee to the next. In verse 23 Jesus informs the missionaries that they will not have exhausted their safe houses until the coming of the Son of Man. For Matthew's community, this coming may be connected with Jesus' ongoing presence with the community (see Matt 28:16-20) rather than with his final coming in judgment.

Reflection. As missionaries, modern disciples can expect to encounter difficulties in their office, even though they do not stem from synagogue, civil authorities, or family members. Their problems in today's secular society will be more subtle but no less insidious. It will take enormous courage to counter the oppressive forces of greed, power mongering, rejection of the marginalized, etc. The Matthean Jesus, however, directs words of consolation to the missionaries when they face such formidable opponents—they will have the assistance of the Holy Spirit. When forced to reply to their foes, the missionaries will enjoy the presence of the Spirit who will speak through them. The key virtue demanded of them is perseverance. The collaboration of the Spirit with these undaunted missionaries will ultimately win out.

Saturday: Matthew 10:24-33 This passage consists of two components: (1) two proverbs linked to persecution (vv. 24-25) and (2) the fearlessness of the missionaries (vv. 26-33). In the proverbs Jesus reminds the missionaries that, as disciples and slaves, they must anticipate the same fate as their Teacher and Master. What the missionaries must do is to strive to imitate Jesus. If adversaries have accused their Teacher and Master of acting under the aegis of Satan (Beelzebul), how much more his disciples and slaves?

In the midst of these confrontations Jesus exhorts the disciples to be fearless no less than three times (vv. 26, 28, 31). Notwithstanding the hostility, the Good News will go forth. The private instruction of the disciples is to be made public on mission. The disciples should not fear the destroyer of the body but the destroyer of the entire person in eternal damnation.

The missionaries should exhibit total confidence in a loving and concerned Father. The disciples are infinitely more valuable than the cheapest bird (sparrow) for which God provides significantly. Indeed the Father knows the smallest details about them, even the number of hairs on their heads. Hence with all courage they are to bear witness before implacable courtrooms. Then in the final courtroom scene Jesus will provide them with the necessary testimony. To disown Jesus before human tribunals, however, is to have Jesus disown them before the heavenly tribunal.

Reflection. Modern disciples sometimes experience the frustration of ministry and sense that their God has abandoned them. They come to know the anguish of dealing with people and feel that the God of consolation has left them. They receive insults and derision for their work and conclude that their God of love has neglected them. These modern disciples are similar to the disciples in today's passage who also know the anxieties of mission. There were those who could not or would not tolerate their message. But at the same time there was the reassuring message of a compassionate and concerned Father. He took good care of the sparrows—obviously he would take a greater interest in them. He paid attention to all the details of their person, including the number of hairs on their heads. Hence they had no reason to fear. Perseverance in bearing witness to Jesus would eventually win out. To share God's care is to know God's care.

The Fifteenth Week of the Year

Monday: Matthew 10:34–11:1   This passage is composed of three sections: (1) the great demands of fidelity and commitment (vv. 34-39), (2) the rewards of following Jesus (vv. 40-41), and (3) the conclusion of the mission discourse (11:1). In outlining the great demands imposed by commitment, Jesus announces that he does not bring peace but division. Ironically such division will surface in family relationships. Quoting Micah 7:6 once again (see 10:21), Jesus underlines the strife between the younger (son, daughter, and daughter-in-law) and the older (father, mother, and mother-in-law) generation. To be worthy of Jesus, one cannot love family members more than Jesus. The cross becomes the symbol of the lengths to which committed disciples may have to go. In the following of Jesus no price is too high. Matthew then offers the paradox of Christian discipleship. By seeking yourself, you lose yourself, but by losing yourself, you find yourself. This is a formulation of the death-resurrection experience of Jesus.

In discussing the rewards for following Jesus, Matthew lines up possible recipients of the disciples' dedication: (1) apostles, (2) prophets,

(3) the righteous, and (4) the little ones. To welcome any of these is to welcome Jesus and, ultimately, the Father. To share one's goods with prophets and the righteous (the latter are the more prominent members of the community) is to be assured of the appropriate reward. Last but not least are the little ones, most likely the ordinary members of the community. Not to overlook them is to be duly rewarded.

Reflection. Finders keepers, losers weepers. Some modern disciples believe that they truly find themselves by keeping to themselves. By limiting the horizon of their ego, they may feel they have made it. In today's passage, however, Matthew's advice to missionaries is to lose themselves for the sake of the kingdom. They will find out who they really are by losing themselves. On the other hand, they will never discover themselves by seeking themselves. Matthew emphasizes the little ones, the ordinary members of the community, as special objects of such finding and losing. To discover the value of such ordinary people is ultimately to discover themselves. The cup of cold water is the price of such a discovery. In effect, "finders keepers, losers weepers" does not really measure up to Jesus' standard of discipleship.

Tuesday: Matthew 11:20-24   In this passage Jesus reproaches Galilean cities in which he worked most of his "deeds of power." These deeds announced the coming of the kingdom and the need for total conversion (repentance). Unfortunately the Galilean cities of Chorazin and Bethsaida failed to respond to Jesus' miracles and their inherent message. As a result, on the day of judgment the pagan cities of Tyre and Sidon will fare much better. If these same works had been performed in them, these Gentiles would have reacted appropriately with the symbols of repentance (sackcloth and ashes).

Worse than Chorazin and Bethsaida is Capernaum, the base of operations for Jesus' Galilean ministry. Borrowing the text of Isaiah 14:13-15 directed against the king of Babylon, Jesus solemnly pronounces its condemnation of being brought down to Sheol/Hades rather than being exalted to heaven. If Jesus had worked these same deeds of power in infamous Sodom, the quintessence of depravity in the Old Testament, it would have existed to the present. On the day of judgment, Sodom will have an easier time than Capernaum.

Reflection. Disciples can be duped into thinking that their spiritual status will ward off any and every kind of condemnation and punishment. Matthew, however, takes the opposite position. He recalls for his Jewish audience the disasters God visited upon Tyre, Sidon, Babylon, and Sodom. In effect, he is attempting to deflate the smugness of his audience that regarded the destruction of these cities as God's just punishment. After all, God could visit such just afflictions on them as well. For both Matthew's audience and modern disciples, the deception of being spiritual elite can have dire consequences. Both audiences must continually respond to Jesus' activity. The only fitting response is repentance and conversion demonstrated on a daily basis.

Wednesday: Matthew 11:25-27   This passage consists of: (1) the Son's praise of the Father as revealer (vv. 25-26) and (2) the Son's revelation of the mutual knowledge of the Father and himself (v. 27). In the first two verses Jesus admits that the Galilean ministry has not gone well. The religious experts have rejected his message, but the outer fringes of society (the tax collectors, poor, etc.) have accepted it. This is his Father's plan, a plan that does not exclude human malice. In verse 27 Jesus acknowledges that he has a special relationship with the Father—a relationship that far transcends adoptive sonship. (This special relationship between the Father and the Son is reminiscent of the Fourth Gospel where the Father and Jesus are one [see John 10:30].) In turn, Jesus shares this mutual knowledge with those whom he chooses. Hence disciples gain access to the intimacy between the Father and the Son.

Reflection. It is all about communication. In this passage Jesus discloses that he is indeed the one who reveals the Father. Disciples may look upon this intimate disclosure as the very heart of Christianity, namely, sharing with others through the Spirit the revelation that Jesus gives of his Father. Such participation grounds believers in the very mystery of the Trinity. In short, the mission of disciples is fundamentally communication. Those who have received the Good News of the triune God are not to hoard it as a miser's booty. In their everyday life, in their meetings with friends and acquaintances, at their jobs, etc., disciples are to exercise this profound task of communication. God has elected to make them his spokespersons. It is all about communication.

Thursday: Matthew 11:28-30 See Wednesday of the Second Week of Advent.

Friday: Matthew 12:1-8 In this chapter Matthew develops the ongoing opposition of Jesus' adversaries. In this passage the opposition revolves around the command to keep the Sabbath holy. Specifically the Pharisees regard the disciples' plucking of heads of grain as a violation of the Sabbath rest. In reply, Jesus refers to David's actions in 1 Samuel 21:1-6. In that incident David and his men were permitted to eat the holy bread placed before God ("the bread of offering") because of their hunger and the unavailability of other bread. Hence David and his men could break a divine law without divine offense. Jesus also points to the practice of the priests in the temple—they work on the Sabbath but remain guiltless. At this juncture Jesus presents himself as something greater than the temple. Finally Jesus cites Hosea 6:6 where mercy supersedes sacrifice. If the Pharisees had really grasped the meaning of this prophetic text, they would not have reproached Jesus' disciples. As "Lord of the sabbath," Jesus designates himself as the final arbiter and interpreter of the Law and the Prophets.

Reflection. This passage challenges modern believers and their interpretation of laws. All too often they may think that all laws are the same so that no hierarchy of values prevails. They may also fall into the trap of obeying the law merely to avoid dire consequences. This episode reveals Jesus as one who invokes the role of mercy in legal interpretation. It also shows him as one who searches for the inherent values in laws. Perhaps the following rule of thumb may assist disciples in their approach to law, whether ecclesiastical or civil. They should do what is right because it is right, not because they will be rewarded. They should avoid what is wrong because it is wrong, not because they will otherwise be punished.

Saturday: Matthew 12:14-21 This passage opens with the Pharisees' plot to eliminate Jesus after his Sabbath cure of the man with the withered hand. Aware of this, Jesus withdraws and cures all in the crowds following him. At this point Matthew introduces a fulfillment of Scripture passage, citing the first Suffering Servant song (Isa 42:1-4). He

does so to stress that Jesus' meekness proceeds from God's will as speci-
fied in the Scriptures. As servant (the Greek word also means "son"),
Jesus is the chosen and beloved of the Lord who will proclaim God's
saving intentions to the Gentiles in the aftermath of Israel's rejection
of his message. Despite his people's disavowal, he will not respond with
revenge or hatred but with meekness, not crying aloud for publicity or
attention. In his gentleness he will not break a bruised reed or quench
a smoldering wick until he achieves the ultimate victory in his death-
resurrection. Once this vantage point is reached (see Matt 28:19), the
Gentiles will place their hope in him.

Reflection. This emphasis on the meekness and gentleness of Jesus
against the background of the first Suffering Servant song must strike
a sensitive chord for believers. It poses this challenging question: how
should they respond to violence, violence that plagues and cripples not
only individuals but also entire nations? In this passage, though his
enemies conspire to take his life, Jesus leaves and proceeds to address
the needs of those following him. He will achieve his ultimate victory,
not through military hardware, but through gentleness that in the end
will involve suffering and death. Modern believers must give answer to
a way of life that is nothing less than a way of death in which power and
violence unfortunately serve as the final arbiters of human conflict. How
do bigger and better tools of annihilation fare in the shadow of the
cross?

The Sixteenth Week of the Year

Monday: Matthew 12:38-42   In this passage some scribes align
themselves with the Pharisees to request a sign from heaven of Jesus.
In their mind such a sign will authenticate the claims he has made. Jesus
responds (1) by labeling the sign-seekers an evil and adulterous generation and (2) by promising only the sign of the prophet Jonah. "An evil
and unfaithful generation" conjures up the Old Testament images of
disobeying God and violating their covenant bond, respectively. For
Matthew, the three days and three nights refers to Jesus' time in the
abode of the dead that will be followed by his resurrection, the great
sign that will shatter the insatiable appetite of death. Continuing the

Jonah story, Jesus contrasts the reaction of the Ninevites to the prophet's message with that of his own audience. The irony is that Jesus is something greater than Jonah.

Jesus takes up another biblical allusion to condemn the sign-seekers. The queen of Sheba traveled from Arabia (v. 42: "the ends of the earth") to be dazzled by King Solomon's wisdom. Ironically these scribes and Pharisees enjoy the presence of Jesus, the very quintessence of divine wisdom, but refuse to listen. Like the Gentile Ninevites, this Gentile queen will condemn the sign-seekers at the final judgment.

Reflection. Compelling proof and substantiating evidence sometimes plague even the most faithful of disciples. There seems to be an insatiable appetite to know for certain and to be assured. In today's episode Jesus states categorically that his resurrection satisfies all such queries and searches. His resurrection entails much more than revivification—it is the conquest of death itself. It is that transforming experience whereby Jesus becomes immortal in power and glory. By his resurrection Jesus is the firstborn of the dead (Col 1:18) and the trailblazer (Acts 3:15) who holds out to his sisters and brothers the hope of new life. His experience of resurrection provides the compelling proof and substantiating evidence not only that God sent him but also that he is humanity's paradigm and model. The empty tomb symbolizes a full life for his extended family.

Tuesday: Matthew 12:46-50 Blood relationship versus doing the will of Jesus' heavenly Father is central in this passage. Here Matthew draws a sharp contrast between insiders and outsiders. Twice (vv. 46, 47) he mentions Jesus' mother and brothers standing *outside*. To underline this contrast further, Matthew shows Jesus posing a question about his true family and then gesturing to that family. For Jesus, blood relationship does not constitute one a disciple. In fact, Jesus has already taught that a disciple must break family ties (10:37). And that is precisely what Jesus does here. Rejecting blood relationships, Jesus insists that only doing the will of his heavenly Father admits one *inside* the family circle. Such a person thereby becomes Jesus' brother, sister, and mother.

Reflection. Belonging to clubs, associations, societies, etc., is a common human phenomenon. People thus acquire a certain title or dignity and promise to observe the rules and regulations of the group. Jesus, however, places the relationship with himself on a much higher level. By doing the will of his heavenly Father, believers join Jesus' family, becoming his brother, sister, and mother. This family relationship high-lights at least two aspects. First, it emphasizes the intimate nature of discipleship. Those committed to observing the Father's will enter the family circle and share the honor and dignity of being family. Second, it stresses the heinousness of not doing the Father's will. All acts of disobedience constitute nothing less than dishonoring the family name and jeopardizing the bond of trust and love. This passage insists to the nth degree that disciples must practice noblesse oblige.

Wednesday: Matthew 13:1-9   This chapter marks a new stage in Matthew. Jesus has now met with resistance. This lack of response makes him resort to the veiled language of parables. Actually the intent of the parables is to teach, to challenge, and to confront. Although Matthew has changed the intent of the parables, this parable itself does suggest a point in the ministry of Jesus when resistance and lack of response prompt a realistic appraisal of the law of loss and gain in the kingdom. Jesus counters the despair of the ministry by pronouncing this parable of hope.

The parable itself is the parable of the seed, not the sower. Apart from verse 3 and the later interpretation in verse 18, the parable deals only with the natural inevitability of failure and success in sowing. There are three states of loss: immediate (path), gradual (rocks), and ultimate (thorns). There are three degrees of gain in the good soil: thirty, sixty, and one hundred (hence as diverse as the losses). Significantly the par-able spells out how things go wrong (path, rocks, thorns), but not how they go right. The parable points to the law of growth and decline in the kingdom. Although one can understand better how things go wrong, one is challenged to hope in that mysterious process whereby they go right. God's mysterious plan is at work and good results do come, although the bad ones are more readily explained.

Reflection. To develop hope is to cultivate mystery. Believers are some-times seduced into thinking that only the present counts. They are encouraged to believe that nothing can really be changed. They are exhorted to hold that there is only one way to go—the party line. They can thus become victims of despair. In this debacle only hope will rescue them. For Matthew, this theology of hope becomes central. Disciples are writing off Jesus and some are no longer walking with him. Jesus responds to this situation by noting the natural process of failure and success. The mode of failure is readily explainable; the mode of success is rarely intelligible. Yet despite the obvious failures, God is at work. To hope is to let God act in his own mysterious fashion and not impose human restraints. To develop hope is to cultivate mystery.

Thursday: Matthew 13:10-17   In this passage Matthew explains why Jesus speaks to the crowds in parables. Unlike the disciples, the crowds have refused to listen to Jesus' message. Because Israel has failed to respond to Jesus' offer, they will lose their special privileges. Jesus goes on to cite Isaiah 6:9-10 according to which God mysteriously controls the flow of history, including human sinfulness. In verses 16-17 Matthew has Jesus quote a saying that congratulates the disciples for their seeing and hearing. While Israel's ears have grown hard of hearing and their eyes have closed shut, the disciples' eyes and their ears hear the fulfillment of the longing of Israel's prophets and righteous people.

Reflection. This passage focuses on the perennial problem of seeing and hearing the Good News of Jesus. It is one thing to see and hear that message physically. It is quite another thing to internalize it and make it the springboard for daily living. This poses the following question: who really live the Good News? Perhaps the canonized saints come immediately to mind. Admittedly the church has recognized their heroic virtue. But maybe disciples should look closer to home and consider the married couples who deepen their mutual commitment each day, the parents who lavish unstinting love on and attention to their children, the single people who devote all their energies to help others. And the list goes on and on. These and similar believers have so absorbed the Gospel message that they reflect it unwittingly in their everyday actions. These are without doubt the disciples who see and hear.

Friday: Matthew 13:18-23   This passage provides the allegorical interpretation of the parable. As such, it decodes the parable, applying it to the various dispositions of people toward the proclamation of the kingdom. Most likely it illustrates the experience of at least some early

Christians. The first type of person hears but does not really understand. Then the devil comes along and snatches the Word away. The second type receives the Word with exuberant joy but lacks real roots. In times of trouble or persecution such a person literally collapses. The third type hears the Word but the attraction of wealth and concern for worldly success choke the Word, resulting in no yield. The fourth type, however, hears the Word, understands it, and initiates a course of action, producing yields "a hundred or sixty or thirtyfold" (v. 23).

Reflection. In this allegory believers encounter three cases of failure and one case of success. They are challenged to ask to which category they belong. Do they fail to understand the message of the kingdom? Do they last only for a while and then falter? Are they too much the victims of money and power? In attempting to answer these questions, they may opt to understand them in terms of their failure to share the Word with others. Such an approach may keep them from a purely egotistical interpretation of the passage. Hence an invaluable gauge of response or lack of response is the answer to the following question: to what extent do they make Jesus' message available or unavailable to others?

Saturday: Matthew 13:24-30   The parable of the wheat and the weeds (darnel, a poisonous weed) is unique to Matthew. In the first exchange the owner is aware that the weeds represent the work of an enemy. Two problems thus arise: (1) how to save the wheat and (2) how to outwit the enemy. In the second exchange the owner resolves the two questions. With regard to the first, he will allow both wheat and weeds to grow together until harvesttime. With regard to the second, he will use the weeds for fuel. What was originally designed as a disadvantage has now become an advantage.

The parable reflects Jesus' understanding of the kingdom. The kingdom is not an ideal union of only the perfect; it includes, rather, both good and evil. Firm and resolute action is called for, but it is a type of action that recognizes that violence will be counterproductive and that force will endanger the common good. In the kingdom, therefore, both patience and forgiveness are required. The final separation of good and evil is left to the last judgment.

Reflection. Disciples sometimes feel that they are used by others and think that violent retaliation is the order of the day. They are betrayed by others, even loved ones, and conclude that only revenge is the proper reaction. They are often hurt by the words and remarks of others and judge that to hurt them in turn is the right antidote. In this parable Jesus speaks to these experiences. He realizes that the kingdom is no utopia. Both good and evil coexist, but not peacefully. Confronted by attacks, he yet recommends the policy of the wise farmer: overcome evil by good. To check one's wrath when confronted by the weeds means to protect the common good. To refuse to yield to rage implies hope for future repentance. For Jesus, only the patient and forgiving can sing, "We shall overcome."

The Seventeenth Week of the Year

Monday: Matthew 13:31-35   The parables of the mustard seed and the leaven underline the contrast between humble beginnings and unexpected endings. Although the mustard seed does not really become a tree, the exaggeration contributes to this contrast. Referring to Daniel 4:10-22 for its use of birds, the parable of the mustard seed understands the tree as God's universal kingdom that provides cover for all peoples. Since yeast or leaven symbolized corruption for both Jews and Christians (see 1 Cor 5:6-8), Jesus' use may suggest the outcast sinners he has gathered about himself. The passage concludes with a formula quotation from Psalm 78:2. This depicts Jesus as the wisdom teacher par excellence. Jesus thus articulates mysteries hidden from all creation, even though some find his parables obscure.

Reflection. These parables address the needs of modern disciples. At times they allow themselves to become depressed because their output is so meager, so inconsequential. Apparently they employ the scale of values that derives from the business world. Jesus, however, strongly suggests that they continue to walk in faith and to imagine what God's grace can accomplish. While they are not to exclude their own efforts, they must always calculate the impact of divine grace whereby the seemingly infinitesimal brings about mind-boggling, not faith-boggling results.

Tuesday: Matthew 13:36-43   This passage opens with Jesus' return to the house that probably symbolizes his break with Israel, a break that will permit Jesus to devote more time to the needs of his disciples. In this allegorical interpretation of the parable of the wheat and the weeds, Jesus decodes the various components, e.g., the sower of good seed = the Son of Man; the field = the world; the weeds = the children of the devil; etc. As the Son of Man, Jesus is the exalted One who presides over the world until the last judgment. Harvest time serves as a traditional image for judgment. Interestingly the angels, not the Son of Man, will function as the agents of this judgment. Evildoers will experience the furnace of fire whereas the righteous will enjoy divine glory, becoming luminous beings in the kingdom of the Father. Although the original parable of the wheat and the weeds underscores the need for patience and tolerance, the allegory focuses on the role of final judgment.

Reflection. This passage insists that both the world and the church are curious mixtures of both good and bad. Both are under God's threat of judgment and hence both can respond in repentance while there is yet time. In recalling Matthew's own interpretation of Jesus' original parable, disciples should perhaps accentuate the positive. While they admit that evil must necessarily be punished, they should recall that the best way to overcome evil is to do what is good. They are called upon, therefore, to overcome the calamities of their world by the contagious reality of doing good. Why should they let the devil have all the lines?

Wednesday: Matthew 13:44-46   The parables of the buried treasure and the pearl are unique to Matthew. Both deal with the advent of the kingdom and radical commitment to it: the selling of everything one has. Both have the same sequence: finding, selling, buying. Yet at the same time they are different. In the first parable, the farmer is not seeking but happens to find the treasure. In the second, the merchant is seeking and finally finds the pearl. In the first, there is a certain shock in that the farmer hides the treasure and goes off to buy a seemingly ordinary field. In the second, there is less shock since the merchant goes about his purchase quite openly.

In the treasure parable the first stage is normalcy, namely, the routine work of a farmer whose whole future is plotted out by his circumstances. The second stage is the discovery of the treasure that then creates a new world and new possibilities. The third stage is the reversal of the past whereby the farmer is obliged to sell everything he has. The fourth stage is the new activity of the farmer made possible by the discovery. He is no longer programmed as before. This fourth stage is the world of new possibilities grounded in the person of Jesus.

Reflection. Believers also seek happiness in a world of comfort but often find monotony. They search for satisfaction in a world of pleasure but sometimes find discontent. They look for power in a world of affluence and not infrequently uncover disillusion. In such circumstances Jesus' parable of the buried treasure speaks volumes. Here Matthew pictures the farmer in a world of drab monotony whose future is determined. But the discovery of the treasure offers the possibility of a new life. He reverses the past by selling all that he has. He joyfully addresses the challenge of his new world. For Matthew, only the kingdom as rooted in the person of Jesus gives true meaning and direction to one's life. For Matthew, only the Jesus-treasure satisfies.

Thursday: Matthew 13:47-53 The parable of the dragnet is also unique to Matthew. It is linked to his explanation of the parable of the wheat and the weeds in 13:36-43 by means of a temporary mixing of good and evil, a final distinction, and appropriate punishment. It is also connected to Matthew's discourse on the last judgment (24:1–25:46). Here as there, Matthew teaches that evil will be rejected and punished. Hence, while the good fish are put into baskets, the bad fish are thrown out.

In verse 52 Jesus describes his disciples by way of a parable. Every scribe trained in the Law and the Prophets who also understands his message is like the head of a household. He brings forth both the new (Jesus' message) and the old (the Law and the Prophets). For Matthew, such a scribe is the Christian ideal.

Reflection. Perhaps this parable of the dragnet can remind modern disciples that they are not necessarily the final arbiters of what is valuable and what is useless. Instead of regarding certain people as a priori useless, they do well to recall that God has the capacity to make what is useless into something quite valuable. God thus enjoys the liberty of the potter (see Jer 18:1-6) to fashion whatever object he desires. This is also the task of believers. Instead of passing judgment, they should endeavor to transform and shape those who seem to be of no consequence. In so doing, they join the ranks of the divine Potter who reworks the clay into a new creation.

Friday: Matthew 13:54-58   Borrowing this account from Mark, Matthew has shortened it and left out mention of the disciples and the Sabbath. In so doing, Matthew has focused the spotlight solely on Jesus. He shows that Jesus lacks the proper credentials when he returns to his hometown and preaches in the local synagogue. There is such a great disproportion between his simple family background and the great notoriety of his wisdom and miracles. The Nazarenes' reaction to Jesus supports the proverb that familiarity breeds contempt. Ironically the townspeople are mistaken about Jesus' family. As Matthew has shown in 12:46-50, Jesus' true relatives are those who do the will of his heavenly Father. In the end Jesus experiences the typical fate of the prophet, namely, rejection by his own. Owing to the Nazarenes' disbelief, Jesus does not perform many deeds of power there.

Reflection. This passage may recall for believers their sharing in Jesus' prophetic mission by reason of their baptism. They too are called to be his spokespersons in today's world. This passage must challenge them to ask to what extent they are willing to exercise that office. By consistently choosing good over evil, they proclaim Jesus' message about the kingdom. By acting justly, they announce Jesus' viewpoint on the dignity of the human person. In these and similar modes of conduct they will experience ridicule and rejection. Nonetheless, by dismissing such false reactions to their prophetic ministry, they advance Jesus' plan for the kingdom. They will also find consolation in the fact that God chooses to use them—with or without great credentials—to accomplish the mission of the church. While the prophetic office is indeed demanding, it is also rewarding.

Saturday: Matthew 14:1-12   Matthew arranges his text so that the account of the death of John the Baptist in this passage follows upon the rejection of Jesus in 13:54-58. Here Herod Antipas, the tetrarch of Galilee and Perea, is suffering from the pangs of guilt. He persists in thinking that Jesus is really John back from the dead. This explains for the tormented ruler why Jesus performs miracles. This conclusion provides the link to the account of the Baptist's martyrdom in which Matthew depicts John as the unflinching exponent of fidelity to the prophetic call. Aware of that call, he does not hesitate to condemn Herod's sin of incest. Only the fear of the crowds initially prevents Herod from executing John. After his oath to Herodias' daughter, however, he can save face only by acceding to Herodias' wish to have the head of the Baptist on a platter. After burying their master, John's disciples inform Jesus about the whole affair.

Reflection. John the Baptist exemplifies the criticizing dimension of prophecy. It involves saying it the way it really is and thus pointing out the evils that fester in the community. The Baptist's heroic resistance must move modern believers to look at their own community's woes and make them known. Some of society's programs are presumed to be just, even though they hurt countless people. Bearing in mind John's fearless opposition to Herod Antipas, modern disciples are encouraged to take a long look at the problems confronting their community, make them known, and anticipate some form of retaliation. As spokespersons for God, modern prophets must exhibit no little courage as they struggle to make the community whole again. Silence will not ordinarily achieve the goal—only the relentless prophetic voice will.

The Eighteenth Week of the Year

Monday: Matthew 14:13-21 (Matthew 14:22-36 can be used in Year A)   This account of the feeding of the five thousand alludes to the manna in the desert (Exod 16:1-8), Elisha's feeding of one hundred men from twenty barley loaves (2 Kgs 4:42-44), and the Eucharist (Matt 26:26: blessing, breaking, giving). Jesus is interpreted as a new Moses and a new messianic king. Like Moses, Jesus provides bread in the desert. Like the messianic king, Jesus hosts a banquet that looks to the final banquet of the kingdom.

Jesus' withdrawal points to a new period in his ministry as he separates from his enemies until the moment of the passion. Matthew emphasizes here the compassion of Jesus that leads him to heal, not teach, as in his source Mark. This compassion also carries over to feeding the crowd. By dropping the disciples' question and Jesus' counterquestion in Mark,

Matthew portrays Jesus as totally in charge of the situation. Then, like a Jewish father presiding over the family meal, Jesus blesses the food, i.e., praises and thanks God for it. Matthew heightens the effect of the miracle by adding to his source Mark that the five thousand do not include women and children.

Reflection. Some disciples are tempted to regard living as a very private enterprise—it concerns them but no one else. They consider living as seclusion from the rest of humanity—they wish to be insulated from the problems of others. They look upon living as their *individual* way of serving God—they disapprove of serving God by attending to *common* ills. On the other hand, Matthew presents Jesus as opposed to everything that oppresses and depresses the human spirit. For Matthew, Jesus' life has meaning only insofar as others find meaning in their own lives. In this passage Jesus withdraws only to discover a frustrated, dejected humanity. For Jesus, to be moved with pity means to heal, to be concerned means to provide food, to be filled means to fill others. Here Jesus fulfills the expectations of the messianic king: he offers life to his people and by offering life finds his own reason for living. In Matthew, for Jesus to live is to let live.

Tuesday: Matthew 14:22-36 (Matthew 15:1-2, 10-14 may also be used, especially in Year A when Matthew 14:22-36 is used on Monday)   Matthew adds to Mark's account of Jesus' walking on the water the tradition about Peter. This is probably Jesus' first postresurrectional appearance to Peter (see John 21:7-8) that Matthew has inserted into the time of Jesus' ministry to show both the divine presence and the Christian's dilemma of being caught between faith and doubt.

The scene borrows from the Old Testament: (1) Yahweh walks on the waters of chaos (Job 38:16; Isa 43:16); (2) Yahweh reaches out to rescue one captured in death's flood waters (Pss 18:16-17; 144:7); and (3) Yahweh indicates his presence ("it is I") and intent to save (Exod 3:14; Isa 45:18). The tradition implies the following: (1) when chaos overwhelms the church, Jesus is there; (2) when fear overtakes the community, Jesus reacts: "Do not be afraid!"; and (3) when faith gives way to hesitation, Jesus is still willing to stretch out his hand. Unlike Mark, Matthew has the disciples reflect the faith of the Christian community. Jesus is not merely another miracle worker; he is the Son of God.

Here Peter represents the conflict between faith and doubt. "Little faith" captures the dimension of doubt and wavering. Yet Jesus heeds Peter's request by stretching out his hand and the others' request by entering the boat. For Matthew, Jesus does not abandon his church even when the situation appears hopeless. Jesus will continue to stretch out his hand and save.

The passage concludes with Jesus' landing at Gennesaret. When word of his arrival spreads throughout the region, the people besiege Jesus for healing. Here Matthew emphasizes his enormous power: *all* the sick are brought to him and *all* who touch the fringe of his cloak are healed.

Reflection. Some people perceive other people's discouragement, yet are content merely to shrug their shoulders. They notice other people's doubts, yet are happy to leave them with their doubts. They hear of other people's frustration, yet are reluctant to make such frustration their own. Against this background Matthew presents Peter struggling with discouragement, doubt, and frustration. He demonstrates little faith, hovering between belief and disbelief. Yet the Lord stretches out his hand to save Peter. But Peter's renewed faith is not for himself alone. In Matthew, Peter is the rock of the church: he affords solidity and strength to those who experience discouragement, doubt, and frustration. In Matthew, Peter learns that to believe in God is to reach out to others.

Wednesday: Matthew 15:21-28   Matthew changes Mark's ethnic identity of the woman ("Syrophoenician") to "Canaanite." He probably does so to emphasize the enmity between Jews and Gentiles from the time of the conquest. What this Gentile woman is seeking to achieve in this episode is more than the cure of her daughter—it is the recognition of women's place (and Gentile women as well) in Matthew's community. There are those in the community who insist that Jesus send her away. When Jesus discourages her with his limited view of mission (only Israel), she persists. When Jesus poses the harsh parable about the children (Jews) and dogs (Gentiles), she is unrelenting as she counters with the observation about the crumbs. In the end Jesus lauds her faith and accedes to her wish for her daughter. Ultimately the woman also finds her rightful place in worship and the study of the Scriptures (v. 22: "Have pity on me, Lord"; v. 25: "Lord, help me").

Reflection. Disciples take pride in the name *Christian* but know that sometimes their life does not always match the name. They may rejoice in being regular churchgoers but recognize that their daily lives are not always consistent with their attendance. They are happy to read church documents but must admit that their conduct does not always reflect the view of Jesus' church. Against this background Matthew presents the Canaanite woman as the embodiment of Christian faith. Though belonging to two minorities (she is not only a Gentile but a Gentile woman), she dares to seek Jesus out. When others try to rebuff her, she persists. When Jesus discourages her with his limited view of mission, she is unrelenting. When Jesus poses the harsh parable about the children and the dogs, she counters with the observation about the crumbs. It is this type of faith that Matthew holds up to his community. The woman's actions embody what faith is all about, namely, to cling to Jesus through thick and thin. Matthew has the Canaanite woman teach that to follow Christ is to live up to that name.

Thursday: Matthew 16:13-23   In constructing this scene, Matthew uses some special material that probably originated in a postresurrectional appearance to Peter. Whereas Peter identifies Jesus as the Messiah in Mark and the Messiah of God in Luke, in Matthew Peter adds "the Son of the living God." For Matthew, therefore, the Son of Man is not only a *son* of God as Davidic king (see Ps 2:7) but *the* transcendent *Son* of God. In verse 20 Matthew concludes this part of the scene by repeating Mark's command of silence but also by making explicit the title of Messiah.

Jesus proceeds to reward Peter for his perception, since it is based not on weak human nature ("flesh and blood") but on a revelation received in faith from the Father. Jesus confers on Peter the grace of leadership. The title "rock" evokes the unshakableness he will provide for Jesus' church. "The gates of the netherworld" refer to the abode of the dead with its insatiable appetite and power. The keys, as seen in Isaiah 22:22, represent the authority of a prime minister and, as seen in Matthew 23:13, the power to teach the way to the kingdom. The rabbinic background of binding and loosing implies both authoritative teaching and disciplinary power.

Peter cannot accept the implications of Son of Man as propounded by Jesus. To say Messiah/Son of God is to say glory and majesty. Jesus must, therefore, reproach Peter as a stumbling block to God's plans. Peter now plays the role of Satan that Matthew described in the temptation in the desert (4:1-11). Like the devil, Peter opts for the easy, manipulative way of buying people off rather than a suffering and death program. As rock, Peter must communicate Jesus' teaching, not human plans and programs.

Reflection. Some believers enjoy *being over* people but do not relish *being under* the obligation of serving them. They rejoice to have a nameplate and a title but are rather loath to implement that name and title for others. They are happy on making it to the top but resent having to provide for those under them. Today's passage, however, provides a different take. Jesus makes Peter the leader of his church. By being over the others, he is under the compulsion to serve and assist them. He is the rock: he affords solidity for the entire edifice. His strength is to be their strength. Because of the keys, Peter is authorized to teach the way to the kingdom: the teacher relates in terms of those taught. He has the power to bind and loose: his authoritative teaching and disciplinary power must promote the common good, not Peter's personal good. To be over Christ's church is to be under the obligation of serving. To be over is to be under.

Friday: Matthew 16:24-28 In this passage Matthew teaches that Jesus' fate becomes the disciple's fate. To follow Jesus is to reject the world's security measures. To lose oneself for Jesus' sake is, paradoxically, to find oneself. To gain the whole world but to destroy oneself in the process does not turn a profit. But to sacrifice oneself now for Jesus' cause guarantees more than survival on the last day when the glorified Son of Man returns to reward the concrete activities of the disciple.

This passage concludes with Jesus' statement that some of his disciples will not die until they see the Son of Man coming with his royal power. While this saying may have originally referred to the expectation of an imminent second coming by some early Christians, for Matthew it must have another meaning. Perhaps Matthew is thinking of the anticipation of that second coming when Jesus solemnly assures the disciples after his resurrection that he will be with them always to the end of the age (28:20).

Reflection. At times disciples expend much time and energy on their future security but neglect to provide for others in the present. They spend their talents on creating tax shelters and nest eggs but refuse to meet the needs of family and friends now. They use up their time and gifts to ensure their financial gains but are unconcerned about the loss of love. In the final analysis, they contend that not to find and not to gain mean to lose. Opposed to such strategies, Jesus chooses to blaze the path to glory along the route of suffering and death. He opts to create a Messiah image out of the common clay of pain. By thus losing himself for his Father and his community, he finds himself so drained that he can be filled with the Spirit on Easter Sunday. The apparent loss becomes an unimaginable gain. In Jesus, losing is finding.

Saturday: Matthew 17:14-20   Matthew introduces the father of the epileptic boy as a believer since he kneels before Jesus and addresses him as "Lord." He then describes his son's condition, remarking that he is a lunatic, namely, one affected by the moon. He also notes that the disciples were unable to cure him. Jesus responds by accusing Israel of infidelity in that it rejects his miracles and overall message. At this point Matthew relates the cure of the boy in short order: the rebuke of the demon, its expulsion, and the instantaneous healing. Next Jesus considers the question of the disciples about their inability to heal the boy. He characterizes them as people of little faith. Thus they understand and assent but do not trust God wholeheartedly. To describe the proper response of faith, Matthew has Jesus refer to the mustard seed that is minute and unimpressive. A faith like the mustard seed is capable of moving even mountains.

Reflection. Without question disciples accept doctrines and statements but to what extent do they accept the person of their God? Are they satisfied with "I believe this truth," or will they go on to declare, "I believe in this God"? Hence there is a significant difference between comprehension and trust. The Matthean Jesus acknowledges that his disciples understand but adds that they are people of "little faith" (see also Matt 6:30; 8:26; 14:31; 16:8). Jesus is thus implying that their faith must grow, that it must advance beyond understanding and assent, and must reach the level of trust. Modern disciples must also engage themselves in this growth process. They must progress beyond the recitation of church formulae and attain that plateau where the person of their God becomes so paramount that trust takes center stage. Perhaps they can take their experience of total trust in other human beings and use it in assessing their trust in God.

The Nineteenth Week of the Year

Monday: Matthew 17:22-27   This passage consists of two scenes: (1) the second prediction of the passion (vv. 22-23) and (2) the question about the temple tax (vv. 24-27). In the passion prediction Jesus fends off any possible political interpretation of his messiahship. The passive formulation (v. 22: "to be handed over"; v. 23: "will be raised") suggests that the Father functions as the agent of the whole course of events. The distress experienced by the disciple registers their understanding of the Father's plan.

In the second section Matthew deals with a problem in his community, namely, payment of the temple tax. If subjects are not obligated by laws affecting foreigners, then Jesus and his disciples are not obligated by the temple tax since they belong to the kingdom of heaven. The Matthean Jesus, however, does not stop there since there is the question of another value, namely, the claims of love. Since the members of the kingdom of heaven must also avoid unnecessary scandal, they should pay the tax.

Reflection. Disciples must always consider the impact of their actions on others. They must demonstrate their genuine liberty by sometimes curtailing its use. The issue about the temple tax speaks to this point. Although Jesus and his disciples, as members of the kingdom of heaven, are not obligated to pay the temple tax, they do so in order not to give offense. Believers should recall the sage advice of Paul regarding the eating of meat sacrificed to idols. Although idols do not exist, the faith of the weaker members of the community may be shaken by the actions of the stronger members. Paul concludes: "But when you thus sin against members of your family, and wound their conscience when it is weak, you sin against Christ" (1 Cor 8:12).

Tuesday: Matthew 18:1-5, 10, 12-14   In this chapter Matthew constructs his fourth great sermon, namely, advice to a divided community about church life and order. Here Matthew addresses problems in his church and offers advice for correcting them and thus establishing healthy community life. The passage consists of two sections: (1) true greatness (vv. 1-5) and (2) the parable of the lost sheep (vv. 10, 12-14).

In the first section Matthew teaches his community that greatness in the kingdom of heaven does not depend on rank or position but on childlikeness. In that society children had absolutely no value—they were utterly dependent on others. It is that quality that Christians should have toward their God.

In the second section Matthew insists that the community must provide for the little ones, namely, those unimportant disciples who can all too easily go astray because they are neglected. To make his point, Matthew introduces the parable of the shepherd who leaves the ninety-nine sheep on the mountains and searches for the one sheep that has gone astray. In turn, disciples must search for the Christian sheep that has wandered away from the fold and thus violate purely human calculations by leaving the ninety-nine. The one endangered sheep thus takes precedence over the rest. Such relentless care for the one sheep does not spring from an impersonal command but from the will of the Father.

Reflection. Disciples must establish priorities. They must pose the question about which community members demand their greatest attention. In resolving this issue, they can readily consider the parable of the lost sheep. Purely human thinking would suggest that it is safer to stay with the ninety-nine sheep than to go searching for the one stray. Jesus, however, supports the search for the stray. Hence it is the weaker members who require greater attention from the community. Rather than being hooked on the pursuit of honors and power, genuine disciples must exercise vigilance in helping the weaker members find their way back home. It is worth noting that such a policy is more than a mere recommendation. Matthew states that this is the will of the Father.

Wednesday: Matthew 18:15-20   Verses 15-17 show the order to be followed in dealing with a sinful member of the community (see Lev 19:17-18; Deut 19:15). The first step is a purely private correction that saves the reputation of the individual. If that fails, a few more witnesses are brought in to prevail upon the sinner. If that is unsuccessful, the admonition of the full assembly of the local community is the final step. If the person ignores the full assembly, he or she is to be excommunicated and regarded as a nonmember (Gentile) or a public sinner (tax collector). Verse 18 attests that God ratifies such a decision of the local community.

Verses 19-20 were originally concerned with the efficacy of common prayer. In their present place they relate to the decision of the local community. Size is insignificant. The presence of merely a few is sufficient to ensure the hearing of the prayer. Christians gathered around the person and words of the Lord are Christ. The risen Lord is present whenever the community gathers.

Reflection. Believers sometimes look at church organizations and conclude that, as individuals, they are unimportant. They observe church hierarchy and reason that, as individuals, they have nothing to give. They witness church activities and think that, as individuals, they are inconsequential. Opposed to this mindset is the thrust of today's passage. Matthew's community is not a sinless community. Belonging to that community, however, implies being involved. In the case of personal wrong, being involved means correcting the sinner in private and, if necessary, gathering others to win back the wayward member. Being involved implies joining in common prayer, especially in situations where the whole community is called upon to act as a body. Being involved implies that realization that the least private act is by its very nature ecclesial. To be a believer is to be involved.

Thursday: Matthew 18:21–19:1   See Tuesday of the Third Week of Lent.

Friday: Matthew 19:3-12   This passage consists of two components: (1) Jesus' teaching on divorce (vv. 3-9) and (2) Jesus' teaching on celibacy (vv. 10-12). In the first section the Pharisees approach Jesus with malicious intent to inquire about the grounds for divorce. Jesus rebuffs them with a question that cites Genesis 1:27 and then quotes Genesis 2:24. Essentially Jesus' response raises this question: what does the Creator intend in the beginning? The implied answer is that the Creator makes humans male and female for a permanent, not a temporary, union. Jesus next adds that no one can undo the bond that God has thus created.

Observing that Jesus' reply eliminates divorce, the Pharisees pose the question about Deuteronomy 24:1-2 that specifies drawing up a certificate of divorce. Jesus responds that Moses permitted divorce because of the Israelites' hardness of heart, i.e., their unwillingness to abide by God's will. Jesus concludes this dispute with the Pharisees by stating that a man who divorces his wife and marries another commits adultery. As in 5:32, Matthew adds an exceptive clause (v. 9: "unless the marriage is unlawful"). This probably refers to incestuous marriages that Christians contracted before baptism (see Lev 18:6-18). Hence the exceptive clause is not really an exception to Jesus' absolute prohibition of divorce.

In the second section Jesus' stringent stand against divorce prompts the shocked disciples' statement about the inadvisability of marriage. In reply, Jesus acknowledges that celibacy is a special gift from God for only some people. Such people do not include those who are eunuchs by reason of birth ("because they were born so") or castration ("because they were made so by others") but only those "eunuchs" who embrace celibacy for the kingdom of heaven.

Reflection. While the debate about the possibility of divorce in the church continues unabated, disciples may find inspiration in Jesus' teaching about marriage. Dismissing the question about the legality of a man divorcing his wife, Jesus chooses to focus on this central issue: what is God's intent in the very beginning? The citation about male and female (Gen 1:27) reflects the institution of marriage as the high point of God's creative energy on the sixth day. The quotation about a man being joined to his wife and becoming one flesh with her (Gen 2:24) emphasizes the partnership aspect of marriage. By clinging to his wife, a husband does what Israel does when it clings to Yahweh. Thus the husband is supportive, respectful, faithful, and loving. This image, therefore, rejects any purely individualistic notion of marriage—the dimension of a married team is paramount. The intention of the Creator remains central.

Saturday: Matthew 19:13-15 Having discussed marriage and celibacy in the preceding account, Matthew now takes up the family, specifically children. To approach Jesus is to be able to enter the kingdom. Here the Matthean Jesus offers that invitation to children, namely, people without rights and status who must cling resolutely to others. Only those who cling in this way to Jesus are worthy of the kingdom. What stands out in this passage is Jesus' attitude toward children, i.e., regarding them as persons and presenting them as models worthy of imitation, especially in their reception of the kingdom of heaven.

Reflection. The Matthean Jesus challenges believers to adopt the attitude of trust and confidence that people without rights and status must have. To that extent, disciples are bidden to be children. In a world with so much emphasis on individualism, self-esteem, and personal growth the words of Jesus are indeed refreshing: "the Kingdom of heaven belongs to such as these" (v. 14). Believers, therefore, must embody this aspect of the kingdom. After the manner of children, they must reflect the dispositions of trust and confidence and dependence on the Father.

The Twentieth Week of the Year

Monday: Matthew 19:16-22 In Matthew's account of the rich young man the inquirer addresses Jesus as "teacher," a title that the evangelist reserves for nonbelievers. He asks about what good deed will earn him eternal life. In this passage Matthew equates eternal life with entering into life (v. 17) and being perfect (v. 21). Jesus counters this question with the remark that only one (God is implied) is good. When asked about specific commandments, Jesus recites five of the Ten Commandments, adding love of one's neighbor. When the young man asserts that he has kept all these commandments and inquires as to what is yet lacking, Jesus replies with a devastating call to perfection. The young man must sell his possessions and give the money to the poor. This will ensure treasure in heaven. Thereafter the young man is to follow Jesus. Upon hearing such demands, he walks away in great pain since he is extremely wealthy.

Reflection. All too often this passage has been invoked to establish a distinction between "ordinary" Christians and those who take the evangelical counsels of poverty, chastity, and obedience. Such a distinction seems to draw a line between "first-rate" and "second-rate" Christians. Modern disciples can derive hope from this passage in that keeping the commandments ensures entering into life. Believers can use the young man's reluctance to follow Jesus because of his great wealth to ask what obstacles prevent them from following Jesus more closely. In addition to wealth, such obstacles may include the insatiable appetite for power, the unfettered drive to achieve fame and distinction, the unreasonable pursuit of pleasure, and the like. After investigating the extent of such obstacles in their lives, believers can opt to eliminate or at least lessen their powerful grip. Following Jesus never takes a detour around Calvary.

Tuesday: Matthew 19:23-30   In developing the theme of the rich and the kingdom, Matthew has Jesus equate eternal life with entering the kingdom (v. 23) and being saved (v. 25). Jesus employs the example of the young man to demonstrate the difficulty of the rich being saved. With more than a touch of hyperbole, Jesus compares this impasse to a camel going through the eye of a needle—an utterly impossible feat. Thinking that riches indicate God's favor, the disciples are dumbfounded and pose the question: "Who then can be saved?" (v. 25). Jesus glances at them and remarks that salvation means God's free gift, not human achievement. Jesus' reply prompts Peter's question about their reward in view of having left everything and followed him. Jesus goes on to assure the Twelve that on the last day they will function as judges of the twelve tribes of Israel. Having suffered persecution at the hands of their own people, they will experience a reversal in the age to come when they share in Jesus' power and status. In verse 29 Jesus speaks not only about the Twelve but also about all those who encounter loss of whatever kind for his name. They will receive a hundredfold and acquire eternal life. Many of the first (the powerful, etc.) will be last while the last (the disciples, the poor, etc.) will be first.

Reflection. Discouragement and despair plague believers. They expend enormous energy in leaving everything and following Jesus. Too often, however, their efforts seem fruitless as the power-grabbing and pleasure-seeking people make it to the top while they fall hopelessly to the bottom. Their shrill cry for justice drowns in a sea of opposition and vicious retaliation. They pose the same question as Peter: "What will there be for us?" (v. 27). The response of Jesus is the same now as it was then. Reversal will be the order of the day as the first become last and the last become first. In their shocking world of disappointment and failure disciples must continue to hope. Such hope rests on a twofold basis. First, it resides in Jesus' comforting words of assurance that will effect this reversal. Second, it is found in Jesus' experience of passion, death, and resurrection. The shame and pain of Good Friday give way to the glory and exoneration of Easter Sunday. Calvary is never God's final word.

Wednesday: Matthew 20:1-16   Jesus' original parable seems to be verses 1-13. It may be divided as follows: (1) the hiring of five groups (vv. 1-7) and (2) payment of the groups, beginning with the last (vv. 8-13). The unexpected move (v. 8b) introduces the reversal of expectations described in verses 9-13. It is clear that the landowner has committed no injustice. He does appear, however, more as one who offends expectations than as one who is exceptionally generous. On this level the parable teaches that the believer is to accept God's radical freedom, i.e., his ability to give in the face of human calculations and expectations. The believer is to allow God to order the world in God's own way.

Verses 14-16 are probably the work of Matthew himself. In connection with the disciples and their reward in 19:27-30, the parable reminds Matthew's audience that Jesus possesses the radical liberty to call and reward others simply on the basis of his goodness. Leadership positions in the community and outstanding service do not preclude God's freedom to give to others. The "good" Jesus (Matt 19:17) will come back as the Son of Man to render judgment as the "generous" one (v. 15). But the judgment will not be based on human calculations.

Reflection. Believers sometimes see former sinners attain positions of leadership in either church or state and note a certain lack of logic. They observe people less talented than themselves succeed in their careers and register a note of complaint. They may witness disaster in their own lives and express programmed self-condemnation. They must admit they cannot grow because they fashion God in their own image.

Opposed to such modes of thinking is Matthew's parable of the workers in the vineyard. There Matthew's community includes those who begin to work at dawn. They are in leadership positions and have served the community well. But there are also the eleventh-hour members of the community who lack the credentials of the first group. Matthew's advice is to underline God's radical capacity to give, apart from credentials. It is also the challenge to accept Jesus as the giver of gifts and not the celestial dispenser of tit-for-tat theology. The Matthean Jesus is a Jesus who transcends human calculations and expectations, a Jesus who proves in his person that to grow is to accept a God of surprises.

Thursday: Matthew 22:1-14   Jesus' original parable may have comprised only verses 1-5, 8-10. It may have envisioned a defense of Jesus' practice of eating with sinners. Matthew enlarges the original setting of an ordinary meal by speaking of a royal wedding feast, a common image of God's final union with his own in heaven. Borrowing from the parable of the unjust tenants (21:33-43), Matthew expands the parable in verses 6-7 to create a panorama of salvation history. While seeing the first group of servants as Old Testament prophets (v. 3), he probably envisions the second group as Christian missionaries to the Jews (v. 4). Israel rejects both groups, however, so that the king is forced to burn their city (Jerusalem in AD 70). In answer to the question as to who are worthy to share in the final heavenly banquet (v. 8), Matthew has the Gentiles brought in from outside the city. It is not, however, a perfect group, consisting, as it does, of both bad and good.

Verses 11-13 were originally a separate parable that Matthew now connects with verses 1-10. Not everyone who accepts the call lives up to its implications. The man not properly dressed suffers eternal rejection. Not only Israel but also the church come under God's judgment. Verse 14 is an originally separate saying that tells members of Matthew's community to take their call seriously. Though the Lord invites many, he chooses only a few. One must continue to respond to the initial call in order to take part in the final banquet.

Reflection. Though baptized members of the Christian community, believers may tend to equate baptism with final salvation. Though mature Christian adults through confirmation, they may stunt their growth through lack of generosity. Though they promise to be faithful to other people in marriage, jobs, etc., they may act as if the promise without performance assures lasting union with God and his community.

In response to such tendencies, Matthew labors to point out that enjoying the final banquet with Jesus' community requires ongoing effort. He offers the example of Israel. They rejected the Word and their city was destroyed. In the new kingdom composed of both Jews and Gentiles, however, the call must be lived each day. To disregard the implications of the call is to be improperly dressed for the wedding and thus to be rejected forever. The invitation to Christian living is only a beginning. Only ongoing fidelity assures final election. In Matthew's community, only the faithful have reserved seats.

Friday: Matthew 22:34-40   Unlike Mark who presents the question of the Great Commandment as a friendly discussion among scholars, Matthew sees it as a violent attack of the Pharisees on Jesus. Here a lawyer addresses Jesus with the title "teacher"—hence, for Matthew, the mark of a nonbeliever. Unlike Mark who has the scribe applaud Jesus' reply, Matthew has the lawyer set out to trip Jesus up.

The Great Commandment implies a commandment or commandments that give meaning to all the others. Out of the 248 positive commandments and the 365 prohibitions of the Torah, Jesus selects two: (1) love of God (Deut 6:4-5) and (2) love of neighbor (Lev 19:18). Jesus thus implies that there is a certain order or gradation in the legal corpus. Unlike Mark, Matthew likens love of neighbor to love of God. He also adds that these two commandments are the basic summary of all the Scriptures (v. 40: "the whole law and the prophets"). For Jesus, this combination is absolute. There can be no real love of God without love of neighbor.

Reflection. For not a few believers, laws are impersonal, third-person statements. Hence their law-keeping tends to be impersonal. At times they may regard laws as infringements on their liberty. Therefore, they may seek out loopholes to protect their personal interests. Since laws threaten punishments in case of nonobservance, they may obey only because of the possible dangers to themselves. In their legal observance, they become victims of their own ego. Jesus, however, selects from the entire Torah love of God and love of neighbor as the very core of divine revelation. Religion can no longer be the observance of a dry, disjointed list of dos and don'ts. Religion must relate legal observance to people, namely, God and neighbor. For Jesus, not to find one's neighbor in the law is not to find meaning in human existence. Law devoid of concern for others is no longer law. Jesus insists that law-keeping is people-keeping.

Saturday: Matthew 23:1-12   See Tuesday of the Second Week of Lent.

The Twenty-first Week of the Year

Monday: Matthew 23:13-22   This famous speech in Matthew reflects, for the most part, a situation in the life of the community, namely, the conflict between Pharisaic Judaism and Matthew's church. To be sure, Matthew ignores the positive qualities of Pharisaic Judaism. What he chooses to do is to focus on the state of his own community. Thus Matthew finds among his own people many of the same faults that he recognizes in his Pharisaic opponents.

In his first woe (v. 13) Jesus criticizes the scribes and Pharisees for shutting people out of the kingdom of heaven. Instead of making entrance into that kingdom easier, they exacerbate the situation by their teaching. In the second woe (v. 15) Jesus attacks the missionary efforts of his opponents. They go to all lengths to convert just one Gentile who then becomes twice as damnable as the missionaries themselves. In the third woe (vv. 16-22) Jesus inveighs against a form of casuistry that finds some oaths binding and others not so and that sees the binding oaths based on items of lesser value (the gold and the gift on the altar).

Reflection. Modern believers may quickly come to the conclusion that this passage is out of date and, therefore, irrelevant. On second thought they may see Jesus' third woe as a challenge to reassess their priorities. They may ask on what basis they declare something to be of value or without value. Is that basis a perception deriving from the Good News or one evolving from their own prejudices? For example, they may think that private prayer has lost its significance since they focus solely on the liturgy, i.e., the official public worship of the church. They may also believe that devotion to the saints no longer enjoys any relevance since only Jesus deserves their full attention. While some may contend that these examples pale in significance when compared to Jesus' third woe, disciples must nonetheless strike a healthy balance between public and private prayer as well as worship of God and veneration of the saints.

Tuesday: Matthew 23:23-26   In this passage Jesus criticizes Pharisaic scrupulosity in matters of trivial importance and their gross disregard of matters of significant importance. In his fourth woe (vv. 23-24) Jesus considers the duty of tithing, i.e., offering one-tenth of one's produce in support of the temple. The scribes and Pharisees faithfully observe the tithing of the smallest herbs (mint, dill, and cummin) but neglect "the weightier things of the law: judgment and mercy and fidelity" (v. 23). Justice and mercy focus on obligations to one's neighbor while faith may refer to one's total commitment to God. Pursuit of the trivial to the exclusion of the essential finds apt expression in the metaphor of straining a gnat but swallowing a camel. In his fifth woe (vv. 25-26) Jesus addresses the issue of the external versus the internal. The scribes and Pharisees meticulously follow the ritual washing of utensils (the external) while remaining unconcerned about greed and self-indulgence (the internal). Clearly the internal has priority—it is what makes the whole person clean.

Reflection. The fourth woe speaks to the ongoing need for believers to distinguish between the trivial and the essential. While the trivial has some value, the essential has far greater value, namely, justice, mercy, and faith. In practice, believers must begin with their basic priorities, e.g., their obligations to spouse, family, fellow workers, and the like. They must expend their greatest energy and amount of time in loving, supporting, encouraging, and aiding this primary circle. In so doing, they put first things first. Having met these obligations, they may expand their horizons to include others, e.g., their entertainment circle. By establishing such priorities, they do not confuse straining a gnat with swallowing a camel.

Wednesday: Matthew 23:27-32   In the sixth woe (vv. 27-28) Jesus addresses concern for what is outside but neglect for what is inside. The scribes and Pharisees are like whitewashed tombs: they are beautiful on the outside but corrupt on the inside. On the outside they look righteous to the public but on the inside they exude only an abundance of lawlessness and hypocrisy. In their lawlessness they mount rebellion against God. In their hypocrisy they merely pretend to be righteous. In the seventh and final woe (vv. 29-32) Jesus decries the scribes and Pharisees as the offspring of their ancestors who murdered the prophets and the righteous. By building monuments to the prophets and the righteous, the scribes and Pharisees attempt to separate themselves from their murderous ancestors. For Jesus, however, they share the evil genes of their forefathers. Jesus goes on to announce that they will complete or fill up what their ancestors began when they murder him, God's final Prophet.

Reflection. Hypocrisy continues to raise its ugly head, even for believers. For some reason, people like to pretend to be what they are not. They wish to appear righteous and God-fearing, even though they may lack these qualities. The image of whitewashed tombs captures their efforts to disguise the truth. In the final analysis, today's passage is an appeal for honest self-evaluation. Shedding any and every attempt at pretense, disciples must look deep within their hearts. First, they must acknowledge themselves for what they truly are, namely, weak human beings who would like things to be otherwise. Second, they must initiate a plan to offset the pretend game. They must present themselves to others as they are—warts and all! Building from that vantage point, they must pursue a life of integrity and honesty. Ultimately people will recognize such qualities and will register due esteem and admiration.

Thursday: Matthew 24:42-51   In chapters 24–25 Matthew has Jesus deliver his fifth and last great sermon, the so-called eschatological discourse. It focuses on the coming new age, the events that precede it, and the lifestyle of the disciples during the period of waiting. In verses 42-44 Jesus calls for unmitigated vigilance since the coming of the Son of Man will be as unexpected as a thief breaking into a house.

In verses 45-51 Jesus offers the parable of the faithful and unfaithful slave. By means of this parable Matthew speaks to the leaders of his own community—they are the slaves who have been put in charge of their master's household. They are to be watchful, therefore, in honoring their obligations to the community. Here Matthew emphasizes the theme of delay (v. 48). The faithful slave is judged to be truly blessed. As a result, he will assume greater responsibility in taking charge of all his master's possessions. The unfaithful slave, however, capitalizing on his master's delay, punishes his fellow slaves and succumbs to gluttony and drunkenness. Such a slave will have a rude awakening upon his master's return. He will be dismembered and suffer eternal damnation.

Reflection. This parable speaks volumes to modern disciples. They too have assumed different types of leadership in the community. The lingering question is: will they faithfully discharge their office or will they abuse it in order to take advantage of others? The delay of Jesus' second coming enhances their temptation to neglect their duties to spouse, family, and the community. After all, they live in the twenty-first century and do not sense any inkling of the end of the ages. In this impasse they are urged to honor their commitment after the manner of Jesus. Wholehearted service to others must remain their relentless pursuit. Leadership status always involves unflagging attention to the needs of the community.

Friday: Matthew 25:1-13 Although it is difficult to reconstruct the precise wedding customs involved in this parable, it is likely that the bridegroom is returning with his bride from the home of her parents. The bridesmaids are to be part of the joyful procession upon the arrival of the couple. The wise bridesmaids, anticipating the delay, make provisions for such an emergency. The foolish bridesmaids, on the other hand, demonstrate complete lack of foresight. At the arrival of the couple, only the five wise bridesmaids can take part in the procession and thus share in the festivities.

Within the context of Matthew's theology, Jesus is the one who will return at the second coming, when the wedding feast (the consummation of the kingdom) will take place. Delay of the return, however, should engender watchfulness, not negligence. Not to be prepared is not to be known by the bridegroom. Those who live in the present must still reckon with the future.

Reflection. Wisdom means a full life for others. Some believers may equate wisdom with knowing all the answers. They may identify life as success or getting ahead. They may interpret a full life as great success or really getting ahead. Yet they may reject a full life for others. For them, wisdom is a purely personal venture. In today's passage, however, Matthew highlights responsibility, prudence, and fidelity. In his community the truly wise are those who meet the needs of others. In the parable the wise bridesmaids take their responsibility seriously. Because they provide for the needs of the bridegroom and his entourage, they are known, recognized, and thus admitted to the wedding celebration. Wisdom means a full life for others.

Saturday: Matthew 25:14-30 In order to keep his business productive, a wealthy businessman entrusts his excess capital to three servants before setting off on a journey. During the time of his absence the servants are to invest the money and increase the master's profits. The first two servants make use of the exorbitant interest rates and so double the original sum. Their fidelity in small matters leads the master on his return to entrust them with greater matters. Furthermore, they are invited to share the master's intimacy (vv. 21, 23: "Come, share your master's joy"). The third servant, however, refuses to run any risks. He simply buries the sum and unearths it at the master's return. His recital in verses 24-25 paradoxically accentuates the demanding nature of the master.

This parable stresses the demands of judgment rather than the imminence of judgment. For Matthew, gifts imply action, even coping with risks. The disciples who accept the implications of gifts will gain even more. Those who refuse to interact with their gifts, however, will lose what they have. The price of such refusal is awesome indeed: the darkness with its concomitant pain. It would not be surprising to have an indication here of what Matthew expects from the leaders in his own community.

Reflection. Some believers bask in their talents but may often be loath to use them for others. They may take pride in their gifts but may be content to let them lie idle. They may rejoice in their latent abilities but may prove reluctant to develop them. Yet gifts necessarily envision others. In this impasse Matthew presents both a positive and a negative view of giftedness. The first two servants are enterprising. The master challenges them to use their gifts to his advantage. They are rewarded because they have employed their abilities for him. The third servant, on the other hand, is totally inactive. Refusing to react to the master's recognition of his gifts, he is content to atrophy. As a result, no one benefits. By remaining unproductive, the gift ceases to be a gift. Modern believers must take this theology to heart, namely, to be gifted is to be gift.

The Twenty-second Week of the Year

Monday: Luke 4:16-30 Unlike Mark and Matthew, Luke presents the rejection of Jesus at the start of his ministry, not later. This scene in the Nazareth synagogue, therefore, anticipates the fame of the Spirit-filled prophet. In the synagogue service Jesus reads the text of Isaiah 61:1-2 but omits the phrase "bind up the brokenhearted," substituting instead Isaiah 58:6, namely, "liberty to captives." His prophetic message entails bringing good news to the poor and announcing the jubilee year (see Lev 25:8-55), i.e., the time when all debts were cancelled and all property restored to the original owners. Jesus states that he has fulfilled the message of Isaiah through his Spirit-filled presence. This synagogue speech is, in effect, his inaugural address. But ironically this initial positive reaction in the synagogue soon turns to persecution.

The synagogue crowd is astonished that Jesus can proclaim the fulfillment of such a great message, given his hometown lack of credentials. In turn, Jesus reacts by presenting himself as a prophet rejected by his own people. He then illustrates the universalist thrust of his mission by citing the miracles of Elijah (1 Kgs 17:7-24) and Elisha (2 Kgs 5:1-27). Their relevance is that they benefited pagans. The Good News rejected by the Jews will be preached to the Gentiles. Rejection now turns to indignation as the audience attempts to kill Jesus; however, he simply walks through their midst. Thus the Spirit-filled proclaimer of the new era must go down the path that leads through hostility and pain to exoneration. This scene is truly programmatic.

Reflection. Believers share in Jesus' prophetic mission through baptism but suffer pain and thus wonder whether they can survive. They experience failure and inquire if they can still enjoy success. In this frame of mind today's passage is relevant. People in the Nazareth synagogue do not want to hear that Jesus will inaugurate a new age with his prophetic message. For them, it is bad news that this message is intended not only for the Jews but also for the Gentiles, so bad that Jesus must suffer psychologically. The Father sustains Jesus, however, by not permitting the opposition to destroy him at this point and by helping him through the crises in the garden and on the cross. Believers thus learn that God supports his prophets.

Tuesday: Luke 4:31-37   In this episode Luke, following his source Mark, provides a general statement about Jesus' teaching on the Sabbath and the reaction of the Capernaum crowd, namely, astonishment because of Jesus' authority (vv. 31-32). Luke then proceeds (vv. 33-37) to narrate his exorcism in the synagogue. He describes the demoniac as being under the power of an unclean spirit. He adds to Mark that the demon throws the man down before the crowd but he survives without experiencing any harm. Toward the end of the episode Luke connects the exorcism with the Sabbath teaching by repeating the crowd's astonishment in general and their amazement at Jesus' authority.

Reflection. Good can overcome evil. At times believers may become disheartened as they observe the power of evil in the world. Sometimes it seems to be such a menacing power that it gains the upper hand all too readily. In this situation today's passage offers some dimension of hope. Here the spirit of evil recognizes in Jesus the spirit or power of good (v. 34: "the Holy One of God"). In this confrontation good triumphs over evil as Jesus orders the expulsion of the demon. For most disciples, evil usually does not emerge with sinister or diabolical features. It expresses itself subtly but nonetheless realistically in forms of injustice, prejudice, greed, etc. Armed with Jesus' example and the influence of his Spirit, today's disciples can change the power or control of evil by stripping away its destructive veneer. They can achieve this by overcoming evil with good.

Wednesday: Luke 4:38-44   This passage consists of three scenes: (1) the cure of Peter's mother-in-law (vv. 38-39), (2) the evening healings (vv. 40-41), and (3) the departure from Capernaum (vv. 42-44). In the first scene Peter's mother-in-law reacts to her cure by immediately serving those present. While such service corroborates her complete restoration to health, it also becomes a paradigm for other Galilean women who will similarly serve (see 8:2-3). In the second scene Luke presents Jesus as both healer and exorcist. He also notes the titles employed by the demons, namely, Son of God and the Messiah. In the third scene Luke introduces the people's attempt to prevent him from leaving their area. In response to these efforts, Jesus announces his intention to preach elsewhere. What is significant in this reply is that Jesus feels compelled to announce the Good News of the kingdom.

Reflection. Believers must take note of Jesus' compulsion or constraint to share the message of the kingdom. At times disciples can be lulled into thinking that only the hierarchy receives such a Spirit-driven mandate to proclaim the Good News. As Jesus' sisters and brothers, however, all believers are necessarily involved in spreading the Word. As members of his extended family, they are privy to the details of that message. In going about their daily schedule, they communicate the inherent value of every person, the goodness of God's creation, the wonder of God becoming human, the giftedness of all people, and the like. To share these family insights with their world is to proclaim with Jesus: "for this purpose I have been sent" (v. 43).

Thursday: Luke 5:1-11   In this account Luke has used his sources to dramatize the implications of Peter's call. Unlike Mark, Luke first has Jesus preach from Peter's boat. Luke then adds the miraculous catch of fish that, in turn, provokes Peter's reaction. At first Peter addresses Jesus as "Master," but after the catch he appeals to him as "Lord." Peter realizes that he is now in the presence of the One sent by God. He is constrained to ask Jesus to leave because his own sinfulness clashes with the holiness of God's envoy. (This acknowledgement of sinfulness probably stems from a postresurrectional story of the first appearance of Jesus to Peter.) At this point, Jesus addresses only Peter. He offers him a lifelong career as a unique fisherman in God's employ.

The conclusion of the account is important for Luke's theology. In both Mark and Matthew the disciples leave their nets and Zebedee. In Luke, however, they leave *everything*. It is, therefore, a question of radical renunciation. For Luke, the message is this: be detached from possessions and place yourself at the service of your neighbor.

Reflection. All believers realize that they are called by God but may feel they don't have the proper credentials for ministry. They duly realize that others need them but must admit they don't have a clean record. They may sense that they can still contribute something but their history of failure discourages them. Given such a scenario, believers should consider the role of Peter in today's passage. In the light of Jesus' first postresurrectional appearance, Peter recognizes the presence of the Lord and the enormity of his denial. Aware of his sinfulness, he seeks to have the Lord withdraw. Instead, Jesus invites him to take up a new and more engaging career. By responding to that call, Peter demonstrates for disciples of all times that God rehabilitates his chosen.

Friday: Luke 5:33-39   In this passage Luke presents Jesus in a controversy in which unnamed opponents question him about not instructing his disciples to fast. Jesus responds to their problem by means of two parables (a piece from a new garment and new wine) and a proverb (preferring old wine to new). All these components contrast the old with the new. As a whole, the passage poses the issue of relating the old way of Jewish piety with the new way of Christians in the time after Jesus' departure. Whether Christians are feasting or fasting, they are a new reality. Any effort to combine the new and the old does not really take into consideration this new reality and must inevitably lead to the destruction of both. Jesus' opponents have tasted the old wine but refuse the invitation to taste the new. They will not risk the challenge of Jesus' new community.

Reflection. The opponents' rejection of the new wine may strike some believers as a cut-and-dry issue. As a whole, they surmise the Jewish community has rejected the Christian invitation and, as a result, both Jews and Christians must go their separate ways. Against such a negative mindset, Vatican II's Declaration on the Relation of the Church to Non-Christian Religions (*Nostra Aetate*) states otherwise. It expressly notes that Jews and Christians share a rich spiritual patrimony, that the beginnings of Christian faith are already found among the patriarchs, Moses, and the prophets, and that the church continues to draw sustenance from these roots. Perhaps Paul captures best the sense of the document when he writes: "as regards election they [the Jews] are beloved, for the sake of their ancestors; for the gifts and the calling of God are irrevocable" (Rom 11:28-29).

Saturday: Luke 6:1-5   In this passage that Luke borrows largely from Mark, the issue revolves around the observance of the Sabbath. Although this observance stems from God's will in Genesis 2:3, nonetheless, it must cede to other considerations, in this case human hunger. Jesus defends the disciples' plucking the ears of grain and rubbing them in their hands by citing the action of David in 1 Samuel 21:7. Since the priest in the sanctuary made an exception for David and his men to eat the bread of offering, then the Sabbath observance also permits exceptions. Jesus' statement that he is lord of the Sabbath not only defends the disciples' action but also implies that he is greater than David.

Reflection. This passage adds to Luke's growing discussion of the question: who is Jesus? In healing the demoniac in 4:36, Jesus emerges as one with power and authority. In curing the paralytic in 5:24, he appears as one who can forgive sins. In this passage he is viewed as one greater than David in that he is lord of the Sabbath. Believers must marvel at Luke's ability to draw out certain features of his main character. The least common denominator in all of these scenes is that Jesus reaches out to help and, in this case, to defend others. The thrust of all these activities is the fulfillment of his inaugural address in the Nazareth synagogue, namely, that the Spirit of the Lord empowers him to touch the lives of the most frail and fragile. While believers are all too aware of the human quest for power to dominate others, they must take to heart Jesus' interpretation of power, namely, the promotion of the common good through service. Power, authority, and interpretation of law have as their goal the defense and protection of the most vulnerable.

The Twenty-third Week of the Year

Monday: Luke 6:6-11 In this passage Luke narrates another Sabbath controversy, in this case the cure of a man with a withered right hand. Luke depicts Jesus as very much in control of the situation as he knows the very thoughts of his opponents. Having ordered the handicapped man to come and stand, Jesus poses the question about whether it is lawful on the Sabbath to do good or to do harm, to save life or destroy it. Glancing at his opponents, Jesus commands the man to stretch out his hand. Once he does so, his hand is restored. Jesus' question underlines the freedom that his disciples will inherit when they face similar situations of doing good or saving life. The question also catches the spirit of Jesus' ministry, namely, his anointing by the Spirit to assist the poor, the captives, the blind, and the oppressed (4:18). The scene closes on a rather ominous note, however, as Jesus' opponents become infuriated and discuss plans about handling the "Jesus situation."

Reflection. Luke describes Jesus as a person with a specific game plan that he methodically executes. Luke has formulated that plan in Jesus' inaugural sermon in the Nazareth synagogue (4:16-30) in which the Spirit-driven prophet speaks about reaching out to the marginalized. Today's passage provides but one more example of the execution of that plan. It easily appeals to modern disciples and their program for the marginalized in their lives. The passage suggests that their assistance to the down-and-out and their aid to the disheartened and discouraged are not merely random acts of pity. Rather, they represent the concerted and methodical efforts of believers to carry out their baptismal commitments. In alleviating the neglected and rejected, they breathe the Spirit that was manifest in the Nazareth synagogue. They too have plans and programs to transform the world by doing good, not harm, by saving life, not destroying it.

Tuesday: Luke 6:12-19

Tuesday: Luke 6:12-19　This passage consists of two elements: (1) the choice of the Twelve (vv. 12-16) and (2) the crowds following Jesus (vv. 17-19). In the first part Jesus creates a small group of special disciples, namely, the Twelve. Luke demonstrates the significance and seriousness of this selection by having Jesus spend the night in prayer. Jesus calls the Twelve "Apostles," indicating that they are to function as his emissaries and witnesses. The number twelve also plays a significant role in that it recalls the twelve tribes of Jacob/Israel and thus the beginning of a new Israel. While Luke thus supplies the foundation of a new Israel, he cannot overlook the reality of the cross as he closes the list with the mention of Judas the betrayer.

In the second part Jesus descends to a plain or level place where a great crowd of disciples and others from all Judea, Jerusalem, and the pagan cities of Tyre and Sidon comes to listen to him and be healed. The emphasis on listening prepares for the forthcoming sermon in verses 20-49. Luke also notes that all in the crowd are anxious to touch Jesus since power emanates from his very person.

Reflection. One of the great emphases in Luke-Acts is the role of prayer, particularly the role prayer plays in the ministry of Jesus. In this passage, for example, Jesus passes the night in prayer on the mountain before selecting the Twelve. All believers must consider prayer an indispensable element in their lives and ministries. Prayer implies that disciples must withdraw from the clamor and din of daily events to commune with their God. In turn, such withdrawal allows believers to reassess their priorities and evaluate them in the light of God's will. Prayer creates an atmosphere of focus on God and union with him, not focus on self with its egocentric demands. Prayer makes believers all too aware of their human weakness and frailty and their need for divine guidance and energy. Given this overarching role of prayer, it is hardly surprising that Luke begins his gospel with the prayer of devout Jews in the temple (1:10) and ends it with the prayer of the disciples in exactly the same place after Jesus' ascension (24:53).

Wednesday: Luke 6:20-26   Having set the stage in verses 17-19, Luke now has Jesus deliver his Sermon on the Plain (6:20-49) that is comparable to Matthew's Sermon on the Mount (5:1–7:29). In the first three beatitudes (vv. 20-21) Luke has Jesus reflect the joy of the early ministry of Jesus. By announcing the enviable lot of the poor, the hungry, and the sorrowing, Jesus proclaims that the messianic kingdom has arrived in his very person. The lot of these people is enviable because Jesus claims for himself the Davidic prerogative of providing for them. On the other hand, the fourth beatitude (vv. 22-23) reflects the hostility of Jesus' enemies toward the end of his ministry. Thus the lot of those followers who share the prophetic fate of Jesus is now declared enviable.

Luke himself is probably the author of the four woes (vv. 24-26). (Note the abrupt change between verse 26 and verse 27.) They reveal the situation in Luke's community that was composed in large measure of the poor. These woes change the meaning of the beatitudes. The lot of the poor, the hungry, and the sorrowing is enviable because they do not exist for the present world and their condition will be reversed in the afterlife. At the same time, the woes are a strong appeal to the wealthy and powerful to meet the needs of the poor and the weak.

Reflection. Believers observe that not a few of the beautiful people are too often the stars from the entertainment world, but unfortunately such people frequently pursue only their own interests. Believers also experience the reality that the beautiful people are often the powerful and the wealthy, but often such people address only their own personal needs. Against this state of affairs stands the Christian tradition that those who make others blessed are really the beautiful people. In today's passage Luke speaks to this theme by the addition of his four woes. They are nothing less than a call to human involvement. They are the invitation to the wealthy, the sated, and the joyous to reverse the condition of the poor, the hungry, and the sorrowing. Luke's community stands in need of those who will proclaim others blessed by rendering them service. For Luke, these are the truly beautiful people.

Thursday: Luke 6:27-38   In this section of the Sermon on the Plain Luke offers three sets of ideal norms. In the first set (vv. 27-31) Luke mentions love of enemies, nonretaliation, and generosity without recompense. In verse 31 he provides the motivation: "Do to others . . ." In the second set (vv. 32-36) Luke lists loving, doing good, and lending. In verses 35-36 he supplies the motivation, namely, love of enemies and imitation of the compassionate Father. Such imitation functions as a transition to the next topic, namely, the issue of judging that also demands the application of God's mercy.

In the third set (vv. 37-38) Luke has not judging/not condemning, forgiving, and giving/good measure. In verse 38b Luke offers the motivation: "the measure with which you measure will in return be measured out to you." Judging has to do with finding fault or criticizing other followers, not a judicial process. In turn, mercy in judging should lead to mercy in giving. Forgiveness of other disciples will also lead to God's forgiveness. The full or good measure captures the disciple's way of acting, implying a merciful measure in judging, forgiving, and giving. Such generosity will result in a superabundant harvest of divine rewards.

Luke presents these norms as the basic Christian attitudes. They are Christian wisdom, i.e., they are the attitudes expressive of those who are called blessed. As Christian wisdom, they also look to concrete applications.

Reflection. Believers may feel that they have a genuine Christian mindset but their actions may suggest a policy of "You scratch my back and I'll scratch yours." They may think they have a Christian theology but their actions may imply "I'll get even with you." They may be confident that they possess a Christian sense of ethics but their actions may connote "I'm number one." In this predicament Luke's Sermon on the Plain provides a set of norms that gives evidence of Christian wisdom. In effect, Luke is asking the question: who is the person who is truly blessed and, therefore, truly wise? Luke answers that question by citing Christian values. He insists on loving one's enemies, turning the other cheek, and giving one's shirt as well. He advocates giving without a view to receiving and lending without anticipating compensation. He requires compassion and forgiveness. In Luke, Christian wisdom means Christian values.

Friday: Luke 6:39-42   In verse 39 Luke introduces the parabolic saying about the blind leading the blind. Here Jesus warns against becoming self-righteous, i.e., attempting to be better than others while ignoring one's obvious weaknesses. Applying this to the disciples (v. 40), Jesus remarks that the real student is to be concerned about professionalism. He or she should absorb Jesus' teaching and transmit it accurately. These two verses prepare for verses 41-42. The proverbial saying about the speck and the log is a colorful way of saying that moral improvement begins at home. Only after one's own house is in order, should one venture forth to correct others. Correction of others implies previous self-correction. The opposite is hypocrisy.

Reflection. Jesus' parabolic saying about the speck and the log is as timely today as it was in Jesus' time. Believers are not exempt from this innate temptation to reprove others before taking stock of their own failings. Disciples can also create a false image of their own moral superiority that leads them to correct the apparent moral inferiority of others. This passage powerfully challenges disciples to make an inventory of their own faults and failings before presuming to correct those of others. Once they have done so, only then will they see clearly enough to remove the speck from their neighbor's eye (v. 42).

Saturday: Luke 6:43-49   In this passage Luke has two components: (1) a tree and its fruit (vv. 43-45) and (2) the two foundations (vv. 46-49). In the first part Jesus asserts that results tell everything. Thus there is a correspondence between a person's character and actions. For a good person whose will ("heart") is bent on concern for God and fellow humans, goodness will result. On the other hand, from an evil person whose will ("heart") is bent upon the pursuit of self, only evil will result. The will ("heart") is ultimately the determining factor.

In the second part Luke concludes the Sermon on the Plain with the parable of the two foundations. It is not sufficient merely to listen to Jesus' words. Disciples must also act upon them. Such disciples are comparable to a builder who laid a solid rock foundation for his house. When the flood came and the river struck the house, it survived because of its solid foundation. On the other hand, disciples who listen but do not act upon Jesus' words are like a builder who constructed his house without a foundation. When the flood came and the raging river pounded the house, it collapsed for want of a foundation.

Reflection. Believers are gratified to be called Christians but living up to the name is something else. Believers may find it pleasant to be known as regular churchgoers but living out the Sunday liturgy in daily life is another matter. In such a scenario Luke offers a parable on living out the norms of the Sermon on the Plain in daily life. It is a question of producing. Like the good tree, disciples are required to produce good fruit. After all, Christians are to be known not simply by their name but also by their yield. One has a right to expect charity rather than pursuit of self, blessing rather than cursing, encouragement rather than lack of concern. For Luke, productivity is the name of the game.

The Twenty-fourth Week of the Year

Monday: Luke 7:1-10   Luke uses this story to illustrate the faith response expressed at the close of the Sermon on the Plain. He also employs the account to elaborate continuity between Israel and the Gentiles. Whereas Matthew 8:5 has the centurion directly petitioning Jesus, Luke uses Jewish elders who then mention the centurion's kindnesses to Israel.

In the telling of the story, Luke emphasizes two points: (1) the cure of the servant without personal contact and (2) the recognition of the power of Jesus' word. In sending a second delegation, the centurion stresses his unworthiness. Although Jesus does not hesitate to enter a pagan's house, the centurion is nonetheless aware of the Jewish sensitivities involved. Against the background of Roman military discipline, the centurion acknowledges the authority of Jesus' word. To give a command is to see it executed. At this point Jesus must take note of the centurion's faith that outstrips the faith Jesus has experienced among his own people. The statement of the cure (v. 10) attests to the power of Jesus' word.

Reflection. Believers gladly recite the Creed but may not always recite it with others in mind. They may willingly attend liturgy but may not always attend it with others in mind. In this scenario their faith appears more as a private possession than a contagious experience for others. Today's passage works in the opposite direction. Here Luke illustrates Jesus' mission to the Gentiles by healing the centurion's servant. The first delegation, the Jewish elders, argues that the centurion merits the healing of his servant because, though a Gentile, he has done favors for the Jewish people. The second delegation, friends of the Roman officer, argues from the analogy of military procedure, specifically the role of authority. Hence the centurion implicitly acknowledges that Jesus has power over the forces of death. The response of Jesus to the centurion's faith by word and deed demonstrates that faith must have repercussions for others, in this case the people of Israel. To have faith means to share faith.

Tuesday: Luke 7:11-17   In this passage Luke shows that God has visited his people through the ministry of Jesus, particularly to the disenfranchised. Since the dead man is the widow's only son, her existence is most precarious since she has no breadwinner. In this account Jesus' compassion moves him to restore the widow's son to life. It is significant that his concern is directed to the mother, not the son. Realizing the plight of a sonless widow in that society, Jesus also restores life to this desperate widow. Luke also notes the reaction of the crowd. They break out in praise of God because a great prophet has risen among them and God has looked with favor on his people.

Reflection. Believers see the world's rejects and unwittingly may perhaps assume the absence of God. They see the destitute and the underprivileged and may somehow infer the absence of God. They hear of famines in the Third and Fourth Worlds and in some way may reason to the absence of God. Against such an emphasis on the absence of God, today's passage strikes a positive note by stressing the role of compassion. In this account Jesus finds himself in the presence of death and, since a young man is involved, in the apparent absence of God. To complicate matters, the young man is the only son of a widow. Consequently her life will be extremely precarious without a breadwinner. Jesus' reaction is to be moved to pity. By restoring the young man to his mother, Jesus restores belief in the presence of God. Here Jesus teaches that compassionate believers communicate the presence of God.

Wednesday: Luke 7:31-35   Here Luke presents both John the Baptist and Jesus as God's messengers. Their audiences, however, are like children who insist on having things their own way. While the Baptist is an ascetic and, therefore, possessed, Jesus is not an ascetic and, therefore, charged with gluttony, drunkenness, and association with tax collectors and sinners. Luke points out, however, that those who make these allegations against the Baptist and Jesus are really foolish and not as shrewd as they would like to think. They choose to close their minds and hearts and, in so doing, reject wisdom.

Reflection. The insistence on the role of wisdom in this passage offers food for thought for believers. Wisdom emphatically teaches that there is a variety of approaches to God and hence a variety of lifestyles. The Baptist's ascetic lifestyle need not clash with Jesus' less than ascetic approach. It is a question of both/and, not either/or. The ultimate test of wisdom is openness to God's will. It is not a matter, for example, of celibacy being better than marriage. Rather, it all comes down to God's individual call and one's response to that call. Paul expresses this approach when he writes: "let each of you lead the life that the Lord has assigned, to which God called you" (1 Cor 7:17).

Thursday: Luke 7:36-50   In this scene Luke provides a stark contrast between Jesus and Simon. Simon recognizes Jesus as a rabbi, perhaps as a prophet. He neglects the outward signs of a warm Near Eastern welcome and proceeds to sit in judgment on both Jesus and the woman.

For him, the woman is obviously a sinner and, therefore, to be avoided. Jesus, however, welcomes the demonstrations of affection and, therefore, cannot be a prophet. Simon has set limitations on the forgiveness of sins. On the other hand, Jesus recognizes that, though the woman's reputation remains, her life has entirely changed. He consequently welcomes the affection lavished by the woman since her faith has prompted her sorrow.

To make the point clear, Jesus tells the parable wherein gratitude to the forgiver is in proportion to the sins forgiven. The woman is forgiven much, as is obvious from the fact that she has loved much. For Jesus, the kingdom means to set no limits on God's ability and willingness to forgive. Jesus and Simon differ because their understandings of the kingdom differ.

Reflection. Even believers sometimes feel they are obliged to set limits on God's forgiveness. They seem on such occasions to foster the need for elitism. They unconsciously perhaps conclude that they must change the church into the community of the perfect. They are more in the camp of Simon than in the camp of Jesus. In this scene Simon has calculated the kingdom's size and determined the entrance requirements with computer accuracy. He views God as the celestial, impersonal dispenser of justice who has to draw the line and suffocate the human yearning for forgiveness. Simon's kingdom is a kingdom of custom-made and impeccably packaged requirements. Simon and some modern believers have yet to learn that the church is the refuge of sinners.

Friday: Luke 8:1-3   In this passage Luke presents Jesus as one who continues to break down barriers associated with a false understanding of the kingdom. In the previous episode the barrier was the woman's sinfulness. Here the barrier is women in general. Rejecting the usual rabbinical practice of not having women pupils (see 10:38-42), Jesus associates these women with the Twelve. At the same time, Luke is also preparing for the women's role of witness in the passion and resurrection account (see 23:49, 55; 24:10, 22-23). It is worth noting that some of the women, e.g., Joanna, are women of means. It is hardly by accident, therefore, that Luke later speaks of the role played by prominent women in the early church (see Acts 18:1-4, 26-28).

Reflection. This passage must impress upon believers Jesus' attitude toward the kingdom. His view of that kingdom does not exclude women from participating, although in Jesus' time women traveling companions would certainly be viewed as scandalous. This scene challenges believers to accept Jesus' perspective that all are involved in the proclamation of the Good News: women and men, married and celibate, healthy and sick. People's gifts and talents are not purely personal attainments. Rather, they are the patrimony of the community. No matter the gender, economic status, or marital status of such people, their gifts and talents are intended to enrich Jesus' entire extended family.

Saturday: Luke 8:4-15   In this passage Luke introduces three components: (1) the parable of the seed (vv. 5-8), (2) the purpose of parables (vv. 9-10), and (3) the allegorical interpretation of the parable (vv. 11-15). In the parable itself, Jesus notes three cases of failure (the path, rock, and thorns) and one case of success (the good soil). While the three cases of failure are carefully spelled out, the one case of success, though strikingly bountiful, merits no special analysis. In discussing the purpose of the parables, Jesus distinguishes between the disciples and "others." Only the disciples are privy to the more profound and hidden aspects of the kingdom. In the allegorical interpretation of the parable, Jesus interprets the seed as the Word of God and elaborates on the different reactions to its challenge. On the one hand, there are disbelief, apostasy, and the unbridled pursuit of riches and pleasure. On the other hand, there is the total embrace of the Word leading to fruition through generosity and perseverance.

Reflection. This passage must naturally lead believers to inquire to what extent and in what manner they respond to the Word of God. Luke does not provide a checklist to help believers assess their response. Nonetheless, key words in the passage offer some help in this endeavor. These key words include: (1) faith (vv. 12, 13), (2) testing (v.13), (3) constancy (v. 15: "embrace it"), and (4) endurance (v. 15). Believers must examine their faith, i.e., whether they truly accept the person of the revealing God. They must also consider their record during times of testing or temptation. They must also look into their ability to be steadfast and persevering. In the end, the examination may yield more questions than answers. But even this result is a good start for engaging the question of response to the Word of God.

The Twenty-fifth Week of the Year

Monday: Luke 8:16-18 This passage consists of three separate sayings that continue Jesus' proclamation of the Word: (1) not hiding a lighted lamp (v. 16), (2) secrets becoming public (v. 17), and (3) more being given to one who already has (v. 18). In the first saying, just as a lighted lamp does not belong in a jar or under a bed but on a lamp stand to provide light, so too disciples must make the Word of God available to others. In the second saying, what is secret will become public. Hence disciples who know the secrets or mysteries of God's kingdom must not hoard that knowledge but share it with others. In the third saying, disciples cannot be satisfied with merely hearing the Word—they must also understand it. To the maturity of understanding that disciples already have more will be given.

Reflection. This passage underlines the awesome responsibility of disciples with regard to the Word of God. Rather than a purely private gift, their penetration of that Word must become public. Modern believers must function as a lamp to their world. In other words, their hearing and understanding must affect the lives of others. Similarly their personal knowledge of the mysteries of the kingdom must seek a wider audience. Disciples dare not exist in splendid isolation. The whole world must become the beneficiaries of their grasp of the Word of God. The relationship of individual disciples to the larger community cannot be stated more forcefully.

Tuesday: Luke 8:19-21 Luke has completely rewritten this account of the true family of Jesus that he finds in his source, namely, Mark 3:31-35. Earlier the mother and brothers of Jesus (Mark 3:21) thought that Jesus had gone crazy—a remark that Luke drops. Whereas Mark heightens the physical family's exclusion by having them stand outside, Luke remarks that their distance from Jesus is due to the crowd. Whereas Mark has Jesus question their membership in his true family of disciples and gesture to the disciples standing around him, Luke omits both. In Luke, Jesus receives word of his physical family's presence and goes on to observe that his (true) mother and brothers are those who hear the Word of God and do it. Luke thereby includes Mary and his brothers among his disciples. The criterion for discipleship is twofold: (1) hearing the Word of God and (2) putting it into practice.

Reflection. Believers would do well to ponder the role of the Lukan Mary. One can rather easily make the case that she is, for Luke, the model disciple. At the annunciation she is, unlike Zechariah (see 1:20), totally open to God's Word: "Here am I, the servant of the Lord; let it be with me according to your word" (1:38). At the visitation Elizabeth extols not only her status as the mother of her Lord (1:43) but also her vibrant faith (1:45). When the woman in the crowd remarks how blessed is his mother (11:27), Jesus, without denying that declaration, adds something else apropos of Mary, namely, hearing the Word of God and obeying it (11:28). Finally after Jesus' ascension from Mount Olivet, Mary devotes herself to prayer along with Jesus' brothers to await the coming of the Spirit at Pentecost (Acts 1:14). For Luke, Mary has become the embodiment of genuine discipleship.

Wednesday: Luke 9:1-6   In this scene Jesus, having trained the Twelve for some time, has reached a point where they will now share in his own mission. They will now experience the reality of Jesus' proclamation and healing. The meagerness of their provisions stresses their total dependence on God's Providence. (Luke goes so far as to forbid even the carrying of a staff.) Jesus invests the Twelve with power and authority but does not limit it to proclamation—healing the physical and mental ills of the people is also included. In their mission they are to accept the hospitality of those who receive them and be satisfied with it. Like Jesus himself, the Twelve will also experience rejection. In the aftermath of such rejection, they are to shake the dust from their feet, symbolizing the end of all contact with that unwelcoming town.

Reflection. Believers may be easily tempted to think that the missionary efforts in today's passage apply only to the Twelve and other specially chosen people. Hence they are exempt from all such ventures. While certain features, e.g., the meagerness of provisions, may envision a limited group, the missionary vocation as such impacts all the baptized. The mode of proclamation and the manner of healing may admittedly differ but the radical nature of this charge still remains. Disciples fulfill this missionary calling in their families, at the office, in their social life—in brief, in all those situations where proclamation and healing are needed. To provide some time and attention to those wavering in their faith, to offer encouragement to the brokenhearted, to aid the financially strapped, etc., are many different facets of the disciples' missionary vocation. While the church always needs foreign missionaries, it also requires the daily involvement of all home missionaries.

Thursday: Luke 9:7-9   This passage focuses on at least three issues: (1) the question about Jesus' identity by an authority figure, namely, Herod Antipas; (2) Jesus' prophetic stature; and (3) the centrality of the cross. In posing the question about Jesus' identity, Herod Antipas serves as Luke's vehicle for directing attention to the various answers that will soon follow. In rehearsing the possible clues to Jesus' identity, Luke underlines Jesus' prophetic significance. He finds himself in the company of John the Baptist, Elijah, and one of the ancient prophets. In linking John the Baptist with Jesus, Luke anticipates the fate of Jesus. Just as the Baptist experienced hostility from Herod Antipas, Jesus will also suffer opposition (see Luke 23:6-12). Herod Antipas will want to see Jesus perform a sign at the time of the passion. Disciples realize, however, that they can only appreciate Jesus in the setting of Calvary.

Reflection. The question of identity and legacy is always an intriguing one. Like other human beings, believers wonder at times how people will identify them and, in light of that identity, what kind of legacy they will leave. Some may wish to be known as great humanitarians or philanthropists. Others may opt to be remembered as outstanding community leaders or politicians. In this episode, however, Luke finds the only satisfying identity in terms of the cross as the symbol of serving others. By sharing the prophetic company in this passage, Jesus will endure the typical prophetic fate, namely, ridicule and rejection. Luke challenges his own community and today's believers to withdraw to Calvary and discover there the formula for identity and legacy.

Friday: Luke 9:18-22   Peter's confession is one of the key events in the gospel tradition. Luke's mention of prayer enhances its significance. The event presupposes that Jesus has been pondering his own identity and that he has come to realize that only his death will finally usher in the kingdom. The reply of the disciples suggests that he has not discussed his messiahship publicly and, therefore, the general public has not picked up any clues as to his real messianic identity.

Jesus acknowledges Peter's perception but goes beyond it. According to the final form of the gospel tradition, Jesus is here pictured as resolving the question of his identity by using three titles. One interpretation of Messiah was the anointed Davidic king pledged to provide especially for the poor and disenfranchised. The title also took on connotations of power unacceptable to Jesus. Jesus, therefore, combines Messiah with Son of Man and Suffering Servant. In Daniel 7 and the pre-Christian Book of Enoch, the Son of Man is a divine being hidden in God's presence who will be revealed in the end to preside in glory over God's kingdom. According to Isaiah 52:13–53:12, the Suffering Servant represents the best in Israel—he degrades himself as a guilt offering, but is finally exonerated for effecting the survival of the nation. Jesus, therefore, will be Messiah but only as the Suffering Son of Man.

Reflection. Believers are often chosen to bear a title but may not be anxious to fulfill its implications. They may be elected to carry a name but may be somewhat reluctant to uncover its extension. They may be named to discharge a certain office but may be uneasy about searching out its meaning for others. Believers may thus hesitate to interpret their titles, not because of the honors attached but because of the obligations involved. In this quandary Luke provides help as he endeavors to get his community to follow Jesus' manner of interpretation. Jesus will accept the title of Messiah only if it includes the connotations of Suffering Son of Man. In verses 23-24 Luke goes on to apply this interpretive process to all followers. To be chosen to be a Christian follower means to interpret that title in terms of daily shouldering of the cross. For Jesus, in Luke, nomination means interpretation.

Saturday: Luke 9:43b-45   Following the cure of the epileptic boy in 9:37-43a, Luke observes the crowd's amazement at everything Jesus is doing. He then introduces the second passion prediction, limiting it to Jesus' betrayal into human hands. Here Luke chooses to underline the disciples' lack of understanding. The message of Jesus simply eludes them so that they are unable to grasp it. Only Jesus' resurrection will bring the clarity that they obviously lack in this scene.

Reflection. It is a question of the right emphasis. Like everyone else, believers have certain priorities that implicitly, at least, receive their greatest emphasis. Such priorities may include making more money, moving up the corporate ladder, receiving greater adulation from others, and the like. While these priorities have some merit, they may receive undue emphasis. In today's passage Jesus provides a vivid example of the wrong emphasis as everyone is utterly amazed at everything Jesus is doing. The right emphasis would be to marvel at Jesus' forthcoming destiny, namely, his suffering and death. Against this background believers must emphasize those areas in their lives where people need them the most and where they can render the greatest service. It is all about the right emphasis.

The Twenty-sixth Week of the Year

Monday: Luke 9:46-50   This passage consists of two episodes: (1) rivalry among the disciples (vv. 46-48) and (2) the unaligned exorcist (vv. 49-50). In the first episode, Jesus places great emphasis on the role of humility among his disciples. To illustrate this virtue, Jesus places a little child by his side, the ultimate symbol of powerlessness in his society. Identifying himself with the little child because of his mission from the Father, Jesus teaches that, in order to accept him as well as his Father, disciples must be willing to accept and value the weakest member of society. In the second episode, the disciples admit their failure in trying to stop an unaligned exorcist who was casting out demons in Jesus' name. In response, Jesus advocates a twofold attitude, namely, tolerance and respect for persons. Disciples must not only avoid rivalry; they must also cultivate an openness toward others who do not belong to their specific group.

Reflection. A certain elitism can plague believers. By directing all their attention to those "inside" their group, they may disparage those who are "outside" their group. In the second episode, Jesus calls for an attitude of openness, tolerance, and respect for all those "outsiders." Actually the term "outsiders" is not really apropos since such people, like the exorcist, are actually promoting the goals of the kingdom as well. Wherever goodness of whatever category is found, there Jesus is present. Perhaps Jesus expresses it best of all when he says: "whoever is not against you is for you" (v. 50).

Tuesday: Luke 9:51-56   This passage is the beginning of Luke's so-called Travel Document (9:51–19:27). The "taken up" (v. 51) refers to the entire complex of passion, death, resurrection, and ascension. Here Jesus initiates this complex by heading for Jerusalem. In setting his face like flint, Jesus indicates his prophetic determination to attain his objective (see Isa 50:7; Ezek 6:2).

The Samaritan episode is significant for Luke's Gentile mission. Luke implies that this mission already begins during Jesus' lifetime. At this point, however, the Samaritans cannot accept Jesus. This nonacceptance stems from Jesus' Jewish ancestry and perhaps also a reluctance to accept the prophetic fate associated with Jerusalem, namely, his death. In turn, the nonacceptance gives way to misunderstandings on the part of James and John. Their desire to destroy the Samaritans indicates that they have not yet accepted a suffering Messiah.

Reflection. Like Jesus in this passage, believers also experience key moments in their lives, moments when they make irrevocable decisions. For many believers, the wedding day constitutes such a moment. It may also include abandoning one's career to care for an ailing parent, ending an intimate relationship, leaving home to pursue a career, etc. In today's passage, Luke lists some of the characteristics of such moments. One is that the decision marks the beginning of a series of events. Thus Jesus' determination to go to Jerusalem is the beginning of a chain of events that will culminate in his passion, death, resurrection, and ascension. Believers also realize that their decisions will also entail other components. Another characteristic is Jesus' resoluteness—"he resolutely determined to journey to Jerusalem" (v. 51). Similarly believers must demonstrate perseverance in pursuing their own calling. In the final analysis, the metaphor of a journey impacts everyone, both believers and nonbelievers. Believers, however, can draw strength and hope from their guide Jesus.

Wednesday: Luke 9:57-62   As Jesus begins his trek to Jerusalem, Luke brings together three sayings that capture the rigor of discipleship for those who are "proceeding on their journey" (v. 57). In other words, disciples must accept a demanding invitation as they join Jesus on the journey. In the first saying (v. 58), Jesus announces that discipleship is no easy matter—unlike the foxes and birds, Jesus and his disciples experience absolute homelessness. In the second saying (v. 60), Jesus emphasizes wholehearted and prompt commitment by speaking of the dead burying their own dead. In the third saying (v. 62), Jesus insists on immediate and absolute dedication by excluding anyone putting his hand to the plough and looking back. This final saying recalls Elisha's call by Elijah in 1 Kings 19:20. Unlike Elijah, Jesus permits no turning back.

Reflection. Believers may prefer at times to qualify and limit their commitment. For example, they vow loyalty in marriage but are tempted to make it less than total. They promise unswerving devotion to their family and friends but are later prone to deviate. They profess complete fidelity to Christian principles of justice but are soon exposed to compromise. In such wavering circumstances, today's passage is right on target. As Jesus makes his way to Jerusalem to consummate his prophetic mission, he invites others to join him as disciples. But to follow him is no popularity contest. It means to have nowhere to lay one's head. It means to allow no delays but to follow spontaneously. It means to refuse turning back and thus to accept the course ahead. It means to accept the person of Jesus and thus to set one's face like flint toward Jerusalem. For the Lukan Jesus, the disciple's way is only one-way.

Thursday: Luke 10:1-12   Toward the end of the first Christian century, Luke's community has become largely Gentile. In this gospel scene he anticipates the thrust of Acts: the proclamation of the Word to the Gentiles. Unlike Mark and Matthew, Luke also has the mission of the Seventy(-two). The reading can be either "seventy" or "seventy-two." It is likely that the number symbolizes the seventy nations in Genesis 10 (or seventy-two according to the Greek Bible). Luke thereby establishes continuity for the missionaries of his own time. They too have a mandate from Jesus and so participate in his mission.

There is a great sense of urgency in this charge. The harvest does not last long. The missionaries must forgo the barest necessities, even omitting the common courtesies of Near Eastern wayside conduct. The opposition (the wolves) will attempt to minimize their efforts. Yet God will provide for them in their crises. Moreover, in keeping with the Gentile community, the missionaries need not fret over nonkosher foods. In Jesus and his missionaries God is present to the people and their needs. Indeed Luke proposes different forms of that presence: word of mouth communication of the Good News, healing of the sick, and bestowal of peace. With regard to the rejection of their message, the missionaries are not to act like James and John in Samaria (see Luke 9:54). They are to use the prophetic symbol of repudiation. Hence by shaking the dust from their feet, they declare themselves free of the fate that follows upon rejection of the Word. Sodom—a biblical synonym for depravity—will have it easier on the day of judgment.

Reflection. Believers sometimes falsely think that only priests, brothers, and sisters receive the missionary vocation. They may be duped into thinking that the Word about the kingdom is the exclusive domain of the clerical and religious institutions. They may accept the stifling report that they less-than-clergy-and-religious, and hence ordinary, folk cannot really make a difference. Against this way of thinking today's passage presents another scenario. In the absence of Jesus and the death of the Twelve, the Lukan community asks how God will meet their needs. Luke replies to this nagging question by showing Jesus charging missionaries of his own community other than the Twelve without specifying particular credentials. Significantly these missionaries not only proclaim the Word about the kingdom; they also heal the sick and bring peace to households. The missionary endeavor embraces all those capable of representing Jesus.

Friday: Luke 10:13-16   In this scene of woes directed against Chorazin, Bethsaida, and (implicitly) Capernaum, Luke has added to the mission charge in 10:12 where Jesus states: "it will be more tolerable for Sodom than for that town." Luke reminds his readers in these accusations against towns that Jesus himself evangelized of their grave responsibility. The message of the missionaries now confronts them with its challenge to accept or reject their message. To accept their message is to accept Jesus himself. To reject it is to reject Jesus and his Father. In the latter case Tyre and Sidon (pagan cities) will have an easier time at the judgment than they.

Reflection. In this passage the chain of command plays a central role, namely, the Father, Jesus, and the missionary. Believers would naturally find it easier to accept Jesus and his Father rather than the missionary. The missionary, however, ultimately represents Jesus and his Father and, therefore, speaks with authority. Such a missionary confronts believers in a variety of situations outside the official place of worship. At work, at play, at home, etc., this missionary is the so-called ordinary person who has so absorbed Jesus' message that she or he, most likely without realizing it, challenges other believers through example to practice justice, to support the value of human life, to reach out to the hurting, and the like. To heed the message of such an unpretentious and un-assuming missionary is to accept the message of Jesus and his Father.

Saturday: Luke 10:17-24   This passage consists of two components: (1) the return of the Seventy(-two) (vv. 17-20) and (2) Jesus' praise of the Father and the special status of the disciples (vv. 21-24). In the first part, the disciples upon their return reveal their great delight. To their remarks about the demons, Jesus replies that they did indeed counteract Satan's influence. In verse 19 Jesus adds that he has put his own power into their hands. The basis of this jubilation, however, should not be the ability to contain the demons but to retain their proper relationship with God (see Rev 20:12).

In the second part, Jesus expresses delight in his relationship to the Spirit of God and to God himself (the Father). He praises his Father for revealing his mysteries, not to the intellectuals but to the little children, namely, his disciples. The special knowledge gained by the disciples is Jesus' relationship to the Father and their relationship to him. In comparison to their contemporaries, namely, the intellectuals, the disciples enjoy a unique status because they have been privileged to share the Son's special revelation. Owing to this experience, they clearly outstrip many prophets and kings of old.

Reflection. This passage highlights the unique status of the disciples because of their special insights. In addition, it challenges modern believers. This special knowledge shared with believers is not intended to be a purely personal gift reserved only for the recipient. Rather, this knowledge must become so contagious for believers that they feel compelled to share it with others. In turn, such sharing need not take the form of a solemn proclamation from a bully pulpit. Instead, this sharing takes place in the seemingly insignificant scenes of daily life. Whenever believers reach out to the marginalized, provide for the indigent, encourage the disconsolate, etc., they share their special relationship with

Jesus. One must also include the nonbelievers who perform these same ministries but without realizing explicitly their link to the revealing Jesus. The Good News knows no boundaries.

The Twenty-seventh Week of the Year

Monday: Luke 10:25-37   In this passage Luke has taken the question of the Great Commandment from Mark 12:28-31 (along with a sayings source) and added to them the parable of the Good Samaritan. The whole complex consists of four components: (1) the question concerning eternal life (vv. 25-28); (2) the lawyer's question about the meaning of "neighbor" (v. 29); (3) the parable itself (vv. 30-35); and (4) question (v. 36), answer (v. 37a), and admonition (v. 37b).

In the question about eternal life Luke has the lawyer cite two Old Testament texts (Deut 6:5 [love of God] and Lev 19:18 [love of neighbor]) that Jesus then approves. The lawyer's question (v. 29) picks up the key word "neighbor" from Leviticus 19:18. In both instances "neighbor" means someone who receives help from another. In the parable itself "neighbor" means someone who provides assistance for another. The detailed description of the Samaritan's involvement challenges the lawyer to combine "Samaritan" and "neighbor"—something exceedingly difficult for a Jew (see John 4:9). In effect, for the lawyer the combination is a contradiction in terms. Jesus' question in verse 36 summons the lawyer to select which of the three (priest, Levite, or Samaritan) meets the definition of "neighbor." Instead of saying "Samaritan," the lawyer replies: "The one who treated him with mercy" (v. 37a). Finally Jesus admonishes the lawyer to go and do likewise.

Reflection. Believers at times pose questions about the corporate image. They may observe the organization of their community and are perhaps led to think that this is the corporate image. They may note the judicial processes of their community and are perhaps led to infer that this is the corporate image. They may see the power possessed by certain members of their community and are perhaps led to conclude that this is the corporate image. In today's passage, however, Luke proposes that compassion is the corporate image. He rejects a narrowly defined set of norms centering on the question: who is my neighbor?

Instead, he promotes an open, unlimited lifestyle based on the question: to whom can I be a neighbor? For Luke, a Christianity that defines itself in terms of limitations refuses to define itself in terms of Jesus. For Luke, compassion is the corporate image.

Tuesday: Luke 10:38-42   In this scene Martha welcomes Jesus, the divine visitor (note the title "Lord"), as a guest. Luke's intention is not to disparage Martha and her household chores. Rather, his intention is to show that discipleship preempts all other concerns. In a world where women did not receive Torah instruction from the rabbis, Luke relates that Jesus and Mary function as teacher and disciple. Mary's posture (see Acts 22:3) and the insistence on the words of Jesus suggest religious instruction. "There is need of only one thing" (v. 42) seems to fit Luke's emphasis on priorities (see Luke 18:22). In this instance discipleship is primary, running the kitchen is secondary. Against the Jewish background of excluding women from Torah instruction, Luke finally argues that Jesus' message is for women and men alike.

Reflection. Believers sometimes worry because their calling may keep them from making it to the top. They may fret because in their vocation the gold medal is necessarily out of reach. In this quandary about priorities, today's passage provides no little insight. Martha is anxious because the kitchen seems to be the top priority. Mary listens to Jesus because discipleship preempts all other concerns. Mary has perceived a priority where Martha has not. The kitchen is not unimportant, but Jesus' message is all important. God's plan is the top priority.

Wednesday: Luke 11:1-4   In Luke's Hellenistic world all prayer is basically impersonal and prayer of petition is of doubtful value. To his predominantly Gentile Christian audience, Luke proposes Jesus as the model of prayer (see 3:21; 6:12; 9:18, 29). It is significant that Jesus himself is at prayer prior to instructing the disciples. The disciples thus experience God as Father because they share in Jesus' experience of God as Father. The disciples are thereby drawn into the family circle.

In his version of the Our Father Luke differs somewhat from Matthew's version (6:9-13). Instead of "Our Father in heaven" (Matt 6:9), Luke has simply "Father" (v. 2). Matthew adds the petition about doing God's will (6:10)—something not found in Luke. Whereas Matthew has: "Give us *this day* our daily bread" (6:11; emphasis added), Luke has: "Give us *each day* our daily bread" (v. 3; emphasis added). While Matthew speaks of the forgiveness of debts (6:12), Luke speaks about the forgiveness of sins (v. 4). Matthew concludes with the addition of deliverance from the evil one (6:13)—a petition not found in Luke.

Reflection. At times believers may experience God as a cold, impersonal power, impervious to their needs. They may regard him as the celestial administrator and themselves as so many customers with bad credit. They may find God to be aloof, tucked away from the real world of their problems. Opposed to such tendencies is Jesus, the Lukan model of prayer. At the deepest possible level, Jesus recognizes God as Father. This Father is so eminently real to Jesus that his every care becomes the care of his Father. In the temptation-ridden moments of his ministry, Jesus knows that he will have a hearing. He does not have to fake it. He shares the tragedies and disappointments of his ministry with One who can and will make a difference. This is the attitude that Luke proposes to modern disciples. To pray is to be part of the family.

Thursday: Luke 11:5-13   This passage consists of two parts: (1) the parable of the unexpected guest (vv. 5-8) and (2) the efficacy of prayer (vv. 9-13). In the first part, to exemplify the petition in the Our Father about asking for daily bread *each day*, Luke offers the parable of the unexpected guest (a parable unique to Luke). Although the relationship is that of friends, the lesson of persevering prayer is clear. The bond of friendship and the virtue of perseverance ultimately win out.

In the second part, Luke returns to the father-son relationship. If human fathers provide for their sons, with all the more reason will the Father provide for his children. Instead of giving good things (Matt 7:11), the Father here gives the Holy Spirit. Luke is probably envisioning persecuted Christians who need strength to withstand their ordeal. The caring Father appreciates the predicaments of his family.

Reflection. Believers not infrequently find it difficult to continue to pray for certain intentions because God never seems to listen. Day in and day out they bombard this God with their prayers but all they receive in return is divine silence. In such circumstances, the parable of the unexpected guest may provide some help. Like the unexpected guest, believers must persist in petitioning God—they dare not take no for an answer. Admittedly this God does not find an adequate image in the friend who eventually delivers because his wife and family will otherwise get no sleep. For Luke, however, God is more than a friend—he is a Father who realizes the needs of his family. Unrelenting prayer to him will eventually result in more than three loaves of bread.

Friday: Luke 11:15-26   Having exorcised a demon from a speech-impaired person, Jesus provokes the reaction of some people that he is in league with Beelzebul or Satan. In response to this reaction, Jesus employs two images: (1) the divided kingdom and (2) the fallen house. These images connote dissension and anarchy since Jesus' exorcism represents a frontal assault on the power of evil. Jesus then strengthens his argument by appealing to the practice of their own exorcists, i.e., they would have to be in league with Beelzebul or Satan too. Using an Old Testament figure of speech ("the finger of God"—see Exod 8:19), Jesus relates his own activity to God's former agents and announces that the kingdom of God has arrived in their midst. In verses 21-22, while Beelzebul or Satan may be viewed as "a strong man," Jesus is "one stronger than he" who has come to defeat him. In verse 23 the phrases "with/against me" and "gather/scatter" unequivocally state that one cannot remain neutral in reacting to Jesus' battle over the demonic forces.

In verses 24-26 Jesus speaks about the return of an evil spirit to a previously possessed person. In so doing, Jesus cautions his disciples—they are not to be overly confident about the final defeat of evil. It is not enough for a demon to be expelled. The orderly, swept clean house represents the person who can yet experience the return of a demon who will gather even more demons. Such a person must be constantly prepared for such a return by finding protection in God's word.

Reflection. Not infrequently believers like to sit on the fence and remain perfectly neutral. They really don't want to take sides and thus offend one or the other party. The fence thus serves as a bastion of security. In today's passage, Luke presents Jesus taking the opposite stance with regard to his exorcism and possible association with Beelzebul or Satan. His response is quite blunt: "Whoever is not with me is against me, and whoever does not gather with me scatters" (v. 23). In everyday life believers make decisions for or against Jesus. While such decisions do not focus on the origin of Jesus' exorcisms, they often touch on issues like justice, compassion, charity, and the like. Reread in such situations, this passage compels believers to get off the fence, dismiss all neutrality, and opt for Jesus' position. While the Good News is frequently consoling, it is also equally demanding.

Saturday: Luke 11:27-28   This scene is unique to Luke. A woman from the crowd announces the enviable ("blessed") state of the mother of Jesus (for breasts and womb as a circumlocution for mother, see Luke 23:29). In itself the beatitude is ambiguous since it may emphasize the son produced by such a mother. In 1:42 Luke has Elizabeth declare Mary worthy of praise on account of her son but in 1:45 Mary herself is called blessed. The woman in the crowd adopts the stance of Elizabeth in 1:42, namely, that Mary is blessed because of her son. Jesus' reaction is not to deny the woman's statement but to correct it. The basis of the beatitude should be that one has heard God's word and kept it. Thus Mary has completely engaged her person to hear the Word and carry it out. Jesus' statement here is corroborated by Acts 1:14 where Mary forms part of the prayerful Pentecost community.

Reflection. At times believers may so alienate Mary from the real world that it becomes impossible to emulate her in their lives. Today's passage does much to anchor Mary in this real world. Briefly stated, Mary is Luke's model disciple. While her physical maternity is worthy of a beatitude according to the woman in the crowd, Jesus adds a corrective. For Jesus, Mary proves herself worthy of being hailed blessed because she had heard God's Word and kept it. This simple but challenging formula of hearing and obeying becomes the standard for all believers. Hence they too can merit a beatitude by doing likewise.

The Twenty-eighth Week of the Year

Monday: Luke 11:29-32   See Wednesday of the First Week of Lent.

Tuesday: Luke 11:37-41   As Jesus continues his journey to Jerusalem, he utters sayings against the Pharisees and lawyers (scribes). Verses 37-38 introduce this whole series of sayings (11:39-54). In this first episode, Jesus has accepted a dinner invitation from a Pharisee but has failed to wash his hands before reclining at table. Aware of his host's shock, Jesus takes up the issue of the ritual cleansing of cups and dishes. For Jesus, washing the outside of such utensils is simply not enough—one must also wash their inside, i.e., the inside of human beings whence greed and wickedness proceed. Continuing his argument, Jesus refers to the role of God as the maker of both the outside and the inside of these utensils. Jesus concludes this episode by admonishing the Pharisees to dispense the contents of the cup and the dish as alms to the poor. Such almsgiving will effect genuine cleanliness in God's sight that is the original intent of this ritual washing.

Reflection. Believers can also be confused at times about externals. At worship they perform certain ritual actions. In addressing other people, they observe the formalities of etiquette. At meals they follow the conventional rubrics for eating and drinking. Today's passage, however, urges believers to look beyond the external to consider the internal. At worship do their external gestures of standing, genuflecting, etc., correspond to their awareness of God? In addressing other people, do their external formalities make them aware of the sacredness of such people? In following the rules of etiquette at table, do they realize that such external rules relate to their regard and concern for their table companions? Relating the external to the internal is always a daunting but rewarding exercise.

Wednesday: Luke 11:42-46 This passage consists of three woes addressed to the Pharisees (vv. 42-44) and one woe addressed to the lawyers (vv. 45-46). In the first woe against the Pharisees, Jesus accuses them of neglecting justice and love of God while offering tithes on small herbs (mint, rue, and the like). In his second woe against them, he scolds them for their pomposity in seeking out the places of honor in the synagogues and respectful recognition in the marketplaces. In the third woe, Jesus scorns them for their failure to realize what they really are, namely, unmarked graves containing the bones of the dead that carry the risk of contamination for the unwary. Jesus then addresses the lawyers among the Pharisees after one of them remarks that to insult the Pharisees is to insult them as well. Jesus responds with a woe that criticizes them for heaping unbearable burdens on people with their legalistic minutiae but making no effort to lighten their load.

Reflection. How easy it is for believers to be so concerned about pica-yune matters that they forget about the core values of justice and love of God. At times believers cannot see the forest for the trees. In today's first woe against the Pharisees, Jesus reminds believers about a healthy sense of balance. They must concentrate on love of God and love of neighbor and, having satisfied these obligations, only then direct their attention to matters of lesser moment. Healthy believers must acknowledge such priorities in their daily lives.

Thursday: Luke 11:47-54   This passage consists of the second (with added sayings) and third woes addressed to the lawyers (vv. 47-52) and their persistent hostility against Jesus in his discourses (vv. 53-54). In the second woe, Jesus criticizes the lawyers for constructing monumental tombs for the prophets whom their ancestors killed, thereby partici-pating in their sinful deeds. Jesus seems to be implying that they will inflict a similar fate on him, God's last and definitive prophet. God's wisdom, however, will not be compromised. Unless this generation rejects the past, they will bear responsibility for all the injustices inflicted on the prophets from the first (Abel) to the last (Zechariah) murders in their Bible. In the third woe, Jesus attacks the talented lawyers both for not entering the house of wisdom (God's will in the Torah and ongoing tradition) and for preventing others from entering as well. Given Jesus' condemnation, it is not surprising that his opponents lie in wait for him.

Reflection. Today's passage alerts believers to the need to hear the prophetic message and act on it. As God's spokespersons, modern prophets focus on the evils in society and the remedies for eradicating them and thus creating a truly human way of living. One can think of Pope John XXIII who challenged the church to throw open its windows to the surrounding culture and accept the challenge it brings. One can recall Martin Luther King Jr. and his prophetic dream of a truly human community where prejudice and injustice give way to peace and toler-ance. One can bring to mind Mother Teresa of Calcutta and her relent-less crusade to provide for the poor, the ostracized, and the dying. These are but a few of the modern prophets who by word and deed address the conscience of all people of good will. Not to heed them is to court disaster.

Friday: Luke 12:1-7 This passage is made up of Jesus' warning about the leaven of the Pharisees (v. 1) and his exhortation to fearless confession (vv. 2-7). In attacking the hypocrisy of the Pharisees, Jesus uses the metaphor of leaven that, albeit good in itself, operates through a process of corruption that eventually impacts the entire loaf of bread. For Jesus, the Pharisees do not reveal on the outside what they truly are on the inside.

In the exhortation to fearless confession, Luke has gathered together sayings of Jesus from different stages of his ministry. In verses 2-3 Jesus declares that secret words or deeds are not really hidden from God. The real core or center of a person will eventually come to light. In verses 4-5 Jesus addresses his disciples as friends, exhorting them to courageous behavior and confession during times of persecution. Disciples should not fear physical death caused by other humans. Rather, when tempted to sacrifice their values, they should fear God who has the power to cast them into hell. In verses 6-7 Jesus reminds his disciples of God's ongoing care for them. In times of persecution they should abandon all fear. If God's Providence includes provision for seemingly insignificant sparrows and an exact knowledge of the number of hairs on their head, will God do less for the disciples and friends of Jesus? Fear in the face of persecution, therefore, makes little sense.

Reflection. Most believers probably do not have to endure the threat of persecution with subsequent loss of life. Nonetheless, they are often subject to ridicule and disparagement because of the values reflected in their way of life. It is all too easy to capitulate in such circumstances. Today's passage, however, with its insistence on Jesus' friendship and the role of Providence, is indeed encouraging. As friends of Jesus, believers enjoy an intimate relationship with him and can count on his timely support. As daughters and sons of a concerned Father, believers are of inestimable value (v. 7: "worth more than many sparrows"). The love of this Father reveals itself in his knowledge of the number of hairs on their head. In life's daily trials and temptations, believers must always recall Jesus' abiding friendship and the Father's relentless concern.

Saturday: Luke 12:8-12 This passage contains: (1) sayings about allegiance and nonallegiance to Jesus (vv. 8-9) and (2) sayings about the Holy Spirit (vv. 10-12). In the first part, Jesus insists that disciples must acknowledge him before others. In turn, Jesus as the Son of Man will acknowledge them before the angels. Disciples who disown him before others will, in turn, be disowned by Jesus before the angels. In the first saying of the second part (v. 10), speaking a word against Jesus can be forgiven, but blasphemy against the Holy Spirit will not be forgiven. Speaking a word against Jesus may refer to rejection of Jesus in his earthly condition as nothing more than a mere human. The sin against the Holy Spirit, however, is far from clear. This unforgivable sin may be a deep-seated opposition to the role of the Spirit of God and thus alienation from and radical rejection of God himself. In verses 11-12, Jesus promises help for disciples when they are brought to court and made to appear before worldly authorities, whether Jewish or Gentile. In such circumstances, they need not worry about what to say since the Holy Spirit will instruct them.

Reflection. The opening saying in this passage about acknowledging Jesus before others may speak to the needs of modern disciples. For such believers, it is usually not a question of formal acknowledgement before a court of law or similar setting. Rather, it is generally a matter of daily personal conduct that reflects allegiance or nonallegiance to Jesus. Through their honesty, integrity, respect for others, etc., believers demonstrate their allegiance to Jesus. Hence their actions speak far louder than their words. More often than not, their fidelity in the small trials of daily life reveals their standard of allegiance.

The Twenty-ninth Week of the Year

Monday: Luke 12:13-21   Verses 13-15 provide the occasion for Luke's parable of the rich fool. Although recognized as an authority by the people, Jesus refuses to render a legal judgment—he is not the proper arbiter. Moreover, the question is wrong. Jesus points out to the crowd that possessions do not of themselves make for living in the kingdom.

In the parable Jesus describes a man who completely fails to read the situation and act accordingly. The words "myself" and "fool" capture the thrust of the parable. "Myself" implies the entire person—here the rich man with his personal identity. At the same time, "myself" includes an existence that transcends this life. In his pursuit of self, the rich man confuses his entire self with his body. Against the background of Old Testament wisdom literature (see Job 2:10; 30:8), the farmer has violated healthy community life. By envisioning everything solely in the context of his desires, he demonstrates the lack of wisdom needed for true human development. In the game of life, he is a failure.

Verse 21 interprets the parable. The quest of the rich man is an ego trip. It is only a matter of himself—*his* wealth and *his* lifestyle. This verse states categorically that to grow wealthy only for himself is to court death and judgment. Wealth requires concern for others.

Reflection. Believers experience a certain conflict in distinguishing between their values and the world's values. Believers accept the principle that life means celebration, not just getting by, playing it safe, and eking out a living. The world, however, informs them that prudent investments, trust funds, special policies, tax shelters, etc., will properly insure them. While these arrangements have their value, today's passage suggests otherwise. Here Luke pities the devotees of the rich man. To provide for one's future without meeting the present needs of others is futile, empty. To insure oneself for life but then only court death and judgment is the great irony. Jesus must refuse to answer the question of the younger brother because only the right questions are those that concern others. Self-giving is the only viable form of life insurance.

Tuesday: Luke 12:35-38 At this point in his journey to Jerusalem, Jesus switches his topic from concern about earthly possessions to the theme of vigilance and faithfulness. This passage reminds disciples of the constant need for readiness in view of the approaching end time. Such disciples resemble slaves who must perform all their duties properly during the absence of their master—they must be dressed for action with their lamps lit (v. 35). When the master returns from the wedding banquet and finds them alert and prepared, he will reward them by inviting them to a banquet and serving them himself. Whether he comes around midnight or just before dawn and finds them discharging their duties, such slaves will be truly blessed.

Reflection. The early church anticipated Jesus' imminent return but gradually became aware that there was no set timetable. Similarly modern disciples do not expect a sudden second coming of Jesus. Today's passage recommends, however, that they always keep Jesus' return in mind.

To achieve this, Jesus calls for vigilance and readiness. Believers are urged, therefore, to perform their duties and discharge their office by daily vigilance. They are asked to consider their responsibilities to others and carry them out on a regular basis. They truly prepare for the final coming of the kingdom by their watchfulness and readiness. Daily fidelity to their calling as believers is the best preparation for enjoying the great banquet with Jesus and his extended family.

Wednesday: Luke 12:39-48   This passage consists of the following: (1) a section dealing with a vigilant master (vv. 39-40), (2) a second section concerning the manager of an absent master (vv. 41-46), and (3) a final section focusing on an unfaithful servant's appropriate punishment (vv. 47-48). The first section is a remnant of a parable that highlights the vigilance of a house owner who takes steps to prevent a thief from breaking in.

In the second section, Luke speaks, not of a slave or servant, but of a manager or steward. In addition, he has Peter introduce this section by questioning the applicability of the parable remnant in verses 39-40. While all disciples are bound to be faithful, it is especially the stewards or managers, symbolized by Peter, who have the greater responsibility. They are not to use their power to abuse the members of the community. Rather, that power implies communal service, not personal gain.

In the third section, Luke directs his attention to the slave or servant who does not carry out his master's will. His punishment will be in proportion to his awareness of his master's wishes and his culpability. The greater the power entrusted, the greater the responsibility.

Reflection. People often experience power as the means for improving their lot. They may also see it as a reward for faithful service and hence a prize uniquely their own. They may even gloat over their power because others must now meet their needs. Today's parable about the steward or manager, however, urges believers to think and act differently about the role of power by understanding it in terms of stewardship. Fundamentally stewardship is the call to be involved in the running of God's world/their world. Stewardship is the invitation to participate in the management of God's kingdom/their kingdom. Power has value only if the people of the world/kingdom retain their value. Power can tend to reduce people to things. Stewardship, however, tends to retain people as people. Power ultimately means stewardship.

Thursday: Luke 12:49-53 In this passage Luke presents Jesus focusing on the role of decision. He describes his mission in terms of fire. He has come to separate the true from the false, using fire as a purifying agent (see Mal 3:4). His fire will necessarily provoke a decision: in one case, acceptance of his person and message; in another, rejection of his person and message. Jesus' own death goes hand in hand with the fire image. For the third time he speaks about his passion (see 9:22, 44). Water symbolizes anguish and frustration, and baptism relates to his death (see Mark 10:38-39). Jesus, however, cannot hold back his desire for the "baptism" to take place since it will release the Spirit and complete the purifying process.

As anticipated in Simeon's prophecy (see Luke 2:34-35), Jesus' message will result in division, a decision for or against God. The Christ event will divide households. Here Luke relies on Micah 7:6 and its description of family turmoil. He holds both the older and the younger generations responsible but places the older first. The message provokes a decision.

Reflection. Believers accept Jesus' command to love everyone but are tempted to exclude. They acknowledge Jesus' message of fidelity in marriage but are exposed to compromise. They acknowledge Jesus' teaching on justice for all but may attempt a form of peaceful coexistence with injustice. There is thus a discrepancy between the message and the messenger. Here Jesus' person and Jesus' message overlap. Though it touches him deeply, he preaches that the divided household is the uncommitted household. He insists that disciples cannot have it both ways: they must be *for* or *against* the kingdom. Logically, his enemies believe that to kill the messenger is to kill the message. Paradoxically, however, the death of the messenger ensures the ongoing life of the message. The cross on Calvary is proof enough that the messenger must become the message.

Friday: Luke 12:54-59 This passage consists of two components: (1) reading the signs of the times (vv. 54-56) and (2) settling with one's opponent (vv. 57-59). In the first part, Jesus addresses the crowds who have been following him but is dismayed that they fail to understand what is happening in their midst. He admits that they read the weather accurately and thus know when either rain or scorching heat will develop. Unfortunately they cannot read the significance of his presence among them and his message about his Father and the kingdom. In the second part, Jesus urges reconciliation with an opponent by pointing out the dreadful consequences of being dragged into court and ending up in prison. Jesus is thus advising his disciples to make compromises that will eliminate all these conflicts.

Reflection. Believers must also read the signs of the times. Their situations and circumstances are not static realities. Rather, they are the raw materials for making proper decisions about themselves and their communities. Such decisions must be grounded in the seemingly ordinary events of daily life. To read such signs and decide properly ultimately means that they must be rooted in a vision of faith in their God, in their community, and in themselves.

Saturday: Luke 13:1-9   This passage consists of two units: (1) the need for universal repentance (vv. 1-5) and (2) the parable of the fig tree (vv. 6-9). In the first part, as Jesus continues his journey to Jerusalem, people inform him of some Galileans whom Pilate put to death. This information provides the occasion to speak against the view that the fate of these Galileans equals their guilt. To bolster his argument, Jesus cites the example of the eighteen killed at Siloam. What emerges is the constant need to reform. In the second part, the parable of the fig tree likewise shows that Israel must repent now, for tomorrow may be too late. For Luke's community, the words of Jesus point out the implications of their Christian call. They have to be ever alert and hence ever willing to renew their original Christian commitment to follow Jesus.

Reflection. Believers may be tempted to look with longing eyes at the power and prestige of others and conclude that they are truly liberated. They may even admire those who flout convention because of their wealth and infer that they are truly liberated. They may even envy those who enjoy perpetual leisure and reason that they are truly liberated. For Jesus, liberation consists in ongoing fidelity. In Luke, that fidelity takes the form of never ceasing reform. Disciples are supposed to be like the fig tree that produces on time. Such producing on time is the way to maintain the proper relationship between the owner and the tree. By not producing, the fig tree no longer has a claim on the owner. On the contrary, by producing, the believer retains his or her relationship with Jesus. Fidelity, not the assertion of ego, means the experience of liberation. Only the faithful are truly liberated.

The Thirtieth Week of the Year

Monday: Luke 13:10-17   On his journey to Jerusalem Jesus enters a synagogue in an unnamed town on the Sabbath and cures a crippled woman—an event that ignites a controversy about Sabbath observance. Luke observes that the woman has endured this painful condition for eighteen years. In fact, she is unable to stand up straight. By laying his hands on her, Jesus sets her free. Her cure sparks a dispute, however, in which the synagogue leader decries the healing since it occurs on a Sabbath and indeed in a synagogue. Quoting the Genesis creation account, the leader seeks to limit such cures to the other six days of the week. In response, Jesus cites the accepted custom of watering animals on the Sabbath. If it is permitted to provide for animals in this way on the Sabbath, it is certainly permitted to care for a suffering human being on the Sabbath. Having shamed his opponents in this way, Jesus provokes the rejoicing of the entire crowd. It is worth noting that this overcoming of physical evil on his journey to Jerusalem will be followed by a different form of overcoming evil at the journey's end.

Reflection. Believers often face the task of assessing their priorities. They wonder at times whether they should devote more time to earning money or addressing the needs of spouse and family. They question whether they should socialize more and thereby have less time for their parenting roles. Today's passage throws some light on this vexing issue. In this episode Jesus offers a lesson in prioritizing, namely, human beings take precedence over animals. Here healing a crippled woman has priority status over Sabbath observance. For believers, prioritizing means serving others first and themselves second. In cases of doubt, believers should prefer service to others to service to themselves.

Tuesday: Luke 13:18-21   This passage contains two kingdom parables: (1) the parable of the mustard seed (vv. 18-19) and (2) the parable of the yeast (vv. 20-21). In the first parable, Jesus makes a man the protagonist as he takes and in a garden sows mustard seed that eventually becomes a tree with sufficient space for nesting birds. By means of this parable Jesus teaches that from very small beginnings God's kingdom can grow into something unimaginable, a result clearly due to God's power. There is thus a unity between Jesus' ministry and a future manifestation of God's kingdom. In the second parable, Jesus makes a woman the protagonist as she takes yeast and mixes it with three measures of flour so that the yeast affects the whole lump of dough. The hidden yeast is known only from its amazing results. Thus the kingdom in its hidden way also has this leavening effect.

Reflection. At times believers seem to lack the capacity to marvel or be amazed at what God can achieve with seemingly infinitesimal means. Disciples may look at themselves and conclude that, owing to their paltry talents or credentials, they cannot contribute much to the advancement of God's kingdom. This inability to be surprised may take on a form of depression in which evil so predominates over good that the situation is utterly hopeless. Today's parables, however, may provide an antidote to this negative outlook. The mustard seed becomes a tree and the small but powerful amount of yeast leavens the entire batch of dough. Though the beginnings are indeed small, they are not negligible. God has the capacity to transform and energize hesitant believers by utilizing whatever talents they have for the benefit of the kingdom. Awe, wonder, and amazement are intended to be the characteristics of all believers.

Wednesday: Luke 13:22-30   Only fidelity gets one into the kingdom. Luke sounds this ominous note by connecting this scene with Jesus' trek to Jerusalem that will result in the inauguration of the kingdom. Jesus dismisses the bystander's question about the number of those to be saved. It is the wrong question. The right question is this: how does one get into the kingdom? Jesus' answer is in the plural (v. 23: "he answered *them*"; emphasis added), hence a message for Luke's audience. Luke then brings together two originally separate sayings of Jesus about doors. The narrow door (v. 24) means personal responsibility—religious status is meaningless. The closed door (vv. 25-27) suggests personal fidelity—personal relationship is useless. Though the kingdom-seekers properly address the master as "Lord," they will still find themselves outside. Evildoers have not reacted properly to Jesus' Word.

The "all talk, no show" people will catch a glimpse of the residents of God's kingdom. They will see the following guests: patriarchs, prophets, but also outsiders, namely, the Gentiles. To become a guest, one must first heed God's Word. Finally (v. 30) Jesus tells his audience that seating in the kingdom depends on fidelity, not rank. At the same time, Luke tells his audience that they should learn from Israel's mistake.

Reflection. Believers sometimes use the phrase "we're number one" as the measure of success in their business and social lives. Ironically, they may carry it over into their view of Christianity. Thus baptism by itself, mere enrollment in the parish register, or mere attendance at church functions is supposed to make them "number one." Today's passage, however, proceeds differently by urging that to be faithful is to be "number one." Jesus refuses to accept the "all talk, no show" disciples. In an even bolder move, he makes response to his Word the final criterion. To shout the slogans of religion ("Lord, Lord"), to claim Abraham as father, or to insist on old acquaintances does not meet the mark. Jesus dismisses elitism, disallows rank, and disavows status. With impeccable clarity he states his position: "who[ever] comes to me, hears my words, and acts on them" (Luke 6:47).

Thursday: Luke 13:31-35 This passage consists of two units: (1) Herod's desire to kill Jesus and Jesus' departure from Galilee (vv. 31-33), and (2) Jesus' lament over Jerusalem (vv. 34-35). In the first unit, some Pharisees prevail on Jesus to leave Galilee because Herod Antipas, the tetrarch of the region, intends to kill him. In response, Jesus labels this powerful political figure a fox and adds that he will continue to expel demons and work cures until he finishes his work and thus achieves his destiny. Jesus appears to spell out this work and achievement when he states that he will suffer a prophet's fate in Jerusalem to which he has been inexorably making his way.

In the second unit, Jesus pronounces a lament over the doomed city of Jerusalem, a city that kills the prophets and stones those sent to her.

Jesus then compares himself to a mother bird, indicating his intent to save the city. Unfortunately Jerusalem will not react to Jesus' protective wings. All that is left is final judgment on the sinful city and its inhabitants. The statement "you will not see me until the time comes" (v. 35) seems to involve three periods: (1) Jesus' triumphal entry on Palm Sunday (19:38), (2) the women's mourning (23:27-28), and (3) his final coming as judge (Acts 1:11).

Reflection. Believers may suffer from a certain lack of enthusiasm or drive as they reflect on their lives. They watch the days, weeks, months, and years pass by without reflecting sufficiently on their sharing in God's plan during this time. Their lackadaisical attitude generates no great desire to see themselves as active players in the ongoing challenge of life. Simply put, they lack resoluteness and determination. This passage, however, challenges such an attitude. Here the Lukan Jesus will not be deterred from reaching his goal and achieving his destiny. Not even Herod Antipas' murderous intent will prevent him from continuing his prophetic mission and arriving in Jerusalem. He declares this unequivocally: "Yet I *must* continue on my way today, tomorrow, and the following day, for it is impossible that a prophet should die outside of Jerusalem" (v. 33). Intending to fulfill his Father's plan, Jesus will brook no opposition as he proceeds to Jerusalem. Such a resolute and determined prophet challenges all disciples to shake off their torpor, engage themselves in their duties, and become active players in God's plan for them.

Friday: Luke 14:1-6   In this passage a leader of the Pharisees has invited Jesus to share a meal with him on the Sabbath. Luke adds that Jesus is being closely watched. When Jesus notices a man suffering from dropsy, he poses a question to the lawyers and Pharisees in attendance about the lawfulness of healing people on the Sabbath. While his opponents remain silent, Jesus proceeds to heal the man and dismiss him. In justifying his action, Jesus draws their attention to their practice of pulling out a child or an ox on the Sabbath that has fallen into a cistern. The stunned audience is unable to answer.

Reflection. How should believers perceive fellow human beings? Should they regard them only as cohabitants of this planet or isolated individuals with their own personal agenda? Or should they see them as merely anonymous and faceless and hence undeserving of their time and attention? What is clear is that the Jesus of today's passage does not share any of these worldviews. He is opposed to everything that oppresses and depresses the human spirit. He sees his mission as proclaiming liberty to the captives and Good News to the poor (Luke 4:18). In this episode, he notices a man suffering from dropsy and immediately takes steps to cure him despite the legalistic objections of his opponents. For Jesus, this man is obviously more than one additional suffering human. He is a fellow Jew and has a claim on Jesus' time and power. It is all a matter of perception. Love is in the eye of the beholder.

Saturday: Luke 14:1, 7-11 This passage opens with Jesus' invitation to a Sabbath meal given by a leader of the Pharisees. Luke has gathered sayings of Jesus from different occasions (vv. 7-11, 12-14, 15-24) and placed them in this one meal setting. They all answer the question in verse 15: who can eat bread in the kingdom of God? Noticing the scramble for the dais by the religious leaders, Jesus provides an initial answer to this question. In the kingdom there is room only for those who perceive the value of others and accept it joyfully. This is a paraphrase of Jesus' saying in verse 11: "For everyone who exalts himself will be humbled, but the one who humbles himself will be exalted."

Reflection. Believers also like to be invited to the proper social circles where they can masquerade as other people and make the proper contacts. They attempt to get the right table or sit next to the right people, sometimes disregarding others who have an equal or better claim to such places. Jesus' remarks about the scramblers may be instructive. For Jesus, to believe means to be so rooted in God that one perceives a neighbor's true worth and one's own true worth according to God's view. The scramblers perceive little or no worth in their neighbor. Rather, they inflate their own egos to distortion levels and seek to exploit the situation to their own advantage. Faith and dining go hand in hand.

The Thirty-first Week of the Year

Monday: Luke 14:12-14 This scene takes place at the Sabbath meal hosted by a leader of the Pharisees in 14:1-6. Here Luke connects the self-flaunting in 14:7-11 with arranging the guest list. In human relationships people tend to view other people not as people but as objects.

Hence it is a question of inviting only those who can reciprocate at a later date. The guest list thereby becomes a cryptic form of IOUs. In answer to the question about who can eat bread in God's kingdom, Jesus now replies that the one who treats people without a view to a reward here and now deserves to be a guest in that kingdom. One must expect a reward outside history, at a point that only faith can perceive. For Luke's audience, living in a world of "favors returned for favors given," Jesus' saying has no little impact. Faith without expectation of a reward now is the lifestyle of those who will be invited to God's table.

Reflection. Believers are also tempted to view other people as a means to their ends. They can thus use people with a view to getting some personal favor at a later date. Once again the issue revolves around the inherent dignity of human beings. Today's passage provides an insight into how the Lukan Jesus perceives this issue. In speaking to the arranger of the guest list, Jesus is implying that one must uncover the image of God in another precisely as a person, not an object. The host does not detect the image of God in his guests since they are IOUs payable on demand. The host cannot conceive the possibility of God's image in the socially undesirable. In challenging the host, Jesus insists that his disciples acquire a vision of people as made in the image and likeness of God.

Tuesday: Luke 14:15-24   Like 14:12-14, this scene occurs at the Sabbath meal hosted by a leader of the Pharisees in 14:1-6. The parable of the great banquet follows upon a remark by a guest that one is indeed blessed who will eat bread in God's kingdom. Addressing the complacency of the Pharisees and lawyers about their salvation, Jesus tells the parable of an invitation to a great banquet. Jesus seems to be focusing on those Jews whose place in the kingdom may be taken by the so-called outcasts. By the time the summons to attend the dinner arrives, the invitees have a change of plans. Whatever the excuses proffered, the guests are obviously impolite or careless about informing the host of their different plans. Provoked to anger, the host issues an invitation to the outcasts. When this strategy does not succeed in filling the available room, the host extends the invitation to those on the roads and in the lanes.

The parable reveals that God intends to have as many as possible attending the messianic banquet. The parable also makes clear, however, that those who reject Jesus' teaching will eventually experience exclusion from the banquet where Abraham, Isaac, and Jacob as well as all the prophets are guests along with the Gentiles.

Reflection. The question of salvation, namely, admission to the messianic banquet, impacts many people, believers and nonbelievers alike. What, therefore, determines salvation in one case and condemnation in another? Is everything predetermined by God so that people, believers included, have no say in this matter? The parable of the great supper may shed some light on this troublesome question. In this parable Luke seems to establish (implicitly at least) two points. The first is that admission to the messianic banquet hinges on God's invitation. Hence entrance into the kingdom is not purely up to humans, believers included; they must receive the invitation of Jesus, the proclaimer of the kingdom. The second point is that those invited must respond to the invitation, unlike the first invited guests in the parable. In turn, that response must express itself in fidelity to Jesus' message. Through infidelity, those rejecting the demands of the invitation will find themselves outside the kingdom.

Wednesday: Luke 14:25-33   In this passage Luke has Jesus address the high price of discipleship. The opening verse suggests the enlisting of recruits, but the enlisting is set against the background of Jesus' trek to Jerusalem. In answer to the question about the cost of discipleship, Luke has combined three sayings (vv. 26-27, 33) and two parables (vv. 28-32), inserting the parables between the second and third sayings.

"[W]ithout hating" (v. 26) means that Jesus must be uppermost in the lives of disciples so that one's family appears to be despised. Taking up one's cross after Jesus binds the follower to the experience of the passion (see Luke 23:26 where Simon follows *behind* Jesus). Allegiance to Jesus must be so total that possessions do not lessen that bond in any way. It is not the unconditional demand to renounce all property but neither is it an exaggeration for the sake of emphasis. The two parables comment on weighing the cost of discipleship. Both the tower builder and the warring king insist that the follower must calculate the costs, investigate the risks, and estimate the overall demands of discipleship. The price of discipleship is high indeed.

Reflection. By submitting to an exclusive one-on-one relationship with Jesus, believers can tend to insulate themselves by isolating others.

They may falsely claim that following Jesus excludes carrying their neighbor's cross. Ironically, they may find it easier to renounce their wealth for the kingdom than to pronounce themselves interested in other members of the kingdom. In response to such attitudes, Luke refuses to understand Jesus in isolation. In his universalism Luke sees Jesus as the person for everyone. To accept Jesus means to accept the sisters and brothers of Jesus. The radical message of the kingdom is that it is open to all, especially the social outcasts. To follow Jesus to Jerusalem means to follow in a group, not in isolation. To be a disciple of Jesus means to belong to the school of Jesus. In running the risk of following Jesus personally, one runs the risk of following him communally. Allegiance to Jesus means allegiance to others.

Thursday: Luke 15:1-10   The introduction to the two parables in this passage (vv. 1-3) shows that in Luke's community some were demanding stringent requirements for sinners. In these parables Luke does not have Jesus proclaim the Good News. Rather, he has Jesus vindicate the right not to put limits on God's goodness.

In the parables of the lost sheep and the lost coin, the shepherd and the woman, respectively, seem to be worried over what is relatively insignificant: one sheep out of a hundred and one coin out of ten. But the Pharisees and the scribes are guilty of precisely that—they have perverted values. They are more concerned about paltry things than about people, especially sinners. If the finding of one sheep and one coin provokes joy, all the more so the finding of lost humans. To join in the celebration means to join in the recovery of lost values.

Reflection. Believers know the sting of being hurt by others and may react by resolving to hurt them in return. People offend them by their words and they naturally tend to respond by determining to say hurtful words about them. People neglect them and they are tempted to reply by endeavoring to elaborate a plan of counterneglect. Believers live in a world of checks and balances whereby the offense must be returned in kind.

The message of this passage, however, does not endorse a policy of retaliation but one of forgiveness. Those who sin by hurting other people are comparable to the lost sheep and the lost coin. But by searching for the one lost sheep, the shepherd images believers who, putting aside their personal hurt, seek to be reconciled. By carefully looking for the lost coin, the woman reflects disciples who, dismissing their personal anguish, attempt to offer forgiveness. In both instances, celebration is the order of the day. To forgive the faults of others and to be reconciled to them means to enjoy genuine freedom. Those who act in this way are the truly liberated.

Friday: Luke 16:1-8   In this parable that probably ends with verse 8a, Jesus uses the enterprising steward as a model of prudence. When faced with the prospect of losing his position, he begins to juggle the books. Learning of the steward's machinations, the master is forced to applaud his ingenuity. When confronted with crisis, the steward uses all his abilities to safeguard his future. For Luke's audience, Jesus' preaching of the kingdom provokes crises, one of which may well be the prudent handling of material goods.

Reflection. Believers are sometimes tempted to think that to cheat people is acceptable since it increases their wealth. They may contend that to bribe people is equally acceptable since it provides a means to ensure their investments. According to this mindset, people become only figures in their ledgers. In today's passage the steward's enterprising bookkeeping reduces his master's debtors to the level of things. They are valuable commodities only insofar as they absorb the steward's losses. In contrast, believers are to relate the use of wealth to people. It is a question of covenant: the covenant between God and people and the covenant between people and people. The danger is always compromise, namely, the covenant between money and the individual and then the covenant with other individuals only insofar as they enhance the covenant with money. Honest bookkeeping, however, means honest people-keeping.

Saturday: Luke 16:9-15   In this passage Luke provides three applications of the parable of the dishonest steward (vv. 8b-9; vv. 10-12; v. 13) and adds another three sayings, creating an editorial unit about the avaricious Pharisees (vv. 14-15). In the first application, the disciples of Jesus (the children of light) are to employ material possessions prudently and to make friends with those who will welcome them into everlasting dwellings when their wealth dissipates. In the second application, there is a threefold contrast: (1) faithfulness in little things versus big things, (2) working with everyday possessions versus truly valuable items, and (3) responsibility in dealing with another's property versus one's own. In the third application, there is no compromise: either God or wealth. In the sayings about the avaricious Pharisees, vindicating oneself before humans means nothing to God. The genuine evaluation of a person is what God knows. Coveting wealth constitutes the real abomination in God's eyes.

Reflection. Like all human beings, believers are prone to look for criteria to evaluate themselves. Such criteria may include wealth, power, or prestige. According to these criteria the person who has amassed great wealth has truly made it. The person who exerts enormous power and influence over others is a genuine success. The person who enjoys unlimited prestige in the community has really risen to the top. According to the last group of sayings about the avaricious Pharisees (vv. 14-15), however, all these criteria fail because they exclude God's evaluation. The absolute criterion for assessing oneself is God's evaluation, not the porous judgment of fellow humans. "You [the Pharisees] justify yourselves in the sight of others, but God knows your hearts; for what is of human esteem is an abomination in the sight of God" (v. 15).

The Thirty-second Week of the Year

Monday: Luke 17:1-6   This passage contains three sets of Jesus' sayings on: (1) scandals (vv. 1-3a), (2) the obligation to forgive (vv. 3b-4), and (3) the power of faith (vv. 5-6). In the first saying, Jesus points out the inevitability of scandal in the lives of followers. He is fully aware that some of them will commit sin by causing others to sin. The fate of such an agent of scandal is that of a weighted drowning at sea—hence the warning to be on guard. In the second saying, Jesus advocates the need to rebuke an offender. If the rebuke is effective, then forgiveness must follow. Sinning seven times a day and repenting an equal number of times must not be pressed mathematically. It simply means every time—hence the forgiveness of the offended party must be limitless. In the third saying, it is not the amount of faith but the kind of faith that is significant. It must be nothing less than genuine faith. Even if such faith is no bigger than a mustard seed, it is powerful enough to uproot a relatively large tree, like a mulberry, and plant it in the sea.

Reflection. Of all these sayings perhaps the most difficult for believers is the second, namely, the obligation of relentless forgiveness. In essence, to forgive is to break free of the shackles of one's ego, to recognize the repentance of the offending party, and to pronounce the formula of reconciliation, namely, "Despite all that has happened, I still love you." Though forgiveness may naturally grate on believers, especially in the case of multiple offenses, the demands of the Lukan Jesus are all too clear: "And if he wrongs you seven times in one day and returns to you seven times saying, 'I am sorry,' you should forgive him" (v. 4).

Tuesday: Luke 17:7-10 As Jesus journeys to Jerusalem, Luke stresses the link between the service of Christian disciples and their destiny. He seems to be making two points. First, the fulfillment of one's appointed duties is not necessarily a guarantee of one's salvation. After satisfying all expectations, the disciple realizes that his or her destiny is still a matter of grace. Second, any kind of boasting by the disciple is ruled out. The disciple should not anticipate a show of gratitude for merely carrying out what was commanded.

Reflection. The lives of believers are a curious blend of human effort and divine gift giving. This passage powerfully reminds them that their lives as servants are necessarily grounded in service to God and others. Hence they are expected to perform their duties because that is what is expected of them. They can eat and drink only after the master has eaten and drunk. In addition to human effort, however, there is divine gift giving. The ultimate destiny of believers hinges not only on their own attainments but also on divine grace. The traditional formula for salvation still has value: work as if everything depends on you and pray as if everything depends on God.

Wednesday: Luke 17:11-19 In this passage Luke seems to be saying something about the fundamental misunderstanding of Israel. Here nine Jews look upon their cure as something owed them by God. Only the Samaritan recognizes God's great generosity. Thus a Samaritan (for

Luke, a foreigner) becomes a model for Israel and an example of God's overture to the Gentiles.

Jesus does not heal the lepers immediately but merely tells them to carry out the prescriptions of Jewish law. The healing occurs on the journey. The nine Jews, however, continue their journey; only the Samaritan returns. Significantly the Samaritan praises God and then throws himself down before God's instrument. In effect, Jesus' question about the nine appears to relate to the religious leadership of Jerusalem. They have failed to make the proper discovery. They have failed to recognize the manifestation of God's power in Jesus. The faith that leads to healing is not simply the belief that Jesus can heal—the nine had that. It is that dimension of faith that recognizes not only the gift but also the giver. Thus the Samaritan has a double gain: restored health and acceptance of Jesus.

Reflection. Time and again believers feel they've been had. They go out of their way for people, but there is no recognition. Too often they feel they've been exploited. They spend their time, energy, and money, but there is no acknowledgement. People simply accept the gift but never advert to the giver. By contrast, the Samaritan in today's passage knows that he has received a gift—his leprosy is gone. His nine companions are happy with their gift but never get beyond that. The Samaritan's first reaction is to acknowledge the power of God: he "returned, glorifying God in a loud voice" (v. 15). His second reaction is to recognize God's chosen instrument in the cure, namely, Jesus. He cannot rest content until he has isolated the gift and the instrument. Gratitude means the great discovery.

Thursday: Luke 17:20-25   This passage consists of: (1) the question of the coming of God's kingdom (vv. 20-21) and (2) sayings about the revelation of the Son of Man (vv. 22-25). Jesus' reply to the Pharisees does not really deal with the time of the arrival of the kingdom. Rather, his questioners have actually confused the notion of what the kingdom is all about. It is a reality that is not subject to the observation of particular signs. Instead, the kingdom of God is among them. It is either in their very midst, owing to the presence of Jesus himself and his ministry, or within their reach.

Jesus then speaks to the disciples about the day(s) of the revelation of the Son of Man. First, the Son of Man will not come as quickly as they would like (v. 22). Second, he informs them about the manner in which he will not come (v. 23). Third, he instructs them about the way in which he will come (v. 24). Fourth, he introduces the notion of suffering and rejection that must come before the revelation of the day of the Son of Man.

Reflection. Believers are called to help realize the kingdom of God, namely, God's plan to provide for all, especially the marginalized. To be sure, Jesus has taken the initial steps in bringing about this kingdom. It is, however, still in the process of becoming. In that process, believers play a vital role because that kingdom is actually among them. By living the values and principles of the Good News, believers are kingdom builders. By their service to others, they instruct their world about a kingdom within their reach where justice and love prevail over injustice and hatred. In effect, this passage is the clarion call to renew their commitment to the challenge of the kingdom.

Friday: Luke 17:26-37   In this passage Luke continues Jesus' sayings about the revelation of the day(s) of the Son of Man. It contains three units: (1) the days of Noah and Lot (vv. 26-32), (2) the prudent or inequitable aspects of the judgment (vv. 33-35), and (3) the concluding question and answer (v. 37). (Verse 36 is not part of Luke's text.) In the first unit, the comparison of the Son of Man's arrival with the scenarios of Noah and Lot exhorts the disciples to avoid indifference. Whereas people during the time of Noah and Lot were consumed with earthly activities, the disciples should be extremely vigilant. One will not have the luxury of recovering what one owns or has left behind. The fate of Lot's wife should serve as a warning about turning back.

In the second unit, purely human effort will be insufficient in the quest for salvation. Divine judgment will impact both women and men, although the text provides no explanations for the decisions taken. In the third unit, the disciples ask about where all this is going to happen— something they should not inquire about (see 17:23). Jesus' reply about the corpse and the vultures may mean that, just as the vultures invariably appear wherever the corpse is, so the day of the Son of Man will inevitably become manifest.

Reflection. The delay of Jesus' second coming as judge forced Luke to remind his audience of the role of vigilance in their lives. Even though the second coming did not appear to be imminent, his community nonetheless had to be prepared. Such timely advice must also impact today's believers. They too can become so involved in mundane matters that they may overlook their primary concerns. The passage challenges them to focus on such concerns in the midst of their day-to-day activities. Vigilance is still the price of victory.

Saturday: Luke 18:1-8   The parable of the widow and the unjust judge concerns the problem of survival during persecution, a problem also considered in the day(s) of the Son of Man (see 17:22). It raises the question of the attitude of disciples during such times of crisis. Should they simply sit down and wait for Jesus' second coming? The opening verse does not reply that perseverance ultimately fulfills one's prayer but that constancy will counteract capitulation and that God will never cease to support his followers. The parable presupposes that the livelihood of a widow in first-century AD society is precarious. Her virtue, however, is perseverance. She is so persistent that the judge is forced to vindicate her lest her obstinacy completely wear him down.

Jesus applies the parable against the background of persecution and temptation to infidelity (vv. 7-8). God, who is Father, will obviously heed his elect if they continue to cry out. On the other hand, God will be unlike the unjust judge in that he will respond promptly to the needs of his chosen ones. Nonetheless, faith may grow thin before the second coming.

Reflection. The world pledges its word very easily but retracts it just as easily. People vow to serve other people in a variety of professions but sometimes end up serving only some of them and then only for a time. They pledge allegiance "with liberty and justice for all" but may soon distort that pledge by their prejudice. In today's passage Luke reveals an appreciation for the virtue of perseverance in his community. After all, Christian living is not the "in" thing in his society. He argues, however, that perseverance, though difficult, is possible. The God who will sustain them is part of their world. But the danger is that they may cease to be part of his world. Constant prayer is to be their lifeline. God will never tire of listening, though they may weary of calling out. Perseverance is ultimately the "in" thing.

The Thirty-third Week of the Year

Monday: Luke 18:35-43 Basing this account on Mark 10:46-52, Luke recounts the story of the healing of a blind man as Jesus approaches the city of Jericho. The man pleads for mercy, hailing Jesus as the Son of David. While those in front sternly order him to keep quiet, the blind man persists, shouting even more loudly in his plea for mercy from Jesus. As Jesus comes to a halt, he commands the man to be brought to him. Having inquired what the man wishes from him, Jesus restores the man's sight, remarking that his faith has saved him. At the restoration of his sight, there is a twofold expression of praise of God, first by the former blind man and then by the people.

In healing the blind beggar, Jesus demonstrates that he is indeed the Son of David. In this same act, he fulfills his inaugural address in the Nazareth synagogue, namely, "recovery of sight to the blind" (4:18). By placing this episode immediately after Jesus' third passion prediction (18:31-34), Luke shows that the former blind beggar perceives in Jesus what those in front and the Twelve do not. While the Twelve do not grasp the necessity of Jesus' passion and death and perhaps seek to prevent the beggar from approaching him, the blind man understands that Jesus is the Son of David whose mission is to heal.

Reflection. The ministry of praise can elude believers at times. They may witness enormous goodness but fail to applaud the agents of that goodness. They may observe the daily heroism of struggling parents but register no recognition through praise. They may witness the talent and genius of people but repress every inkling to give due notice. On the other hand, today's passage reveals a twofold demonstration of this ministry of praise. First, the former blind beggar cannot contain his exuberance. He must follow Jesus and glorify God. Second, the people join in the man's chorus of praise. Having witnessed this miracle, they are compelled to acknowledge what God has done through Jesus. The ministry of praise seeks more practitioners, believers as well as all people of good will.

Tuesday: Luke 19:1-10 The Zacchaeus story is unique to Luke. He has inserted it between the healing of the blind man (18:35-43) and the parable of the pounds (19:11-17). It is likely that Luke is attempting to make explicit the implicit element in 18:35-43, namely, forgiveness as the granting of salvation.

Luke emphasizes that Zacchaeus is a chief tax collector. Although tax collectors are admittedly sinners (see Luke 3:12), Jesus seeks out their company. Moreover, Zacchaeus is a wealthy man; he is, humanly speaking, unable to enter the kingdom (Luke 12:16-31). Yet Zacchaeus is small of stature and the little people are apt citizens of the kingdom (Luke 9:48). By using the word "today" twice (vv. 5, 9), Luke shows the presence of salvation in the figure of Jesus. Indeed his coming to Zacchaeus' house is part of the Father's plan—Jesus must stay at his house. Jesus' arrival there is thus an instance of Jesus' mercy and forgiveness.

The Zacchaeus story is an example of Jesus' overcoming the objections of the crowd (v. 7). Luke points out that, to be saved, one must accept Jesus' offer of table fellowship, make up for any injustices (v. 8), and welcome Jesus into one's house.

Reflection. Like other people, believers may protest that they love their neighbor but hesitate to forgive their neighbor. They may profess that their neighbor is created in God's image and likeness but are reluctant to be reconciled with their neighbor. They may acknowledge that their neighbor is a new creation (see 2 Cor 5:17) but refuse to speak the creative words, "I pardon you." Their statements are statements of love but their actions are not actions of love. While Luke does not use the word "love" in this passage, he presents Jesus' forgiveness as the result of love. To search out and save is his mission. This searching/saving/loving becomes forgiveness when Jesus becomes a guest in Zacchaeus' house. Salvation means recognizing the presence of Jesus who communicates forgiveness. Jesus' action is the reaction to the murmuring of the crowds. The murmurers cannot forgive because they cannot love after the manner of Jesus. In this passage, as elsewhere, loving means forgiving.

Wednesday: Luke 19:11-28   In this parable Luke intends to counter the mistaken notion that the coming of the kingdom is imminent. To offset this notion, he highlights vigilance but also the obligation of appropriate conduct during the king's journey to a foreign land (the delay of the second coming). To this end, the nobleman gratuitously gives a pound (a significant but not an exorbitant sum of money) to three servants. When the nobleman-turned-king returns, he exacts an accounting from these servants. While the first two increase the sum of money through their industry, the third wraps it in a piece of cloth, earning no profit at all. The king then proceeds to applaud the diligence of the first two servants and award them rule over ten and five cities respectively. He reprimands the third servant, however, and orders his pound to be given to the servant with ten pounds.

In the allegorizing or decoding of the parable, the nobleman-turned-king is Jesus who will ascend to his Father from Jerusalem. By his ascent he will receive the title of king and eventually return in judgment. Upon that return, he will deal with his servants who received the benefits of his message and will avenge himself on those citizens who did not want him to rule over them as king.

Reflection. This passage addresses the conduct of believers during the time between Jesus' return to the Father and the second coming. The account of the three servants raises this question: what is their responsibility as servants during this interim? The obvious answer is that servants must remain faithful to their charge. Such fidelity implies productive servants, i.e., those who make the most of what they have received. Needless to say, not everyone has the same resources. For Luke, however, the decisive point is that believers view themselves as gifted servants, hence as people endowed with gifts and talents for the benefit of others. To make others the beneficiaries of these gifts and talents is to gain a place in the kingdom. Ultimately they do not exist merely for themselves but for others. Productivity is ever a key demand on their time and energy.

Thursday: Luke 19:41-44 Prior to this scene, Luke has described Jesus' triumphal entry into Jerusalem on Palm Sunday (19:29-40). That event generated nothing less than enormous enthusiasm and ecstatic joy among the disciples. The present scene, however, provides a decided contrast as Jesus is compelled to weep over the unfortunate city. Here Luke focuses on the theme of Jesus' rejection by the religious leaders. The city has not recognized Jesus' invitation. Despite the love that Jesus has lavished on the city, he must now announce its coming destruction. Enemies will encircle Jerusalem and set up ramparts. It will experience the typical atrocities associated with ancient warfare. They will dash the inhabitants and their children to the ground and not leave one stone upon another. The city has missed its opportunity for peace.

Reflection. Believers must ask the lingering question whether they will learn from the example of the religious leaders in today's passage. Will today's disciples have the courage to perceive the daily chances to respond to God's unflagging call to repent? This passage challenges them to exhibit their repentance by reaching out to the helpless and vulnerable in their society. It urges them to heed Jesus' message of compassion and self-emptying service. They must seize the day by becoming agents of hope and peace. It is high time to dry the tears of Jesus.

Friday: Luke 19:45-48   This passage consists of two units: (1) the cleansing of the temple (vv. 45-46) and (2) the reaction of the Jewish leaders to Jesus' teaching (vv. 47-48). In the first unit, after the lament over the city Jesus goes directly to the temple and proceeds to drive out the merchants. After the manner of the Old Testament prophets, he decries the transformation of God's dwelling place into a mercantile center. To this end, Jesus cites two prophetic texts: (1) Isaiah 56:7 ("My house shall be a house of prayer"); and (2) Jeremiah 7:11 ("a den of thieves"). By his act of cleansing, Jesus takes over his "Father's house" (2:49) and thus makes it appropriate for his teaching ministry.

In the second unit, Jesus limits his Jerusalem ministry to teaching in the temple area on a daily basis. Luke also lists the Jerusalem authorities (the chief priests, the scribes, and the leaders of the people) and anticipates the passion account by noting their intent to kill Jesus. Luke also observes that these attempts prove unsuccessful because all the people are spellbound at Jesus' teaching.

Reflection. This passage may force believers to consider the significance of worship space in their lives. Thus Jesus' act of cleansing the temple may move them to ponder the role of sacred space. For Jesus, the temple is the place for the proper worship of God, for instruction on the meaning of God's will, and for the special dwelling place of this God. By his prophetic action of purging the temple, Jesus restores it to its intended dignity. This attitude toward the temple may, in turn, lead believers to appreciate their church as the appropriate place for worship, as the locus for discovering God's will for them, and as the area where God chooses to be present in a special way. Worship must finally compel believers to transfer the presence of God in church to his overall presence outside the place of worship.

Saturday: Luke 20:27-40   In this scene the Sadducees, a conservative Jewish sect denying the resurrection of the body and the existence of angels, now question Jesus. They pose the case of a woman who was successively married to seven brothers, citing the levirate law of Deuteronomy 25:5-10, in order to deny the resurrection of the body. If there is a resurrection, then to which of the seven brothers does the woman belong? Jesus replies that his opponents have confused the present age with the future age, i.e., marriage is in view of the present, not the future. Moreover, resurrection is only for those judged worthy (v. 36). Moses was concerned with posterity, but in the resurrection there is no question of death. Aware of their denial of the existence of angels, Jesus observes that those who share in the resurrection become like angels and are sons of God (a title used for angels in Gen 6:2). If the resurrected are called sons of God, then why deny the existence of angels who are called sons of God? At the end some scribes compliment Jesus and desist from asking any further questions.

In citing the passage about the burning bush (Exod 3:6), Jesus shows that God is the God of the living since the patriarchs were long dead at the time of the composition of Exodus. Here Luke adds that all are alive for God. It is possible that Luke is drawing on the noncanonical Fourth Book of Maccabees. In 16:25 the author of that work says that the Maccabean mother and her seven sons, though dead, live unto God with Abraham, Isaac, and Jacob.

Reflection. Believers accept the resurrection of the body but may be tempted to be dropouts from living that belief now. They acknowledge the reality of eternal glory but may be prone to dissociate it from their daily living. They affirm belief in the beatific vision but may be liable to separate it from their actions now. The afterlife appears all too often to be a never-never land that does not impinge on their everyday activities. Against this situation, today's passage has much to commend it. Here Jesus encounters the Sadducees who deny the resurrection and future rewards and punishments. In his reply to their test case, Jesus insists that the resurrection applies only to those judged worthy. To those who insist on Moses' teaching, Jesus responds that there is a relationship between Moses' prescriptions and God's final judgment. Elsewhere (see 14:14) Luke has Jesus teaching that to invite the outcasts to a reception is to reap a reward later on. For Jesus, the afterlife impacts living now.

The Thirty-fourth Week or Last Week of the Year

Monday: Luke 21:1-4   Luke links the account of the widow's mite with Jesus' denunciation of the scribes in the immediately preceding scene (20:45-47) where he accuses them of devouring widows' houses. In this passage Jesus is no less distressed with the scribes. He remarks that the widow, "from her poverty, has offered her whole livelihood" (v. 4). Jesus does not propose a program of giving according to one's means—the widow has given beyond her means! Rather, Jesus laments the situation of the widow who gives what she really cannot afford. In the end, Jesus does not praise her—he pities her because the religious authorities (the scribes) have manipulated her thinking and acting. Ultimately Jesus condemns the value system of the scribes.

Reflection. Believers must find this passage upsetting. Here the widow is the victim of a heinous value system that demands giving beyond her means. Believers must look beyond this text to seek out so-called value systems that manipulate people. In other words, they must ask about those corrupt systems that deny people basic justice, that demean their character as sisters and brothers of Jesus, and that consider them mere chattel, not human beings. This passage is a call to action rooted in baptism. In their prophetic role, believers must say it the way it really is. They must expose the false value systems festering in their midst. The widow in today's passage thus becomes the poster person for this campaign against manipulation of human beings.

Tuesday: Luke 21:5-11   This passage marks the beginning of Luke's eschatological discourse, i.e., it deals with the last things, namely, the fate of Jerusalem and the fate of the world. It typically uses apocalyptic language, i.e., revelatory speech that is highly symbolic. Here a question from one of Jesus' listeners follows Jesus' comment about the temple and its ornamentation.

In verses 8-11 Jesus warns his audience about being led astray. He goes on to speak of false prophets who will come in his name and announce that the time is near. He also mentions wars and insurrections, the clash of nation against nation and kingdom against kingdom, and natural disasters (earthquakes, famines, plagues, etc.). Such speech focuses only on the destruction of the temple and the city of Jerusalem (Luke writes after these events), not the end of the world.

Reflection. It is hard for modern believers to sense the impact that the destruction of the city of Jerusalem and the temple had on the Jewish people. Perhaps the closest they can get is 9/11. The question that seems raised by this passage for disciples is: how does one deal with such disasters? The overly facile answer is to regard these cataclysms as divine punishment for humanity's sinfulness. But more likely believers should probe deeper and ask: what drives people to commit such heinous acts against other people? No doubt the response to this disturbing question will be complex. In any event, it must alert believers to the problems in society that drive such atrocious activity. Apparently the value systems of the world need more than a quick fix.

Wednesday: Luke 21:12-19   In this passage Luke makes it clear that persecutions by both Jews and Gentiles will occur before the destruction of the temple. This will be the opportunity to bear witness. In such crises the proper word and wisdom will be forthcoming, for Jesus will provide them. In the face of opposition from family, friends, and indeed almost any quarter, the faithful will find security. Patient endurance will win out. Even though some may have to offer their lives, they will not thereby lose their real selves.

Reflection. Believers live today in a great age of conformity. They are tempted to conform to the pleasure cult of the media, to adopt a "me first and always" stance, and to be dropouts from community by the sole pursuit of self. Today's passage, however, urges believers to be different. Here Luke insists on a lifestyle that requires fidelity. Persecution and hardship are the arsenal of conformists. To say no to friends and family means to say yes to Jesus. Not to conform is to be different—a nonconformity that may entail death. Paradoxically such nonconformity is conformity to Jesus' style in the face of trial and persecution. To be a believer means to be different.

Thursday: Luke 21:20-28   This section of the eschatological discourse consists of two units: (1) the plight of Jerusalem (vv. 20-24) and (2) the coming of the Son of Man (vv. 25-28). In the first unit, Jesus foretells the plight and desolation of Jerusalem as camps surround the holy city. He announces the impossibility of escape for those who remain within it. Quoting Hosea 9:7, Jesus explains the reason for divine vengeance, namely, Israel's rejection of the Lord and the refusal to heed the prophet's message. The disaster will particularly afflict pregnant women and those nursing. Those who remain in the city will be put to the sword or taken captive to foreign countries. Pagans will trample down the city until the full measure of carnage is complete.

In the second unit, Luke has Jesus take up his second coming at the end of time—it will not occur right after the destruction of Jerusalem. Using apocalyptic language, Jesus announces the cosmic signs (in the sun, moon, stars, and seas) attending the end. These signs will provoke confusion and distress for all nations. Their panic will cause fainting, as the powers of the heavens are shaken. The Son of Man will then come on a cloud with power and great glory. When this event takes place, the faithful will know that their ransom or redemption has arrived. Jesus will come, therefore, as the great liberator.

Reflection. Believers can easily observe the great contrast between these two units. The first concludes with incalculable disaster; the second concludes with the arrival of the great liberator. This contrast must energize believers, prompting them to exercise the virtue of hope. While the disasters and anguish of life are all too obvious, the crowning success of the faithful is not so evident. This passage challenges disciples to live each day in expectation of the second coming of Jesus. At liturgy they proclaim that Christ has died, is risen, and will come again. This last element of the proclamation, however, seems to get scant attention. By focusing on this event, believers gain the strength to spend each day in anticipation of this last day. "Hope does not disappoint us, because God's love has been poured into our hearts through the Holy Spirit that has been given to us" (Rom 5:5).

Friday: Luke 21:29-33 Against the background of the coming of the end time (21:26) and the closeness of the kingdom, Jesus tells his audience that they should learn a lesson from the parable of the fig tree. Just as they know about the signs of summer from this tree, they should also learn the proper lesson about the signs that point to the coming of the kingdom. Jesus then makes two points. The first is that the kingdom is here but not yet fully realized. It is present in the words and works of Jesus but has not fully appeared. The second is the assurance that his words will not pass away until everything has been accomplished. The irony here is that Jesus utters these words shortly before his violent death.

Reflection. In this passage believers can discover another basis for hope. It is the comforting assurance that Jesus' message will not pass away. In the period between the present and the second coming of Jesus, despite the upheavals of history and the constant threat of annihilation, believers continue to experience Jesus in his words. It is this permanency of Jesus' message that inspires hope. In times of doubt and despair, believers do well to recall the words of the prophet Second Isaiah to the despondent exiles in sixth-century BC Babylon: "The grass withers, the flower fades, when the breath of the Lord blows upon it; . . . but the word of our God will stand forever" (40:7-8).

Saturday: Luke 21:34-36 In this passage, Jesus concludes his eschatological discourse with an exhortation to vigilance. The delay of the second coming is no reason for abandoning such vigilance. Hence they should not give in to carousing, drunkenness, or worldly concerns. Constant prayer is also Jesus' recommendation for coping with all the dangers to which his audience is subject. Owing to such prayer and vigilance, they will have no reason to fear appearing before the Son of Man at his second coming.

Reflection. Believers may be tempted to profess that they are already redeemed because they have received the Spirit in baptism. They may maintain that they have already reached Christian maturity because they have received the sacrament of confirmation. They may even feel that they "have made it" for the week because they have attended Sunday Mass. In today's passage, however, Luke offers a different strategy. He attempts to draw the attention of his community away from the precise dating of the second coming. He teaches that, in order to enjoy that moment, they have to make the present sacred. He warns them to avoid self-indulgence and drunkenness. He urges them to practice both vigilance and constant prayer. For Luke, it is never a question of "having made it." Rather, vigilance is the price of victory.

Index of Gospel Passages

BX 2170 .C55 C73 2010
The gospels of the weekday lectionary :
commentary and reflections
178876